MW00983610

077191
(18)
5/14
50—

ART NOUVEAU AND
ART DECO BOOKBINDING

ART NOUVEAU AND ART DECO BOOKBINDING

FRENCH MASTERPIECES 1880–1940

ALASTAIR DUNCAN & GEORGES DE BARTHA

PREFACE BY PRISCILLA JUVELIS

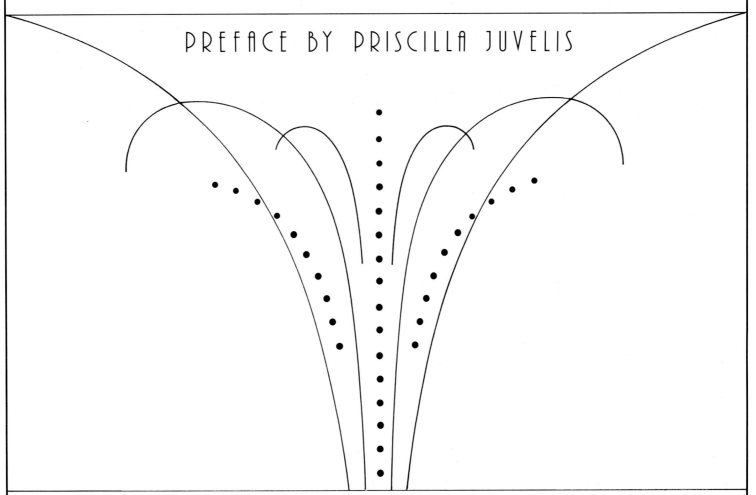

HARRY N. ABRAMS, INC., PUBLISHERS, NEW YORK

To T.K.

Library of Congress Cataloging-in-Publication Data

Duncan, Alastair, 1942–
    Art Nouveau and Art Deco bookbinding.

    Bibliography: p.
    Includes index.
    1. Bookbinding—History—20th century. 2. Decoration
and ornament—Art nouveau. 3. Decoration and ornament—
Art deco. I. De Bartha, Georges. II. Title.
Z269.D86   1988   686.3′6   88–3324
ISBN 0-8109-1881-1

Copyright © 1989 Thames and Hudson Limited, London
Published in 1989 by Harry N. Abrams, Incorporated, New York
All rights reserved. No part of the contents of this book may be
reproduced without the written permission of the publisher

A Times Mirror Company

Printed and bound in Japan

CONTENTS

ACKNOWLEDGMENTS

Gratitude is extended to the following for their co-operation in the compilation of this book: Priscilla Juvelis, Frederick Koch, Robert Rainwater, Félix Marcilhac, Townsend Photo (New York), Christie's Geneva, Habsburg-Feldman S.A., Jean-Loup Charmet, Ralph Esmerian, Frederick Brandt, Steve Andrews, Mr. Molo, Isidra Pastor, and the staffs of the New York Central Library, and, in Paris, at the Bibliothèque Forney, the Bibliothèque Sainte-Geneviève, and the Bibliothèque of the Musée des Arts Décoratifs.

Special thanks are extended to MaryBeth McCaffrey for her co-ordination of the entire project and for her research.

PREFACE

THE ART OF MODERN BOOKBINDING needs no special introduction for the devoted bibliophile. For the uninitiated, however, the bindings included in this important survey of Art Nouveau and Art Deco French binding may come as a surprise. These bindings, though drawn on a rich French tradition, are much more than a continuation of an ongoing craft: they are an art form in themselves. They are inspired by that other twentieth-century phenomenon, the *livre de peintre*, in which original graphics by such modern masters as Picasso, Matisse, or Braque were conceived as an integral creation, rather than as literal illustrations or mere decoration. Not fully appreciated until recently, these books provide an exciting testament to the creative energy of our time.

Interest in these exquisite and highly desirable volumes has risen dramatically. In June of 1982 the enormous public attention aroused by the sale of ninety-one books assembled by the French bibliophile Lucien Vendel and the high prices realized at it served notice that there was a change in the market for designer bindings – especially those on books containing original graphics by the great masters of the twentieth century such as Toulouse-Lautrec, Bonnard, Picasso, Matisse, and Braque. Previous to that time the market for these books was literally a private club, or rather a group of private clubs composed of French bibliophiles who commissioned designer bindings directly from the artist/craftsman.

Although rare books are traditionally the slowest area of the art market to follow a general rising trend in prices, and, conversely, the slowest to fall in a general declining trend, they have seen a dramatic rise in the past six years, particularly in the field of the designer-bound book. With the American entrance into a traditionally European (or French) market, a new collecting era has begun. And the end of these high prices is not yet in sight. As great copies of the key books, like the Bonnard *Parallèlement* in a Bonet binding (ill. 46), or the Schmied *Paysages Méditerranéens* in a Dunand lacquer binding (ill. 86), or a Toulouse-Lautrec *Histoires naturelles* in a Cretté binding (ill. 87), become harder to find, prices will continue to rise. Should the Japanese collectors decide to enter this rarefied market of designer bindings, one can only guess at the result.

Of course, there were any number of other public and private sales of great collections of fine modern bindings prior to the Vendel sale in 1982. As early as 1925 the Descamps-Scrive collection was sold at public auction. That sale catalogue is much sought after by current collectors as a reference work. One interesting entry in it is item 275, which shows a binding by Pierre Legrain and the caption "curieuse reliure de style moderne signée Pierre Legrain." The book sold at the time for FF8000 (in 1925 prices $1,500). Other notable sales were those of Louis Barthou (1935), Daniel Sickles (1948), and Francis Kettaneh (1978).

Perhaps the most important public sale prior to Vendel was the five-part sale of the collection of the great jeweler and connoisseur, Raphael Esmerian, in 1974. Although modern bindings formed only a small part of the sale, they were of such fine quality that Esmerian's books are still a measure for other collections. Several of the books in that sale have come up again for auction. For example, de Gourmont's *Couleurs*, illustrated by Laboureur and bound by Paul Bonet (ill. 37), realized FF20,000 (hammer price) in 1974. It came up again at Christie's Geneva on 13 May 1984 and realized SF40,000 (hammer price). That is, in ten years the price increased from $4,000 to nearly $20,000. Another example of a superb binding from the Esmerian sale is the Schmied *Ballades françaises* bound by Bonet (ill. 34).

Following the 1982 Vendel sale there were a rapid succession of public and private sales at which prices seemed to reach dramatically higher levels with each passing month. One such private sale took place in 1984, when the collection formed by an Argentinian bibliophile was sold to the Sutton Place Foundation. This collection was documented in a catalogue entitled *The Book Beautiful and the Binding as Art* (the first such catalogue to offer color photographs of an entire collection of French bindings with descriptions printed in English). A number of key books in the collection were originally owned by Carlos R. Scherrer (one of Bonet's first important patrons) and passed from Scherrer to a friend's collection on his death. Several of those very special books are included here (Bonet binding no. 46, a particularly significant binding, and no. 56). Another important private sale occurred in 1985 when the Sutton Place Foundation purchased most of the modern binding collection formed by the great jeweler and connoisseur, Henri Vever. Different in scope and content from the 1984 sale, with an emphasis on the Art Deco artist/illustrator rather than the School of Paris artist, it had a number of jewel-like bindings with Dunand lacquer panels, some of which are reproduced in this book (ills. 75, 76, 80, and 204).

By 1984 it was clear that the Americans were competing at public and private sales for the best of the French bindings. Of course, there was competition from the French, but many of the most important prizes went to American, English, and Swiss collectors. One example of a record-breaking price was at the estate sale of Mrs. Florence J. Gould in June 1984. Her copy of Renard's *Histoires naturelles* illustrated by Toulouse-Lautrec and bound by Georges Cretté (ill. 87) realized FF721,500 ($84,500). The price for the Vendel copy of *Histoires naturelles* (1982) bound by Mercier was about $16,176; the price for the Esmerian copy (1974) bound by Cretté was about $8,000!

The years 1985 to 1987 have seen collectors competing for an ever smaller supply of early twentieth-century French bindings. They have now begun to seek later bindings with the same intensity. In May 1987 books of the binder Pierre Lucien Martin were sold at auction in Paris. Martin, considered the successor to Bonet, was always sought after, but few would have predicted the actual hammer prices of FF200,000 to FF380,000 ($35,000-75,000). In 1988 the collection of Léon Givaudan was sold at public auction in Paris, once again achieving record prices which confirmed the continued desirability of Dunand lacquer bindings on Schmied books as well as establishing the value of twentieth-century bindings in general.

Pierre Legrain, Rose Adler, and Paul Bonet, together with Dunand (his lacquers on bindings) seem to be the most popular binders, as reflected in prices attained. Their status and collectability are now without question.

Although price itself is not a criterion for measuring artistic merit, it is a guide to assessing current collecting trends. We invite readers to look and judge for themselves. The charm and elegance of Rose Adler, the taut energy of Pierre Legrain, the daring wit of Paul Bonet, the sheer opulence of Dunand, and the refinement of Creuzevault and Cretté, will captivate the reader as they have captivated countless collectors and connoisseurs.

Priscilla Juvelis

INTRODUCTION

AROUND 1880, the craft of bookbinding in France was enjoying one of the intense periods of creativity that had punctuated its two-thousand-year history.[1] For the first millennium, the book-binder had remained a modest artisan, literally a "binder," whose task was to strap protective boards of cedarwood or beechwood around parchment or vellum leaves. For special commissions, such as those for royalty or church dignitaries, these elementary covers were adorned by jewelers with a mixture of translucent enamels, carved ivory plaques, rock crystal cabochons, and gemstones prised from Antique rings.

The spread of literacy in the Middle Ages increased the demand for manuscripts, which were replicated by scribes in monastic and university libraries. In their search for inexpensive materials with which to cover their volumes, binders resorted frequently to animal hides – deer, chamois, pig, cow, or goat – which they tanned and sometimes dyed.[2] The decoration on these leather bindings remained limited for a long time to the light use of stamped or embossed ornaments such as rosettes, ovoli, and palmetteos. More ambitious compositions, consisting of Romanesque or Gothic architectural elements and ecclesiastical subjects on trellised grounds, were reserved for the ceremonial commissions of Church and State. The most lavish, covered in perishable materials such as velvet and silk, and embroidered with armorial crests, have not survived.

Except for the interchange of decorative motifs, the craft of bookbinding remained largely static until the end of the fifteenth century, when French binders introduced the Oriental technique of gold-tooling. Until then, only "blind" ornamentation (tooling without color or gold-leaf), applied with cold or slightly heated punches or stamping wheels (fillets), had been in common use. The gold gave book covers an added splendor and was quickly adopted for use both on its own and in conjunction with traditional blind-tooling. In the same period, the invention of the printing press commercialized book production.

The Renaissance was the richest epoch of French binding, full of innovation and novelty. A new and vibrant decorative style evolved, in which deep green or yellow-orange morocco covers were embellished with an interplay of crisp linear patterns – lozenges, overlapping rectangles, and cross-hatching – and motifs such as rosettes, fleurs-de-lys, arabesques, and scrolls. Some of these were commissioned by Francis I and Cardinal de Lorraine, but the period's most celebrated bibliophile was an amateur collector from Lyons, Jean Grolier, Viscount d'Aguisy (1479-1565),

who after decades of ardent collecting established a library of more than five hundred sumptuous bindings.

The process of inserting small pieces of colored leather into the leather cover – a technique known in the eighteenth century as "compartment" binding, and later generally as "inlays of leather" – was introduced in this era to improve on the existing, and impermanent, process of using paint to create polychromed effects. The marquetry technique required great patience and precision and was used only for major works. A similar, but quicker and cheaper effect was achieved by glueing the pieces of leather to the surface of the binding. The popularity of these multicolored covers continued in the reign of Henri II.

The religious wars and economic chaos that followed the death of Henri II in 1559 slowed the momentum of the *éditions de luxe* patronized by Grolier. Servile copies of Eastern bindings emerged in which production became increasingly mechanized and mediocre. The period's only technical *tour de force*, introduced in the last years of the century, was "fanfare" binding, in which motifs such as bouquets of flowers appeared to shoot from lobed or oval medallions linked by twisting coils and ropes, to give the effect of a firework display.

The seventeenth and eighteenth centuries were dominated by gold fillet-work in which covers were framed in delicate guilloche, dentilled, and tracery borders centering floral medallions with projecting sprays. Designs were sound and symmetrical, though sometimes over-ornate. Many of the designs from this period were credited to Le Gascon, but too large a number have survived for them all to have been executed in a single workshop. Other notable binders at the time included Du Seuil, the Padeloup family, the Le Monniers, and Derome. Towards the end of Louis XIV's reign, excessive gilding fell out of favor and attention turned once again to the leather itself. Its texture and tactility were emphasized and many austere, plain bindings, known as "Jansenist," were produced.

Late in the reign of Louis XIV, various prominent bibliophiles, members of the French aristocracy, fled across the Channel to escape the new political order. Their departure caused a brief wave of Anglomania, in which Parisian binders drew inspiration from the designs of their counterparts in England in an attempt to retain their exiled clientele.

The French revolution brought an abrupt end to the exuberant ornamentations of the Bourbons, as a spartan simplicity became obligatory to erase the memory of the *ancien régime*. Not only were all books bearing the royal coat-of-arms burned by the mobs who sacked the Elysée Palace, but binders themselves fell under suspicion because of their aristocratic patronage. Moreover, the leather that they needed for their craft was in high demand for soldiers' boots.

The next significant change in the development of bookbinding came during the Directoire period, when binders such as Bradel, Meslant, and Tessier adopted the vocabulary of ornament devised by the architects Percier and Fontaine to mark the new political order. Imperial eagles, lyres, sphinxes, palmetteos, sprays of laurel, and canopic jars were employed on bindings in the same manner that they were used to grace the furniture of Georges Jacob and his sons.[3]

During the First Empire, France became a bourgeois society too impoverished to indulge itself in inessential goods. Bookbinding commissions fell and cover designs and execution became increasingly pedestrian. Production of de luxe volumes yielded to large commercial editions, many of which were housed in half-bindings to conserve the supply of leather. Restoration bindings were likewise undistinguished, as binders resorted to a pastiche of traditional ornamental motifs. These were incorporated into a die-stamp with which the cover was block-printed in a single operation, a far cry from the virtuoso hand-tooling of the pre-revolutionary era. The historicism experienced generally in the decorative arts made its way into binding as France's rich artistic heritage was scoured for romantic imagery. The past soon became the only legitimate source of inspiration.

The copyists of the great masters – binders such as Trautz, Thouverin, Simier, Capé, Chambolle, Niedrée, and Duru – dominated the period between 1840 and 1880. All were suspicious of innovation, as were their counterparts in the decorative arts. For these binders, the craft had reached its zenith by the end of the previous century, and there remained only the need to recreate earlier masterpieces with the same, or improved, irreproachable levels of artisanship.[4] This obsession with revivalism reached ludicrous levels, to the point where some bibliophiles commissioned binders to strip original bindings from books and replace them with exact modern copies.[5]

The German-born Georges Trautz emerged as Paris's most eminent Second Empire binder when he succeeded Antoine Bauzonnet in 1851. His atelier was inundated with commissions for copies of history's finest bindings, which he produced in the same morocco leather enhanced with classical gold fillet-work employed by his predecessors. Despite producing admirable work for thirty years, he remained relatively unknown to the general public and even to some of the capital's foremost book collectors until the 1870s, when he was awarded the nation's Legion of Honor, the first ever such distinction to a binder. The sudden unparalleled celebrity which this generated for him forced his return from retirement at the age of sixty.[6]

It is ironic that Trautz's fame, which culminated in a type of worship inconceivable outside France (contemporary critics called it "Trautzmania"), contributed to the movement towards change that began in the 1870s. Trautz's bindings became so prohibitively expensive when available at auction that new collectors were forced to look for alternatives. In 1874 a society was formed entitled Les Amis des Livres, whose members commissioned limited editions of contemporary works in which authors and artists were invited to collaborate with printers and publishers, thereby reviving the tradition of Grolier in the sixteenth century. Collectors preoccupied themselves increasingly with all aspects of de luxe book production, including typography, paper, layout, and illustrations, turning the antiquated craft into a cult. Some of the most prosperous bibliophiles even went to the extreme of commissioning single copies of their favorite volumes, as in one example of Baudelaire's *Fleurs du mal*, which was illustrated by Paul Gallimond with marginal notes by Rodin, for the collector Eugène Roderigues.

This vogue among new collectors bypassed the annual Salons – the forum where traditional-style bindings were displayed, judged, and commissioned – and gradually made itself felt within the field at large. Elite new book clubs were established, such as Les Bibliophiles Contemporains, founded by Octave Uzanne, one of the period's most articulate proponents of the art and craft of the book.[7] Hand in hand with the new bibliomania came a reaction against neoclassical bindings and an obsessive hankering after novelty. Exclusivity, too, became essential, and top collectors began to insist that their bindings be unique. Predictably, this craving for innovation soon tested the limits of taste as binders searched for new materials and forms of decoration with which to please their clients. Trautz died in 1879, just as this movement gathered momentum, and was succeeded by Francisque Cuzin, a less rigid traditionalist. Within twenty years Trautz was forgotten by all but a few, his bindings at auction around 1900 bringing as much below their true value as they had exceeded it during the height of his popularity.

Within the formal binding community – that of the conventional atelier and its clients – only one binder, Amand, appears to have made a serious attempt during the mid-1870s to initiate change.[8] In response to the disenchantment voiced by some critics with the status quo at the Salons, Amand introduced a range of emblems, or symbols, drawn from the book's text, with which he decorated the spine and front cover. Variations included allegorical figures (part of a pictorial style that was usually known as *reliures emblématiques*), and words or phrases (*reliures parlantes*), the latter often within unfurled banners or vignettes set, in turn, in large floral medallions executed in brightly colored inlays of leather. Amand also applied sections of painted Oriental paper and fabrics to the leather on both the cover and endpapers. Because he was largely unknown, and because the vogue in Paris at the time for Trautz's copies remained undiminished, Amand's attempts to break with tradition were not seen as a threat by book collectors and the Juries at the Salons, despite the fact that he quickly developed a small following. Indeed, five years later he was more or less forgotten, and would probably have remained so, had not his cause been taken up by a much more influential binder, Henri Marius-Michel.

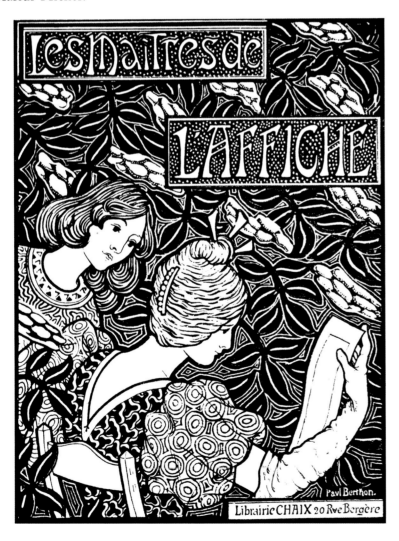

Two examples of 1890s "poster bindings" (*reliures-affiches*): an industrial poster binding designed by Paul Berthon, *c.* 1895 (left), and (above) an Art Nouveau example by Louis Guingot, 1898

Sketch for an ornamental floral binding (*flore ornamentale*), presented by Marius-Michel at the 1878 Exposition Universelle

Marius-Michel, unlike Amand, could not be easily dismissed. He was the son of a noted Parisian binder and had served his apprenticeship with distinction, developing impeccable technical skills and a sensitive, though strictly traditional, use of leather. These attributes, plus his encyclopedic knowledge of the craft, including its history, established him as a formidable figure at the Salons, where, from his debut in 1876, he joined his colleagues in earnest debate on all aspects of binding.

Employed in his father's workshop, where his duties included the reproduction of classical covers enhanced with gold-tooling, Marius-Michel began to formulate and implement his own design philosophies on bindings which he displayed independently at the Salons alongside the atelier's standard repertoire of past master-pieces.

Marius-Michel saw more clearly than most the need for modernization. He was appalled, in particular, by the complacency of his colleagues and the overall stagnation of the craft. The fundamental problem was that binders had always created designs to complement the leather, rather than designs which related to the contents of the book. Although the traditional play of gold- and blind-tooled fillets set off the rich color and tactile qualities of leather covers most effectively, the designs themselves were conceived independently of the text. Marius-Michel believed that a binding's primary function (beyond that of mere protection) was to capture the reader's attention and imagination, and to lure him or her into the text. This would be best achieved by the use of a design which evoked the spirit, or mood, of the work. It was here that Marius-Michel differed from Amand, whose use of emblematic and poster-like designs had overstepped the mark in its lack of subtlety. Amand's designs, depicting figures and events taken from the book, were too realistic and representational, rivaling the illustrations that accompanied the text.[9] What was required was a lighter, more discreet, touch in which the cover design would suggest the text rather than describe it.

Marius-Michel therefore set out to establish a vocabulary of design with which to relate the decoration on his bindings to the subject of the book. He chose the plant in its many forms – flower, petal, leaf, stem, and root – as his principal motif, and developed a style which he termed "La Flore Ornamentale" in which he depicted the plant in a rather formal naturalistic manner. Certain species were considered especially suitable for certain topics. The laurel, for example, was chosen for books on poetry and history; the rose for romances and songs; and the potato flower for stories of the countryside. Other preferred flora were the holly, iris, and mistletoe, all rendered in inlays of leather in a palette of red, blue, and green tones. For small covers, Marius-Michel preferred light compositions of leaves or branches tooled in gold, often within cartouche-formed borders.[10]

In his crusade, Marius-Michel also took issue with the fact that the works of modern authors were bound identically to those of their predecessors. To house the writings of Hugo, Musset, de Vigny, and Balzac in the same covers as those of Racine, Molière, and La Fontaine was incongruous, showing both an appalling lack of creativity and a lack of understanding of the direction in which avant-garde French literature was moving. A modern work required a modern interpretation. The goal, as the critic Henri Beraldi pertinently noted, was "le livre de son temps dans la reliure originale de son temps."[11]

Marius-Michel battled the traditional binding establishment almost single-handedly for five years. To many, his designs were simply shocking, but vital support came in the late 1880s from the writings of Uzanne, Beraldi, Derome, and Gruel, all of whom published works expressing, in varying degrees of urgency, the need for the craft to revitalize itself through experimentation, the cutting of new punches, and a search for inspiration in the book's illustrations.[12] Unfortunately, the initial thrust of Marius-Michel's attacks was weakened by his adoption on occasion of non-traditional forms of book cover decoration, such as incised and *repoussé* modeled panels designed by artists such as Auguste Lepère and Théophile Alexandre Steinlen, which he and other binders incorporated into their front covers. These were viewed by purists as variations on Amand's earlier emblematic and "poster" designs, with the additional criticism that incising and modeling violated the surface texture of leather, so depriving it of its primary allure.[13] But support for Marius-Michel's Flore Ornamentale was eventually won — albeit slowly and begrudgingly — as fellow binders such as Mercier, Gruel, and Lortic began to embrace his philosophies in the early 1880s with varying success. Marius-Michel's cover for Delacroix's *Faust*, published in 1881, received warm praise for its floral ornamentation, and was widely accepted as the turning point in his career. Hailed suddenly as the dean of the new floral esthetic, his former rebelliousness was forgotten. The 1889 International Exposition established him unequivocally as the greatest binder of his time.

The unanimous praise given to Marius-Michel by bookbinding critics at the turn of the century for his role as a revolutionary seems surprising today. Even setting aside the fact that he adhered rigidly to traditional materials and techniques throughout a lengthy career, his floral designs of the 1870s and 1880s appear in retrospect more as diluted precursors of the Art Nouveau esthetic than

as the vehicle which pushed an antiquated medium into the modern age. The floral compositions on his covers do not for the most part fulfill his main claim for them — that they relate specifically to the text of the book they house. Most, in fact, could safely be interchanged from one book to another. In short, although Marius-Michel formulated the new esthetic, he never actually mastered its implementation. The real value of his bindings lies, rather, in their technical virtuosity and majestic weight and size. Every one of his masterpiece bindings, with four or five giant ribs extending equally along its spine and recessed floral panels on its front and back, all exquisitely crafted and housed in a matching cover and slipcase, provides an example of the highest traditions of French artisanship. Yet it is hard to comprehend why they were perceived at the time as such a radical instrument of change.

The truth was that the real revolution in late nineteenth-century French bookbinding was brought about outside Paris by people who were not even bona fide binders. This fact — that change came neither from within the ranks of the binding community itself, nor was born in the nation's capital — contributed in part to the later credit given Marius-Michel by bookbinding historians, who found it difficult to admit that modernization had not come from within.

□ □ □

Due east of Paris in Nancy, the provincial capital of Alsace, a decorative arts movement had sprung up in the 1880s, led by the glassmaker Emile Gallé and a loosely knit group of fellow artists and craftsmen. Under the banner of the Ecole Lorraine d'Art Décoratif (renamed in 1901 the Ecole de Nancy), the group set out to establish a vocabulary of ornament based on Nature — "the fauna and flora of our countryside" — with which to usurp the tired neoclassical motifs dominating the annual Salons. Part of the broader European movement that became known as Art Nouveau, the Nancy school made its debut in Paris at the 1892 Salon of the Société Nationale des Beaux-Arts, held at the Champs de Mars. Included was a comprehensive display of furniture, glassware, ceramics, metalware, fabrics, paintings, and leather, all enhanced with the new style's botanical and entomological motifs. Among the works of tooled and polychromed leather, which included screens, *portières*, furniture upholstery, and box covers, was a selection of bookbindings executed by René Wiener.[14]

Wiener's family owned a stationers in Nancy. He had initially been drawn to binding by two of Nancy's most versatile artists, Victor Prouvé and Camille Martin, who in the 1880s had commissioned him to execute their designs for leather objects. He was not,

René Wiener, designed by **Victor Prouvé**
Album de la mission Moll (author unknown), 1907,
leather with applied and incised copper.
Collection of Félix Marcilhac

René Wiener, designed by **Louis Guingot**
Estampes et livres (Henri Beraldi), 1892, inlays
of leather and blind-tooling.
Courtesy Musée des Arts Décoratifs, Paris

therefore, a professional leatherworker or binder *per se*, but an amateur who through self-application had acquired a high level of technical expertise. Although Prouvé and Martin sometimes executed their own cover designs in leather, it was Wiener who bore the brunt of the outrage heaped on the Nancy group at the Champs de Mars. That he openly solicited designs for almost all of his bindings from such noted contemporary artists as Toulouse Lautrec, Georges de Feure,[15] Paul Elie Ranson, Georges Auriol, Paul Berthon, Eugène Grasset, Léon Rudnicki, and Steinlen, did not lessen the criticism voiced against him by the Parisian bookbinding establishment, or deflect it to the artists themselves. His "poster bindings" (*reliures-affiches*), referred to disparagingly as "Wienerism," achieved great notoriety. Octave Uzanne recorded the reception that awaited Wiener in Paris,

At first the public was surprised and puzzled, while the professional book gilders protested indignantly that this was not real binding at all but a sham, clumsily contrived, and lacking in all the essentials requisite for the proper handling of morocco and the employment of high-class gilding. From their own fastidious point of view these professional workers, imbued with the marvellous principles of the brothers Eve, Le Gascon, Derome, Bozerian, Du Seuil, and Thouverin, were certainly right, for to their eyes a profane, new-fangled, revolutionary style was invading the sacred temple wherein, for centuries past, there had accumulated all the master-pieces of good taste, perfect in technique and execution. . . . Instead, they saw with dismay a strange new style, aiming solely at effect, ignoring finish, caring nought for minute detail, regarding only the general aspect, the *ensemble*. All the old formulae were cast to the winds by the innovators, or else adapted beyond recognition.[16]

Wiener's crime lay primarily in the fact that he was the first to introduce into the bastions of conservatism the new and immensely appealing pictorial style of Art Nouveau that was sweeping all the decorative arts.

Paris's own binders had been continuously debating the same fundamental issue – that of the "binder's binding" versus the "artistic binding" – since Amand had challenged the status quo nearly twenty years earlier. Amand, however, had been almost entirely alone in his promotion of emblematic designs; now, in the early 1890s, a similar pictorial style was attracting a large number of enthusiasts, many of whom were new collectors for whom tradition had no meaning. Binding's old regime felt imperiled, and for good reason. Modernism was encroaching on it, at last, as it had on every other decorative arts discipline.

Unlike the Art Nouveau covers executed by Wiener, no single style was evident in Paris. Charles Meunier, in particular, exasperated the critics by mixing Louis Philippe and Second Empire emblems at random – comedy and satyr masks, plumes, parasols, musical instruments. When he now added to these motifs Art Nouveau cranes, bats, insects, and crescent moons, the charge of bad taste was constantly leveled against him, as it was against others, throughout the 1890s.

The traditionalists, who took as their spokesman Emile-Philippe Mercier, Cuzin's successor as *maître de filets*, asserted that the medium could not be treated as a painter's canvas on which to translate images from the text. Equally, the pure surface of the

Pierre Roche
Loïe (Roger Marx), 1904,
watercolor on parchment

Robert Joly
designed by **Jules Chadet**
c. 1910, leather and gold-tooling

leather should not be violated by incising, tinting, chasing, modeling, or – to many the greatest sin – the insertion of decorative panels. A critic identified the culprits and summarized their misdeeds,

Most of them, Léon Gruel and especially Charles Meunier, for instance, sacrificed everything to make their bindings descriptive, and did it with exaggeration and bad taste. Their bindings likewise sin by an abuse of inlaid metallic and ivory plaques and in particular by the use of embossed and blistered leathers as unpleasant to the touch as they are aggressive to the eye. The materials employed . . . are of a gaudy and showy character which faithfully reflects the taste of the moneyed bourgeoisie.[17]

Other "foreign" materials, introduced with apparent impunity by modernism's protagonists, were equally resisted. The craze for Japonisme, for example, was responsible for many covers in silk and paper printed with simulated leather and wood graining. These began to appear on unique collector bindings, blurring the standard distinction within the craft between industrial and de luxe volumes.

More serious was the revival in popularity of vellum and parchment, by tradition coarse and inferior substitutes for leather. Among the principal users were artist-decorators such as Lepère, L. Rudeaux, Gustave Guétant, Louis Legrand, E. A. Séguy,[18] Pierre Roche, and Steinlen, who responded readily to the paler surfaces of vellum and parchment because of their resemblance to a painter's canvas.[19]

Aligned against the traditionalists were Marius-Michel and a host of binders whose work displayed the entire range of non-conventional styles and techniques: the Flore Ornementale, emblematic and poster bindings, *cartonnage*, and industrial bindings,[20] which their exponents claimed fell under the broad umbrella of "artistic" bindings.

Included in this group were Petrus Ruban, Emile Carayon, Emile Maylander, Romain Raparlier, Joly *fils*, Léon Gruel, and Charles Meunier, all of whom felt that traditionalism was stifling the medium at the very moment that modernism, in the form of Art Nouveau, would revitalize it. They believed, too, that the new style should be perceived differently because it was aiming for a different impact,

We are artists, not trade binders. We are bent on enlarging the scope of a superannuated art, for ever confined within certain narrow limits. We bring new formulae, we aim at expressive ornamentation with boundless possibilities, and with our *artistic* binding we give new life to a craft which hitherto had been bound up in technical restrictions, and had consequently remained very primitive in its forms. We know nothing of the industrial side of the question; but clever craftsmen are not lacking, and when we join forces with them they will devote their practical knowledge, their precision and their finish to the carrying out of our purely esthetic and imaginative work. When they need mechanical assistance in their labors, painters and sculptors and artists generally know where to obtain it, and how to employ it. Why should it not be the same with regard to bookbinding? When we have succeeded in convincing the public, and gradually made clear and established our principles of decorative beauty, we shall find in the binder's workshop all that is required to curb our exuberances.[21]

The progress towards respectability made by artistic bindings at the turn of the century was significantly advanced by Adolphe Giraldon, a gifted painter who applied himself with equal facility to tapestry, fabric, leather, and jewelry design. Giraldon was retained as a binding designer by Henri Couderc, a book collector from Saint-Charmant, who was dissatisfied with the lack of innovation shown by professional binders in their designs for the covers of his recent acquisitions. Giraldon's designs were executed by many of Paris's most noted binders, including Emile-Philippe Mercier, Georges Canape, Affolter, Salvador David, René Kieffer, Charles Lanoë, and Henri Noulhac. The artistic merit of Giraldon's work came to public attention in 1910 when Couderc died and his collection of seventy bindings was auctioned.[22]

At the 1900 Exposition Universelle the jury officially recognized Marius-Michel as the nation's consummate binder by awarding him the Grand Prix and making him a Chevalier of the Legion of Honor.[23] These awards were so much a foregone conclusion that Meunier refused to participate in the Exposition, because, he said, he had no interest in competing for second place. But Meunier did mount an exhibition of his own at the same time at his gallery on the boulevard Malesherbes, which was reviewed by several magazines.[24] Further press coverage of bookbinding was generated in 1902 by the auction in Paris of the Viscount de la Croix-Laval's collection of one hundred de luxe volumes. For the first time, the books in a public sale were catalogued alphabetically by binder, rather than author.[25]

The popularity of artist-decorated books (*livres d'artiste*) grew rapidly between 1900 and 1910 as publishers and private book clubs commissioned prominent modern artists, such as Toulouse Lautrec (watercolors for *Histoires naturelles* by Jules Renard), Pierre Bonnard (lithographs for *Parallèlement* by Verlaine), Raoul Dufy (wood-cuts for *Bestiaire* by Guillaume Apollinaire), and the Beltrand brothers (cameos for *Fioretti* by Maurice Denis), to illustrate their new editions. For the works of such celebrated authors as Colette, Paul Valéry, Oscar Wilde, Edmond Rostrand, Voltaire, and Gustave Flaubert, publishers approached almost every major contemporary artist, including Picasso, Marie Laurencin, Henri Matisse, Georges Rouault, Jean Cocteau, Aristide Maillol, Foujita, Van Dongen, Maurice Utrillo, and Vlaminck, to bring a modern interpretation to both old and new works. Indeed, there does not appear to have been a single painter of merit who did not at some point turn, however briefly, to book illustration. Many works from the era contain a charming bonus, such as a handwritten letter from the author to the book's illustrator, or the original watercolor sketch for the spine, bound into the book's frontmatter.

Publishers and private book club members preoccupied themselves not only with a book's artwork but also with the other elements of its design: typography, layout, quality of paper, and so on.[26] This might have led to the thorny issue of the cover itself, had it not been the French tradition for the bibliophile, rather than the publisher, to determine the design of his binding, which he did in private collaboration with his own binder. So new editions continued to be published, as they had always been, with flimsy paper covers, in anticipation that these would later be replaced by a permanent leather cover of the collector's choice.

In the early years of the century book collecting became more and more popular and attracted many new collectors, often wealthy and distinguished members of the Parisian *haute monde*, such as Baron Robert de Rothschild, Louis Barthou, Descamps-Scrive, de Piolenc and the American ex-patriate, William A. Spencer.[27] New book clubs proliferated, and today the number of clubs flourishing at that time appears astonishing: Les Cents Bibliophiles, Les Amis des Livres, La Société de Bibliophile et d'Editions Littéraires, La Société du Livre Contemporaine, Les Bibliophiles Franco-Suisses, Les XXX de Lyon, Le Cercle Lyonnais du Livre, to name but a few. Some, such as La Compagnie des Bibliophiles de l'Automobile Club de France and La Société des Bibliophiles Médecins, combined seemingly unrelated interests. Editions ranged usually from 25 to 200, depending on the number of members and, for contemporary works, the number of copies reserved for the author and artist-illustrator.

Included in the new wave of collectors were a significant number of women, including the Countesses de Noailles, de Fels, and Greffulhe; Mme Belin; and the American, Mrs. Florence Blumenthal. After World War I, with the emergence of several top caliber women binders in Paris, book clubs set up exclusively for women, such as Les Cents-Une and Les Femmes Bibliophiles, gained greatly in popularity.

The enhanced status of de luxe books after 1900 drew numerous applications to the Ecole Estienne in Paris from teenage boys, many of whom came from families whose fathers and grandfathers had been binders or in book-related crafts.[28] Founded in 1889, the school took its name from Robert Estienne, the 16th-century binder and typographer. A comprehensive programme on the art and craft of the book was (and still is) offered, including typography, type-cutting, decorative composition, linotype, copper engraving, stereotyping, lithography, letterpress, binding, and gilding. Students enrolled at fourteen years of age for a four-year diploma course. Between 1900 and World War I, the teaching staff included several eminent binders and illustrators, including

Henri de Waroquier, Georges Auriol (who created the typeface which bears his name for a 1903 edition of *A Rebours*), and Robert Bonfils. At the time, binding instruction was supervised by Charles Chanat and gilding by Marcel Bailly and his assistant, Pelicier.[29]

◻ ◻ ◻

Bookbinders used the prewar years to greater benefit than their counterparts in other fields of the decorative arts, many of whom were searching for an understated "transitional" style by which to extricate themselves from excesses perpetrated in the name of Art Nouveau.[30] Between 1905 and 1914, decorative bindings became increasingly experimental as the realization overtook binders that they were now constrained less by convention than by good taste. They had, above all, to establish themselves in the eyes of collectors not just as binders, but as *artist*-binders. There was a particular fascination during this period with carved ivory, wood, and bronze plaques, which provided covers with a sculpted and relief dimension. A versatile new generation, most of whom had learned their skills during the 1890s, led the search for new techniques and materials. Among these were René Kieffer, who inserted old roman coins into his covers of *Pétrone et Anacréon* in 1908, and Clément Mère, who interchanged vellum, parchment, and ivory in an eyecatching array of covers. Adolphe Giraldon and Louis Legrand experimented with bronze and enameled copper medallions, while André Mare introduced the first of his translucent and brightly painted vellum covers which were to captivate collectors in the early 1920s. At the same time, artist-illustrators such as Robert Bonfils, George Barbier, André Marty, and Georges Baudin reproduced on parchment the fanciful high-style Art Deco renderings they created for the period's magazines.

World War I brought the binding profession in Paris virtually to a halt. The output of most workshops was severely hampered by the mobilization of both binders and apprentices, many to the trenches in La Marne. There was a disruption not only of the normal flow of work and commissions, but also of the transfer of technical skills from one generation to the next. Even Marius-Michel's studio on the rue Pierre-Nicole was closed intermittently throughout the war (in part due to an illness he suffered at the time). The war and its economy preoccupied most collectors, who set aside the pursuit of their hobbies. Fortunately, two major patrons sustained the craft until it regained its momentum in 1919. One, Henri Vever, had been a bibliophile for many years; the other, Jacques Doucet, a recent convert to modernism, quickly emerged as the craft's most dynamic force and mentor.

Henri Vever (1854–1942) had always been in the avant-garde of new artistic movements. A celebrated jeweler, whose Maison Vever created spectacular gold and enameled *plique-à-jour* jewelry and hair ornaments that rivaled those of René Lalique, the Belle Epoque's master *bijoutier*, Vever was also a writer, historian, and critic whose 3-volume work, *La Bijouterie française au XIXe siècle*, has remained the standard reference on nineteenth-century French jewelry. An enthusiastic book collector for many years — he was at various times an officer of La Société des Cents Bibliophiles, Les Amis des Livres, Le Livre Contemporain and Le Livre Moderne — he retained Jules Chadel, a gifted designer in his employment, to provide modern covers during World War I for the new editions of the works of Proust, Maurois, Valéry, Giraudoux, and Morand that he had recently added to his collection. Volumes illustrated by contemporary artists such as Laurencin, Lhote, Galanis, Laboureur, and Dufy required appropriate modernist covers.[31]

Between 1914 and 1918, Chadel designed approximately one hundred covers for Vever in an engaging pictorial style that is the essence of *fin-de-siècle* Paris. His designs, a mix of flowers, girls, landscapes, and sculpted wood and cameo plaques, have a wistful appeal associated more with the Art Nouveau era than with Art Deco. Various binders executed Chadel's designs, including Joly *fils*, Cretté, Gruel, Canape, Kieffer, Maylander, Lanoë, and Noulhac.[32]

Bookbinding's other great patron at this time, Jacques Doucet, was as eminent a couturier as Vever was a jeweler, rivaled in his profession in the 1890s only by the House of Worth. By 1910, when Paul Poiret eliminated the corset and effectively brought to an end the bustled Victorian look which had popularized Doucet's fashions, Doucet had come to be revered in Paris for his wealth and connoisseurship in art as much as for his clothes. His collection of Old Master paintings, eighteenth-century antiques, and rare books, which he kept in his immense *hôtel particulier* on the rue Spontini, was the envy of the French capital. In 1912, in an abrupt rejection of the past, Doucet divested himself of everything; consigning his furniture and paintings to auction, and donating his library, consecrated to art and its history, to the City of Paris.[33] He moved to 46 avenue du Bois, which he retained the decorator Paul Iribe to furnish in the modern manner. Assisting Iribe was a young trainee decorator, Pierre Legrain.

Doucet welcomed modernism with an ardor equal to that with which he had collected antiques. He later explained his decision as being part of his desire for perpetual rejuvenation, "J'ai été successivement mon grand-père, mon père, mon fils et mon grand-fils."[34] With characteristic energy and meticulousness, he plunged himself into his new venture, overseeing Iribe's selection of contemporary furnishings, which were designed with rich simplicity to complement his newly formed collection of avant-garde canvases by Manet, Cezanne, Van Gogh, Degas, Monet, Seurat, Modigliani, de Chirico, Laurencin, and Picabia. The start of a new library, consisting of literary manuscripts and editions of poetry from the romantics to the present day, was installed in the rue de Noisel. Included were the works of Gide, Claudel, Jammes, Apollinaire, Salmon, Proust, and Doucet's favorite writer, Suarès. Doucet instructed his librarian, Marie Dormoy, to seek out among Paris's top professionals a binder who would bring to these modern works a modern interpretation.[35] It was a fruitless search.

Towards the end of 1916, after two years in the army, Legrain was once again in Paris, and looking for work. Remembering Doucet from the Iribe commission, he sought out the couturier at his home on the avenue du Bois. With typical beneficence, Doucet received the young man and offered him a stipend of 300 francs per month to design maquettes of modern bindings for his new volumes. A makeshift studio was set up in Doucet's dining room, and Legrain began his career as a bookbinding designer, advised in the late afternoons by his patron on Doucet's return from making the round of Paris's contemporary art galleries and ateliers.

It is important to stress that Legrain knew nothing about bookbinding and was unaware of its obsessive traditionalism. Certainly he must have seen the binding displays at the annual Salons, but, trained as a decorator and furniture designer, he probably considered binding an inferior art, or at best, irrelevant. This ignorance of his adopted profession allowed him to make free use of his imagination, to invent a new vocabulary of ornament, and to introduce novel materials expressive of the modern age. Just as the Ecole de Nancy had helped to initiate change in the early 1890s, so Legrain was preparing to propel French bookbinding into the vanguard of modernist design.

With nothing more than his impeccable taste and instinct, and his modest experience as a designer for Iribe, Legrain began to study the ways in which he could transform his adopted medium into a modern art form. Rejecting everything that preceded him — both the floral esthetic of Marius-Michel and the pictorial covers of the artist-binders — he developed a geometric vocabulary of decoration based on the interplay of straight and curved lines. This would symbolize the message of the text: here, Legrain shared Marius-Michel's philosophy that a cover must express the work that it contained, but that it should "evoke not the flower, but its fragrance." Legrain found a new vernacular in the use of abstract geometric motifs, which would prevent the design from becoming outdated (as Art Nouveau's floral compositions already were). The absence of any type of representational decoration would ensure that the design remained pure. As Legrain later explained, "The living forms which each generation sees in its own way age quickly, but the harmony achieved by lines and interweavings never ages. . ."[36] Flowers were now banished, replaced by circles, spirals, arcs, truncated cones, and parallel lines arranged in countless combinations.

Legrain was the first binder fully to perceive a book cover as an integrated whole, rather than as two panels and a spine. Bindings had previously been composed mostly of separate design elements: a front cover, spine, and back. Although the design of the cover and spine were sometimes combined, the three were often perceived individually, and designed as such within their own borders. To Legrain, however, the binding represented a continuous surface on which the design could run from one end to the other, and even, if required, off into infinity. To achieve this, he eliminated the four or five ribs which, by tradition, had adorned the spine, as they impeded the free flow of the design as it moved from front to back.

Perhaps Legrain's greatest contribution to binding was his use of the letters of the title as an integral part of the book's design. Until then, the title had always been positioned on the spine, often in capital letters, so that it could be read when the book was shelved. Although the title was sometimes repeated within a decorative composition on the front cover, the arrangement of the letters remained formal to ensure legibility. In short, the title had never been considered an element of binding design. Legrain saw its potential, realizing that letters of different sizes, colors, and typefaces could be juxtaposed or scrambled together to create dynamic compositions which could even serve as the cover's only decoration. Several later bindings testify to Legrain's brilliance in the use of the title to create a powerful decorative matrix; for example, *Gargantua* (Rabelais), *Lamartine orateur* and *Mirabeau* (Barthou), *Sagesse* (Verlaine), and *Tendres Stocks* (Morand).[37] André Bruel, a Legrain disciple, later provided an eloquent explanation of the reason why a book's title could become a vital decorative tool,

The title of the book plays an almost indispensable part in the decoration of certain bookbindings . . . a large feature, the only feature of certain books which would not have room for any other decorative interpretation than that provided by their title. The author intended the title to be evocative: also the bookbinder can use the title to give it the most appropriate form for the spirit of the book, by a juxtaposition of colors, by linear combination, by carefully chosen and appropriate ornament. Synthesis, the aim is always synthesis! It's the sign of our times.[38]

Legrain's ignorance of traditional bookbinding permitted him a further indulgence: the introduction of "foreign" materials into his cover designs. To leather and calf, for which he had acquired an affinity in his work as a decorator and furniture designer, he added a range of lavish and exotic materials made fashionable at the time by Paris's top cabinetmakers. A novel blend of precious and non-precious materials – gold, palladium, nickel, ivory, wood, mother-of-pearl, and gemstones – were incrusted into the leather, as were skins such as lizard, python, crocodile, and – the era's most sumptuous material – sharkskin. Legrain handled this contrasting mixture of colors and surface textures with extreme delicacy. He treated the surface of the leather itself in a traditional manner, applying gold- and blind-tooled decoration, and inlays of colored leather. The material's tactile properties were exploited to the full.

As with his furniture designs, Legrain left the execution of his bindings to professionals. His first choice for Doucet's commissions was René Kieffer, with whom he worked for four years, after which he collaborated with seven other binders: Canape, David, George Huser, Levitsky, Noulhac, Schroeder, and Stroobants. Legrain supervised production constantly, checking the tones of the leather in juxtaposition and the general harmony of the composition as it progressed.

Legrain's revolution, which had begun in the privacy of Doucet's home in 1917, remained largely undetected for two years, during which time he designed more than 360 modernist covers for his patron's library. The liaison had been an unqualified success, despite the fact that both men were temperamental and strongly committed to their own views.[39] Disagreements had inevitably arisen on the suitability of various designs, which strained the relationship, despite their mutual respect and common goal. At some point during this time, also, Doucet developed a sudden passion for Surrealism and began to pursue this new interest. Perhaps to ease their impending separation and to assist Legrain in developing a new clientele, he exhibited twenty of his bindings at the 1919 Salon of the Société des Artistes Décorateurs.

The 1919 Salons provided the first opportunity for binders to assemble formally after a five-year hiatus, and excitement ran high in anticipation of the opening, which Marius-Michel was expected to dominate with his floral compositions, as he had for a quarter century. Yet it was the exhibit of Legrain's bindings that astonished the binding community, which suddenly understood that it had undergone the most profound renaissance in its history. Even those who could not comprehend the abstractions in Legrain's designs knew instinctively that his covers were of an incontestable originality and refinement. And if the introduction

Pierre Legrain
Petits et Grands Verres (Toye et Adair), 1927, inlays of leather, gold-tooling, and palladium

of strange and exotic materials gave offense, their judicious placement and exemplary execution eased the concern.

In the next years, Legrain drew the patronage of a wide range of eminent bibliophiles, including Louis Barthou, Auguste and Georges Blaizot, Baron R. Gourgaud, Gaston Lévy, Hubert de Monbrison, Baron Robert de Rothschild, René Descamps-Scrive, and the Americans Florence Blumenthal and Daniel Sickles. For his part, Doucet remained an active collector, commissioning modernist covers from Rose Adler, Jeanne Langrand, Geneviève de Léotard, Yvonne Ollivier, Marguerite Bernard, and others, from 1919 until his death in 1929. His collection, bequeathed to the Bibliothèque Sainte-Geneviève in Paris, includes many spectacular 1920s French bindings, especially by Adler, in addition to his large Legrain collection.

It is almost impossible to find a negative contemporary comment on Legrain, even from other binders, who were faced with the dilemma of how to compete with such a radical form of modernism without appearing to imitate it. One critic, however, was sufficiently perplexed, in the face of nearly universal acclaim, to voice his indignation,

Never before has such a consumption of circumferences, of parallel and crossed lines, of barbed wire, of pieces of broken glass, of snail-shaped scrolls, of groups of preposterous letters, of split up and illegible titles, of reptile and snake skins been used to produce something so over-ornate, muddled, and obscure. Lucky Legrain! He can pride himself on having made young girls dream.[40]

What, one wonders, did Marius-Michel think of his young successor? In the early 1920s Marius-Michel remained an imposing presence at the Salons, described by the young Georges Blaizot as proud and genial, with the stature of a ravaged old oak.[41] Stopping in front of a Legrain display, his question to Blaizot underlined the immense, and often irreconcilable, gap between the two generations, "So, young man, you admire that, do you? Decorative art made with a set square, compass, and pen?"[42] In 1924, Auguste and Georges Blaizot took the opportunity to compare how Marius-Michel and Legrain would interpret the same book. On publishing Le Neveu de rameau, unbound copies were sent to both and covers commissioned. Placed side by side the following year, the two volumes showed in the starkest possible manner the distinction between pre- and post-war ideology.[43] Marius-Michel died in 1925, a short time before Legrain was awarded binding's top honors at the Exposition Universelle, providing a neat chronological transfer of sovereignty.[44]

In the early 1920s, perhaps attracted by the fresh image Legrain had given to bookbinding, many women were drawn to the medium. They included both the widows of binders killed in the war and an enterprising generation of young women in search of a fashionable vocation in the arts at a time when many professions in manufacturing were closed to them.[45] As the Ecole Estienne remained exclusively for men, many women enrolled at the city's Ecole et Les Ateliers d'Art Décoratif, a kind of polytechnic college founded in 1894 by the Union Centrale des Arts Décoratifs.[46] Professional book illustrators and artisans were retained to provide expert instruction.

After an inauspicious debut, the School developed gradually, reaching a high level of expertise after World War I. Andrée Langrand, director from 1915, taught the history of art. She was joined two years later by Henri Rapin, a veteran designer and decorative artist, who taught philosophy of art. Binding instruction was offered first by Mme René Sergent, and later by Lapersonne, Choffe, and Geneviève de Léotard. In their second and third year, students were eligible to collaborate on commissions received by the School, which also prepared a selection of bindings for the annual Salon of the Société des Artistes Décorateurs, where examples were purchased by bibliophiles. On completion of the 4-year course, graduates sought employment in the city's main binding workshops, or set out to establish themselves independently. In 1927, increased enrollment forced the School to move to expanded quarters.

Legrain's influence on 1920s binders cannot be overemphasized. Many of the newest generation of binders became immediate disciples, in particular, Rose Adler, who had met Legrain on a visit to Doucet while she was a student at the Ecole des Arts Décoratifs. Adler developed a dynamic personal modern style that was admired both by critics and collectors. The most spectacular of her bindings, many executed for Doucet, are always technically perfect and comparable in artistic excellence to examples by Legrain. Like her idol, she believed fiercely in the need for modern binders to familiarize themselves thoroughly with the contents of the book to be bound, in order to create an accord rather than a direct interpretation.

Adler was the most gifted, but not the only exceptional woman binder. Others adapted to the new grammar of decorative ornament with similar facility. Geneviève de Léotard, Louise-Denise Germain, Germaine Schroeder, Mme Marot-Rodde, Madeleine Gras, and others created startlingly modern abstract compositions. Several women binders showed a preference for calf, which has a smoother, less textured surface than leather. Many of the works of these women have an exquisite delicacy and flow absent from the more formal compositions of their male counterparts. Examination of Marot-Rodde's abstract floral designs, for example, reveals a preciosity and sensuality that male binders did not achieve.

Among the men, two distinct styles evolved after World War I. The first was based on abstract geometric configurations à le Legrain. The proliferation of Legrain-inspired designs, in fact, often made it difficult to determine a binding's authorship. As Georges Cretté noted,

We have renounced the "anecdotal" element. There remain strictly ornamental arrangements. I need not insist here on the prevalence of geometric motifs in modern decoration. . . . Most modern binders make considerable use of them: mosaics of geometrical devices, combinations of lines, dots and circles, are found in the work of almost everyone. One can hardly tell who designed which.[47]

Cretté and Henri Creuzevault evolved into formidable modernists, and René Kieffer, Canape, Emile Maylander, and Charles Lanoë also produced strongly modernist designs.[48] Cretté, Marius-Michel's protégé, allowed a respectable amount of time to elapse before rejecting the master's floral esthetic in favor of his own geometric imagery. Creuzevault was similarly restrained at the start of his career by his traditionalist father, for whom he worked. But both Creuzevault and Cretté developed distinctly personal styles based on crisp linear symmetry and technical excellence.

Pictorial bindings survived in the 1920s due, in large part, to Robert Bonfils and René Kieffer, both of whom employed a light and often fanciful Art Deco graphic style in which subjects were caricatured in silhouette. Bonfils's depiction of young women and vignettes of Parisian night life, in particular, survive as romantic reminders of the Jazz Age. The artist André Mare decorated vellum covers in vivid colors with the full-bodied images which he used as accents on the furnishings that he designed for his decorating firm, Süe et Mare.

To many of today's collectors, the bindings of François-Louis Schmied are the most sensational of the era, particularly when they are enhanced by the lacquerwork of Jean Dunand. Schmied's versatility – he was equally a painter, printer, illustrator, engraver, and binder – has obscured the fact that he was also a highly gifted modernist designer. His linear compositions, executed in a combination of gold- and blind-tooled fillets and inlays of colored leather that utilize the entire surface of the cover, are always exquisitely refined. The panels painted by Schmied to embellish many of his bindings were executed in lacquer and *coquille d'oeuf* by his long-time friend and collaborator, Dunand.

Schmied applied himself increasingly in the 1920s to *éditions de luxe* commissioned by elite book clubs. Several volumes, such as *Paysages méditerranéens, Salammbô, Les Climats, La Création*, and – a perennial favorite – Kipling's *Le Livre de la jungle*, became major projects that could take three or four years to complete.[49] Schmied did not, however, bind all of these himself. Some were published in unbound sheets enclosed in a slipcase to allow the collector to select his own binder. Others were bound by Cretté, or became a collaboration between Schmied, Dunand, and Cretté. On some of these, the decoration – either lacquered panels by Dunand, or watercolors on paper or silk by Schmied – is used on the inside of the cover as doublures, leaving the leather exterior plain, or Jansenist. At a 1927 exhibition at the Arnold Seligmann gallery in New York, several of Schmied's most lavish volumes were listed

Robert Bonfils
doublures, *L'Education sentimentale* (Gustave Flaubert), 1920s, leather and gold-tooling

between $5,000 and $10,000, far beyond the price of any other *livre d'artiste* binding at the time.

After 1925, metal alloys – aluminum, nickel, chromed steel, and palladium (the latter preferred to silver as it did not tarnish) – were introduced increasingly in the search for new, eye-catching effects. There was even a brief discussion on the feasibility of using human skin to bind books of a diabolical or macabre nature, such as biographies of tyrants and chronicles of war.[50] The historian de Crauzat reminded his readers that human skin had fine tanning qualities exploited by eighteenth-century binders, especially in England.

Both Legrain and Doucet died in 1929, closing the chapter on the most dramatic decade in binding's history. Legrain's meteoric career had spanned twelve years, during which time he designed more than 1,300 covers. Due largely to his efforts, book collecting had become wildly popular, so much so that there was a continuous flow of innumerable *éditions de luxe*, produced to satisfy the new market.[51] This was to be sharply reduced in the 1930s, not by any diminution in the popularity of book collecting, but by the New York stock market crash of late 1929, which had serious repercussions in France.

It was a business reversal caused by the deteriorating economy that forced R. Marty, a Parisian book collector, to dispose of his collection at auction in 1930. The sale, held at the Hôtel Drouot,

Paul Bonet
Capitale de la douleur (Paul Eluard), 1934, leather with gold-tooling
and photographic image mounted on board (bound by René Desmules,
gilded by André Jeanne, photography by Chevojon)

and pierced bindings; his first series of covers for Apollinaire's
Calligrammes (1931-32); his first Surrealist photographic
bindings;[55] *irradiantes* (irradiant) bindings (1934-35); and designs
entitled *Les Volutes, Dentelles, L'Ovale* and *Rayonnante* (1937-early
1940s).

Bonet adapted his style readily to the author and work at hand.
Dynamic and delicate designs were interchanged with ease to
achieve the harmony sought between cover and text. As Georges
Blaizot noted,

For Picasso and Apollinaire, he dreamed. For the surrealists, he gave himself
free rein and conjured up internal visions. For Dufy, he smiles and sings softly to
himself. For Segonzac, he is inspired by the bright, clear line of the engraver.
For Laboureur, he wove a bit of lace, or irradiated. For the works of beloved
authors, he seemed to make combinations, to juggle subtly, and the ensemble of
this playfulness was a most surprising synthesis . . . he developed, enriched,
colored with a thousand flames until then unknown.[56]

Bonet retained a team of Paris's most accomplished artisans to
execute these designs, including René Desmules, Clovis Lagadec,
Henri Lapersonne, Maurice Trinckvel, and Charles Vermuyse
(binders); Roger Arnoult, Roger Cochet, Charles Collet, and

included fifty-two bindings by a relatively unknown designer,
Paul Bonet.[52] Book connoisseurs realized that a new genius had
arisen, who, a year after Legrain's death, had inherited his mantle.

Born in 1889, an exact contemporary of Legrain, Bonet began
to bind books as a hobby in 1920. Five years later examples of his
designs, executed by instructors at the Ecole Estienne, were included in the exposition L'Art du Livre Français and again, later in
the year, at the Salon d'Automne. This set the stage for him to
pursue the craft professionally. Between 1925 and 1929 he developed a personal style strongly influenced by Legrain, to whom
he fully acknowledged his debt.[53] In his first designs a cautious
linear style is executed in a strictly traditional manner with blind-
and gold-tooled fillets interspersed with inlays of leather.

The public responded with indifference to Bonet's first displays,
but between 1927 and 1929 Marty became his principal patron.
At the 1928 Salon, Bonet also gained the confidence of Carlos R.
Scherrer, a businessman from Buenos Aires, who spent part of each
year in his Paris office. An ardent collector of bindings, rather than
of books *per se*, Scherrer quickly emerged as Bonet's main client,
acquiring most of his major works in the 1930s.[54]

By 1931, Bonet was firmly established, exhibiting in Brussels
and catering to an expanding clientele. In the same year he created
the first of his major bindings, which were bound by Ferdinand
Giraldon and gold-tooled by André Jeanne. New techniques and
designs quickly followed as Bonet introduced sculpted, all-metal,

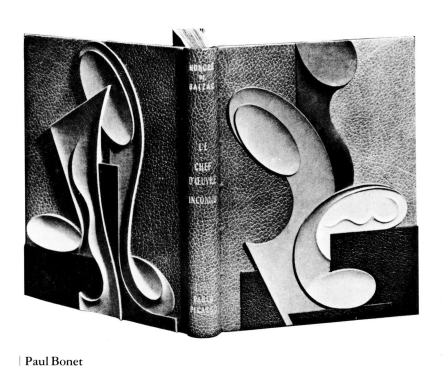

Paul Bonet
Le Chef-d'oeuvre inconnu (Honoré de Balzac), 1944, inlays of leather with sculpted
detailing and gold-tooling (bound by Ferdinand Giraldon, gilded by
André Jeanne)

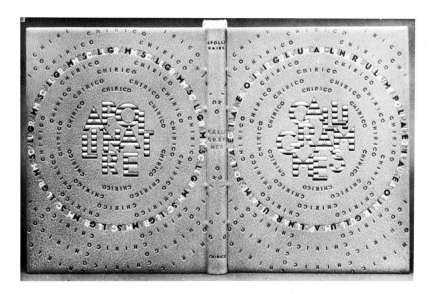

Above left and right
Paul Bonet
Calligrammes (Guillaume Apollinaire), 1943, inlays of leather

Raymond Mondange (gilders); and Egouville, Pierre Boit, and Gustave Miklos (metalworkers and jewelers). The fact that he never executed his own designs drew a criticism from Cretté which todays seems mean-spirited. In a reference to Bonet, Cretté noted, "For me, the rôle of the technician is as great as that of the artist and I never devise a bookbinding design without taking an active part in its execution."[57]

Evident in all Bonet's bindings is the technical virtuosity which he demanded of his artisans. His relief designs, for example, consisted of pieces of wood carved with mathematical precision and fitted together in a delicate puzzle. The leather then had to be fitted tightly over this matrix before gold-tooled lettering and ornamentation were added to produce a work of extraordinary intellectual and technical force. His metal covers, such as several for *Bubu de Montparnasse*, often included articulated joints which required of their makers considerable knowledge of metal technology.[58]

Bonet's ability to reinterpret the same book title seemingly ad infinitum was perhaps his most impressive achievement. Examination of his cover designs for *Calligrammes* (40, 41), *Le Chef-d'oeuvre inconnu, Tartarin de Tarascon* (56), and *Le Bestiaire*, reveals his inexhaustible creativity.[59] As Blaizot noted,

He stood before the complete work each time as though it were a newly discovered book; he studied it anew, and each time he found in the work he had already bound, five, ten, fifteen times, a new emotion, a virgin idea, an unused decorative commentary. His is an extraordinary, magnificent fanaticism. Only a passionately enthusiastic book-binder and book designer could conceive of and reach that absolute. Only an artist so richly endowed with creative imagination could treat over and over again, without fatigue or boredom or repetition, the same problems constantly reappearing. . . . When Bonet refused (as he often did) to repeat a binding, he was no doubt refusing the easy solution, but he was also scorning an order the execution of which might have been immediate (or almost so), economical, or advantageous. This indifference to material gain, this disinterest in money is rare enough to warrant, in passing, deserved praise.[60]

More even than Legrain, Bonet elevated letters to the rank of an individual art form. His compositions for *Calligrammes* and *Champfleury*, in particular, provide endless variations on a common theme in their interplay of single and repeating images.

Although Bonet dominated the 1930s, other binders produced admirable and distinctive work. Creuzevault and Cretté, both of whom in the 1920s had been careful not to adopt a Legrain-like ornamental style, developed a repertoire of formal neoclassical designs in which repeating images, often incorporating recessed or relief panels, dominated. Adler created animated designs with helixes and overlapping ovals in combinations that imparted a feeling of airiness and movement.[61] René Kieffer likewise created handsome symmetrical compositions composed of fillet-work and inlays of leather. His son, Michel, preferred a more austere format embellished, on occasion, with cabochons. De Léotard continued to turn out the fresh linear designs that characterized her 1920s covers. Semet and Plumelle, and Jacques Anthoine-Legrain, Legrain's stepson, preferred a sinuous linear style of ornament.

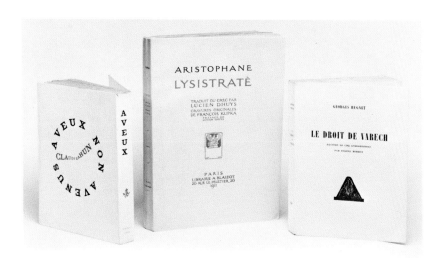

A group of books published in France before World War II, all with
conventional flimsy paper covers

The economic recession of 1934-35 slowed commissions dramatically, causing hardship to several binders, including Bonet, who had to resort in his free time to his old profession of modeling fashion mannequins, and Schmied, who was forced to close his atelier. The earlier saturation of the *livre de luxe* market, sustained by years of speculative investment, took its toll as hundreds of major bindings were forced on the market in quick succession.[62] Several binders, Schmied included, committed themselves to protecting the artistic and monetary value of their creations by buying them back at auction, thereby aggravating their own financial problems.

The market showed a new buoyancy by 1937. That year participation was high at the binding display of the Exposition Universelle.[63] New bibliophiles emerged at the Salons, spurring the younger generation of binders. The American critic Edith Diehl said of the revival, which was virtually extinguished by the advent of hostilities in 1939,

On the eve of World War II there was in France an amazing vivacity, a veritable *vita nuova* among the rank and file of bookbinders, and it was evident that the talent for creating styles, so singularly peculiar to the French, could not fail to make itself manifest in a new art of book decoration. In no other country at that time was there to be found such creative art in the decoration of books as in France, and it made one feel that de Laborde's statement "La reliure est un art tout française" was an excusable exaggeration.[64]

Only the traditionalist binderies found difficulty in procuring business. The Mercier atelier, for example, reduced now to a tiny workroom, complained that it had not received a commission in three years, while the Gruel workshop, which admitted that it had no aptitude whatever for the modern style, continued to adorn its modest output of bindings with the same mix of seventeenth- and eighteenth-century punches employed by Léon Gruel before 1900.

World War II had a destabilizing effect on bookbinding.[65] In its aftermath, binders recongregated at the Salons to make a fresh beginning. Among those who had survived the six-year conflict were Bonet, Cretté, Creuzevault, Adler, Anthoine-Legrain, Moncey, and de Coster and Dumas, who were joined by Henri Mercher, Georges Leroux, Monique Mathieu, and Roger Devauchelle. The originality of Pierre-Lucien Martin, another newcomer, generated a similar excitement to that surrounding Bonet's emergence in 1930. Designs became less structured and symmetrical, more animated and graphic, moving closer to the field of painting. There was also a more flexible attitude to materials. Although leather remained supreme, it was combined increasingly with metals, plastic, and plexiglass.

1 | **Pierre Legrain**
sketch for the cover of *Daphnis et Chloé* (Longus), 1920s, watercolor and ink on paper with pencil notations.
Spencer Collection, New York Public Library

Rose Adler

1890-1959

Adler's work has often been compared to that of Pierre Legrain. Similarities can be seen in both the range of materials and in the designs of the bindings she created in the early 1920s for her chief patron, the couturier Jacques Doucet. Like Legrain she favored nonfigurative geometric compositions executed in brilliant inlays of colored leather embellished with incrustations of exotic materials. She also made full use of the letters of the title by combining them in complex overlapping configurations.

Her later work, after Doucet's death, was more subtle, refined, and simplified and by the late 1930s she had identified herself fully with the avant-garde movement in the decorative arts.

2 | **Rose Adler**
Poèmes (Paul Morand), 1920s, inlays of calf, palladium, and sapphire cabochon.
Collection Bibliothèque Sainte-Geneviève, Paris

Opposite
3, 4 | **Rose Adler**
Ouvert la Nuit and *Fermé la Nuit* (Paul Morand), 1920s, inlays of calf with gold- and silver-tooling.
Collection Bibliothèque Sainte-Geneviève, Paris

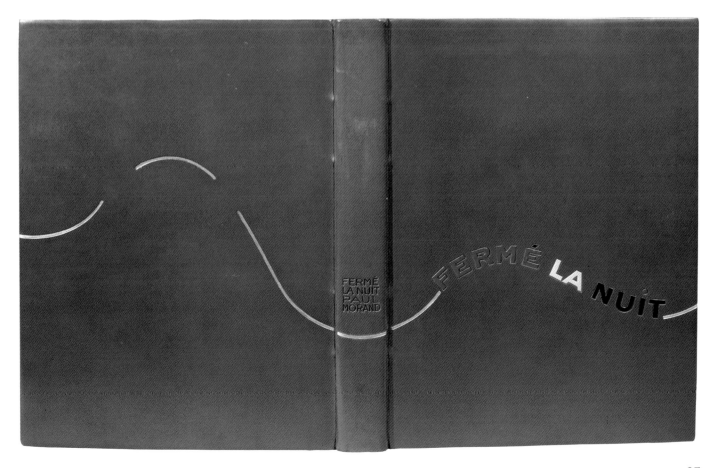

Opposite

5 | **Rose Adler**
Chéri (Colette), 1925, inlays of leather with gold-tooling.
Collection Virginia Museum of Fine Arts

7 | **Rose Adler**
Le Nez de Cléopâtre (Georges Gabory), 1922, inlays of leather with gold- and silver-tooling.
Photograph courtesy of the Sutton Place Foundation

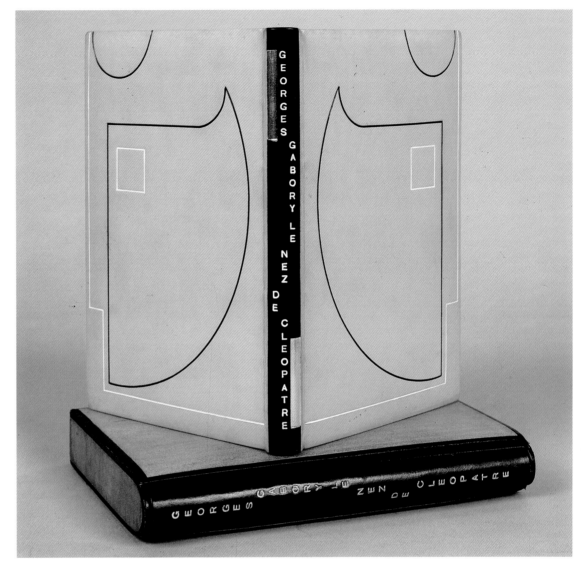

6 | **Rose Adler**
Tableau de la boxe (Tristan Bernard), 1922, inlays of leather with gold-tooling.
Spencer Collection, New York Public Library

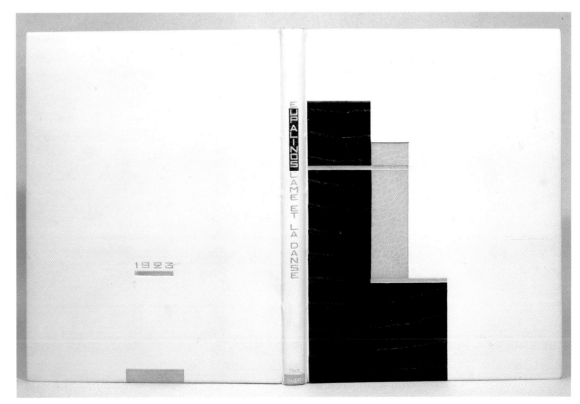

8 | **Rose Adler**
Eupalinos l'âme et la danse (Paul Valéry), 1923, inlays of calf and crocodile, with gold-tooling.
Collection Bibliothèque Sainte-Geneviève, Paris

29

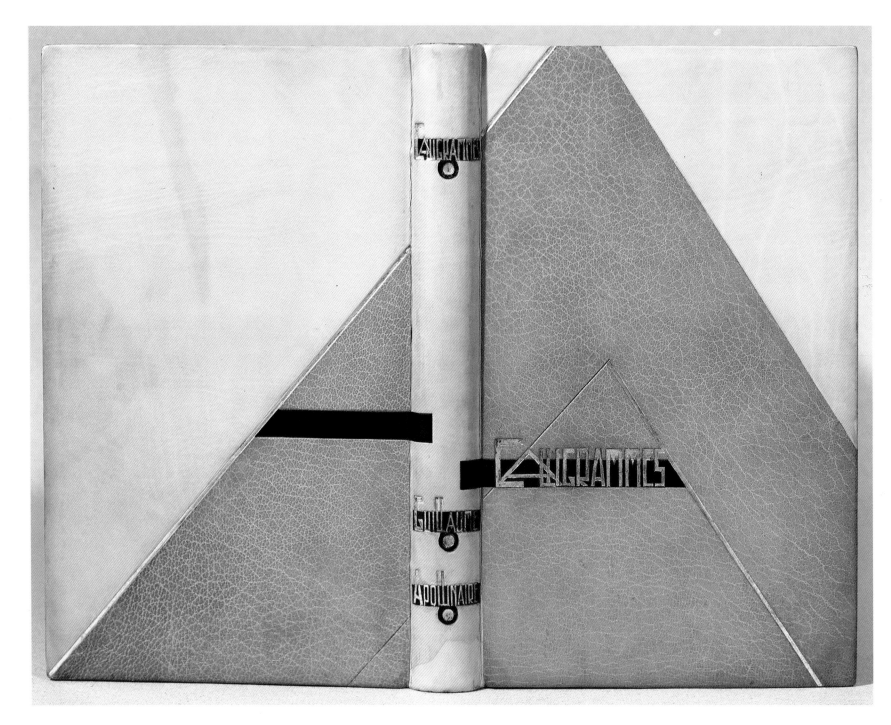

9 | **Rose Adler**
Calligrammes (Guillaume Apollinaire),
1924, calf and inlays of leather, with silver-
tooling.
Collection Bibliothèque Sainte-Geneviève, Paris

10 | **Rose Adler**
L'Envers du music hall (Colette), 1929, inlays of leather and calf with gold- and silver-tooling.
Collection Bibliothèque Sainte-Geneviève, Paris

11 | **Rose Adler**
Aux Fêtes de Kapurthala (Francis de Croisset), 1930, inlays of leather and gold-tooling, with inlaid cabochon.
Collection Bibliothèque Sainte-Geneviève, Paris

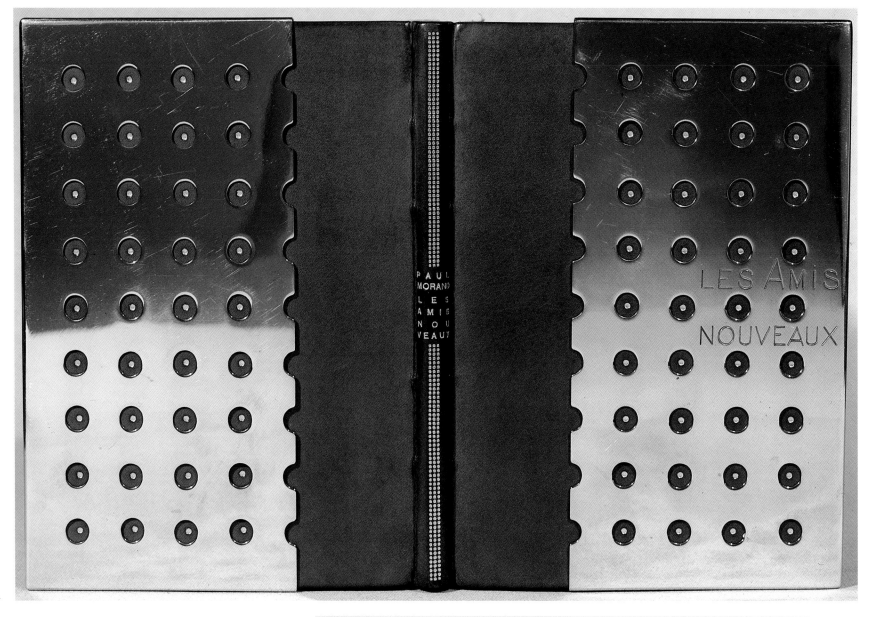

12 | Rose Adler
Les Amis nouveaux (Paul Morand), 1927,
leather, gold-tooling, and pierced
duralumin panels.
Collection Bibliothèque Sainte-Geneviève, Paris

13 | Rose Adler
Suzanne et le Pacifique (Jean Giraudoux),
1930, inlays of calf with gold- and silver-
tooling.
Collection Bibliothèque Sainte-Geneviève, Paris

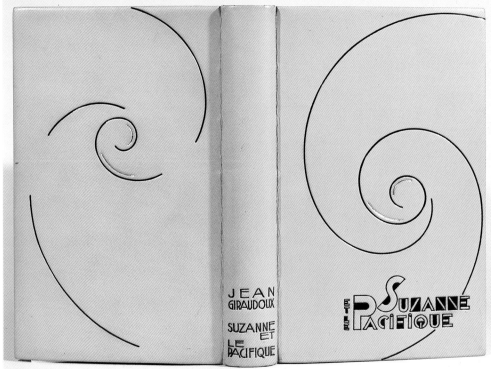

René Aussourd

?-1968

Aussourd learned bookbinding from his uncle, Charles Meunier, and worked as a gilder for Chambolle-Duru before establishing his own studio in 1912. His early bindings were mostly classical, often incorporating Greek key motifs and ivy leaves, but later work became more emblematic and pictorial.

15 | **René Aussourd**
Les Ballades françaises (Paul Fort), 1927, inlays of leather, palladium, and blind-tooling.
Courtesy of Christie's, Geneva

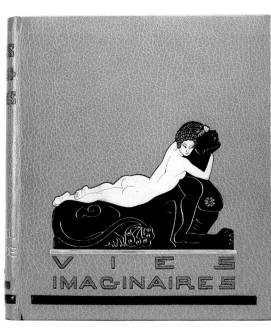

14 | **René Aussourd**
Vies imaginaires (Marcel Schwob), 1929, inlays of leather with gold-tooling.
Photograph courtesy of the Sutton Place Foundation

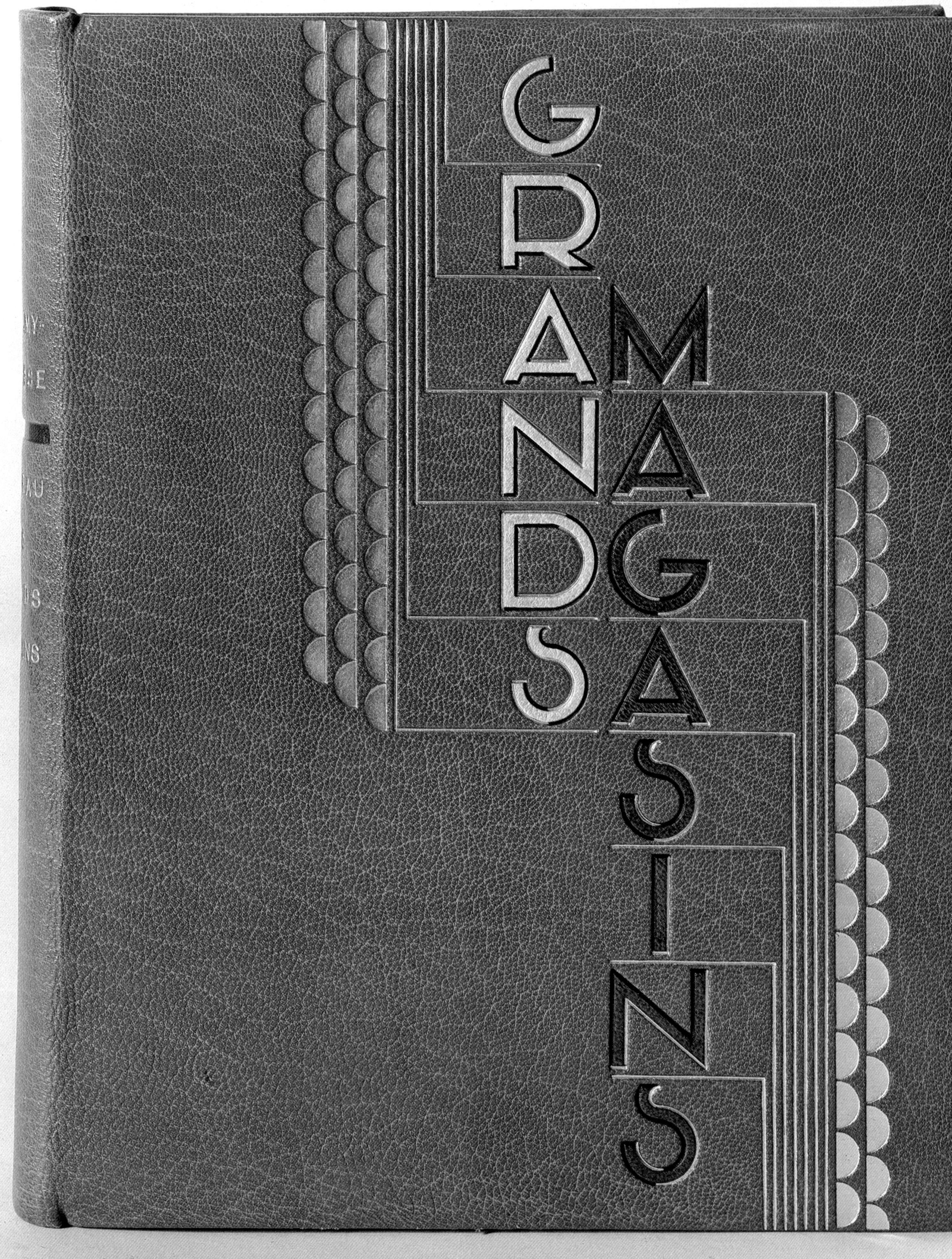
GRANDS MAGASINS

Charles Benoît

Opposite
16 | **Charles Benoît**
Tableau des grands magasins (J. Valmy-Baysse), 1925, inlays of leather with gold-tooling and palladium

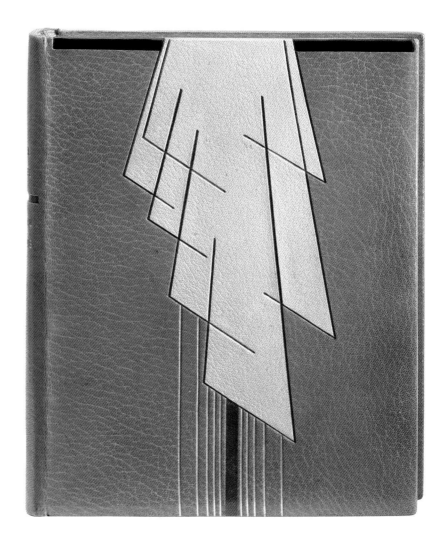

18 | **Charles Benoît**
Tableau du palais (Pierre Lowell), 1928, inlays of leather with palladium.
Courtesy of Christie's, Geneva

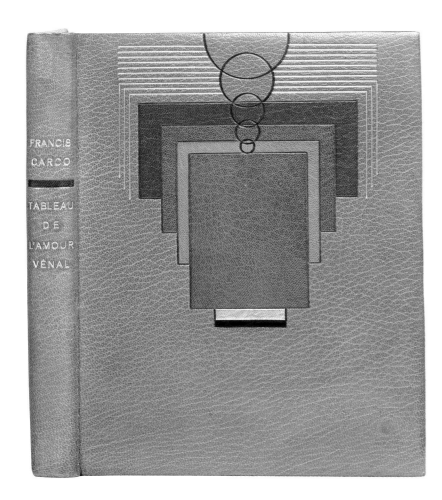

17 | **Charles Benoît**
Tableau de l'amour vénal (Francis Carco), 1924, inlays of leather with gold-tooling.
Courtesy of Christie's, Geneva

HENRI BLANCHETIÈRE

1881-1933

In his early work Blanchetière allied himself to Marius-Michel in his pursuit of a modern binding style inspired by Nature. His rather cautious blend of Art Nouveau flowers interspersed with curved gold fillets gave way after World War I to less traditional covers consisting of symmetrical linear patterns.

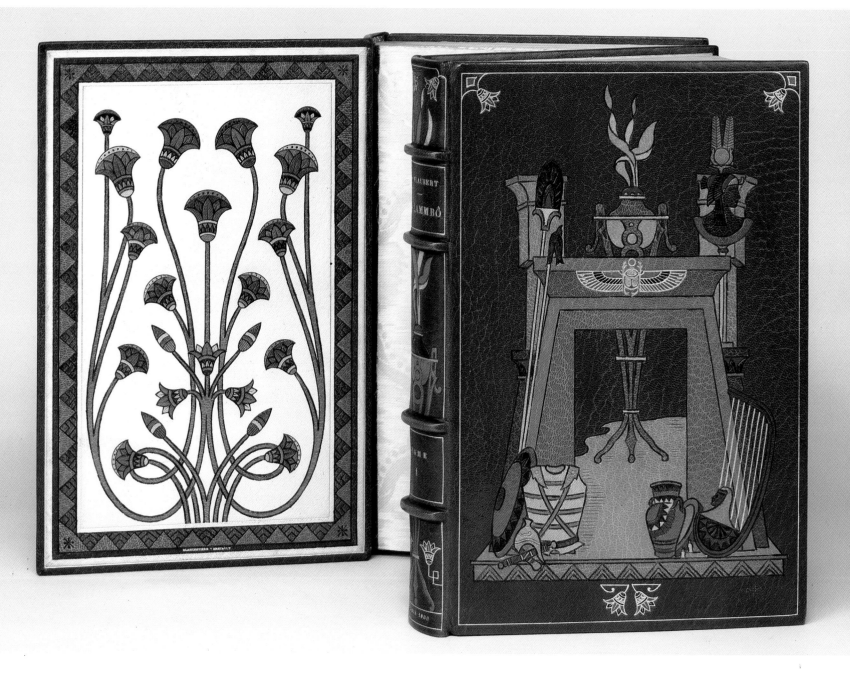

19 | **Henri Blanchetière**
designed by **Joseph Brétault**
Salammbô (Gustave Flaubert), 2 vols., 1900,
inlays of leather with gold-tooling
*Photograph courtesy of the Sutton Place
Foundation*

Paul Bonet

1889-1971

Bonet was in his mid-thirties before he made his debut – in 1926 – as a professional bookbinder. Four years later he was acclaimed as Legrain's successor. Although Bonet readily acknowledged his debt to Legrain, evident in his linear designs of the 1920s, his daring, novel work of the 1930s, in which new techniques and styles followed one another in rapid succession, established him as a master in his own right.

His preoccupation with the letters in a book's title as the principal elements of its design was one of his major contributions to the field.

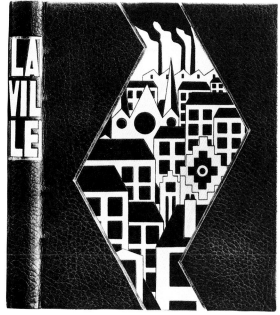

20 | Paul Bonet
La Petite Ville (Yan Bernard Dyl), 1927, inlays of leather (bound by Maurice Trinckvel).
Collection Ralph Esmerian

21 | Paul Bonet
La Ville (Frans Masereel), 1926, inlays of leather and gold-tooling (bound by Maurice Trinckvel, gilded by Marcel Bailly)

27 | **Paul Bonet**
Deux Contes (*Two Tales*: Oscar Wilde), 1928,
leather with lacquer and eggshell panels
(bound by Maurice Trinckvel, lacquer by
Darny-Bui).
Collection Félix Marcilhac

28 | **Paul Bonet**
doublure, *Rue Pigalle* (Francis Carco), 1928,
inlays of leather (bound by Maurice
Trinckvel, gilded by Jules-Henri Fache).
*Collection Lilly Library, Indiana State
University*

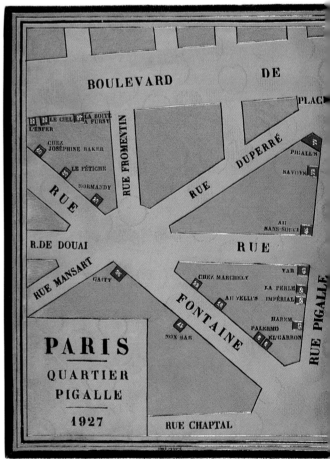

29 | **Paul Bonet**
Mort de quelqu'un (Jules Romains), 1928, inlays of leather, blind-tooling, and palladium (bound by Maurice Trinckvel, gilded by Marcel Bailly).
Collection Lilly Library, Indiana State University

30 | **Paul Bonet**
L'Equipe (Francis Carco), 1929, inlays of leather, palladium, and blind-tooling.
Courtesy of Christie's, Geneva

Above and opposite top

31, 32 | **Paul Bonet**
Les Frères Karamazov (*The Brothers Karamazov*: Fyodor Dostoevsky), 1929, 3 vols., inlays of leather, gold-tooling, and palladium.
Photograph courtesy of the Sutton Place Foundation

33 | **Paul Bonet**
La Ville (Frans Masereel), 1929, inlays of leather, with silver-, gold-, and blind-tooling (bound by Maurice Trinckvel, gold- and silver-tooling by Marcel Bailly).
Photograph courtesy of the Sutton Place Foundation

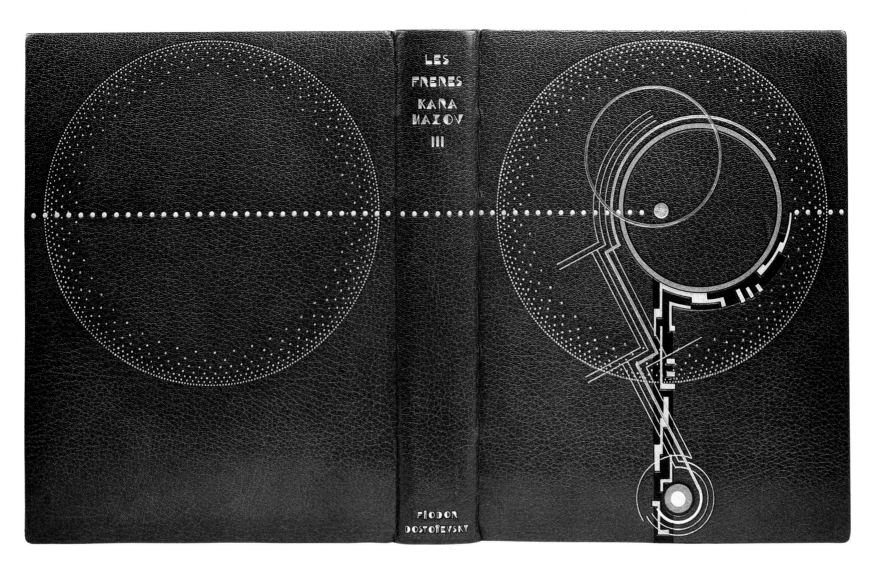

34 | Paul Bonet
Les Ballades françaises (Paul Fort), 1929, inlays of leather, gold-tooling, palladium, and pierced and lacquered duralumin (bound by Maurice Trinckvel, gilded by Jules-Henri Fache, lacquered by Darny-Bui).
Collection Lilly Library, Indiana State University

43

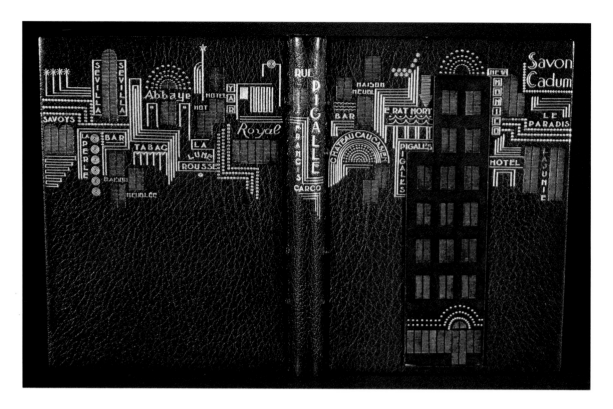

35 | **Paul Bonet**
Rue Pigalle (Francis Carco), 1929, inlays of
leather with gold-tooling (bound by Maurice
Trinckvel, gilded by Jules-Henri Fache).
*Collection Lilly Library, Indiana State
University*

36 | **Paul Bonet**
Histoire charmante de l'adolescente sucre d'amour
(Dr. Joseph-Charles Mardrus), 1929, inlays
of leather, gold-tooling, and palladium,
with circular lacquered eggshell panels.
Courtesy of Christie's, Geneva

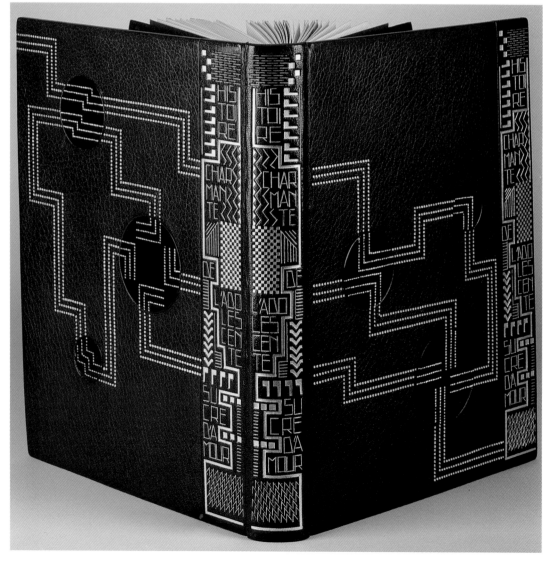

37 | **Paul Bonet**
Couleurs (Remy de Gourmont), 1930, inlays
of leather, gold-tooling, and palladium.
*Photograph courtesy of the Sutton Place
Foundation*

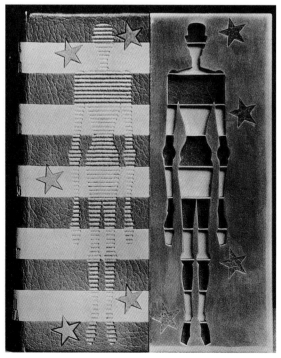

38 | **Paul Bonet**
Les Campagnes hallucinées and *Les Villes tentaculaires* (Emile Verhaeren), 2 vols., *c.* 1930, inlays of leather with gold-tooling. *Courtesy of Christie's, Geneva*

39 | **Paul Bonet**
Colloque entre Monos et Una (*The Colloquy of Monos and Una*: Edgar Allan Poe), 1931, inlays of leather, gold-tooling, and duralumin (bound by Ferdinand Giraldon, gilded by André Jeanne, metalwork by Pierre Boit)

Opposite top left

40 | **Paul Bonet**
Calligrammes (Guillaume Apollinaire), 1930, inlays of leather, palladium, and blind-tooling

Opposite top right

41 | **Paul Bonet**
Calligrammes (Guillaume Apollinaire), 1932, inlays of leather and enameled duralumin

Opposite below

42 | **Paul Bonet**
L'Assassinat considéré comme un des beaux-arts (*On Murder Considered As One of the Fine Arts*: Thomas de Quincey), 1931, inlays of leather, aluminum, and gold-tooling (bound by Gorce, finished by Sellier). *Photograph courtesy of the Sutton Place Foundation*

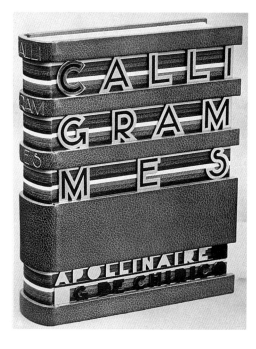

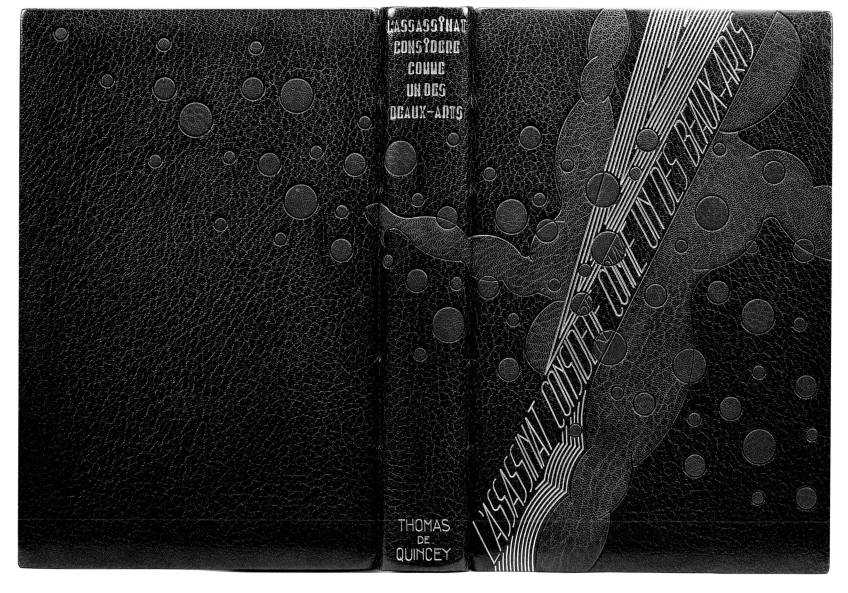

48

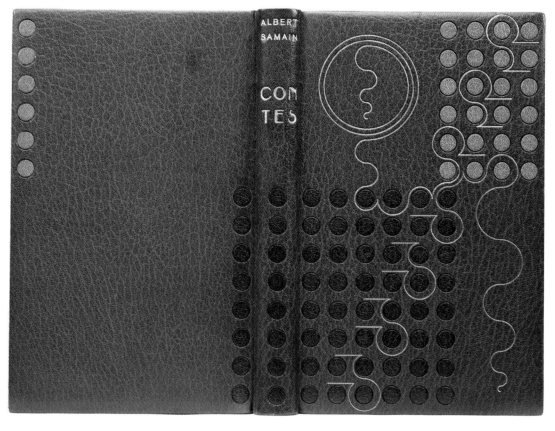

43 | **Paul Bonet**
Lettres Persanes (Montesquieu), 1932,
leather, gold-tooling, and nickeled
duralumin (bound by Ferdinand Giraldon,
gilded by André Jeanne, metalwork by
Pierre Boit).
Courtesy of Christie's, Geneva

45 | **Paul Bonet**
Contes (Albert Samain), 1932, inlays of
leather, gold-tooling, and aluminum (bound
by René Desmules, gilded by André Jeanne).
*Photograph courtesy of the Sutton Place
Foundation*

44 | **Paul Bonet**
Journal d'un fou (*Diary of a Madman*: Nikolai
Gogol), 1932, inlays of leather with gold-
tooling.
Courtesy of Christie's, Geneva

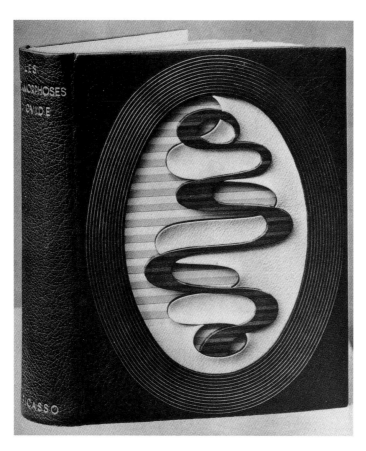

49 | **Paul Bonet**
Les Metamorphoses (Ovid), 1937, inlays of leather with sculpted detailing and gold-tooling

50 | **Paul Bonet**
Discours des misères de ce temps (Pierre de Ronsard), 1938, inlays of leather with gold-tooling.
Collection Humanities Research Center, University of Texas, Austin

Opposite
51 | **Paul Bonet**
Les Climats (Comtesse de Noailles), 1938, leather with gold-tooling.
Courtesy of Christie's, Geneva

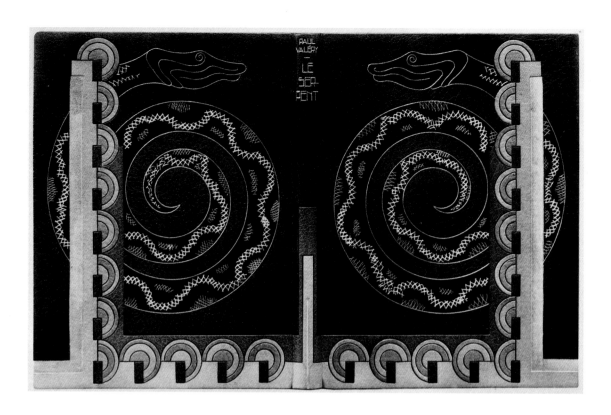

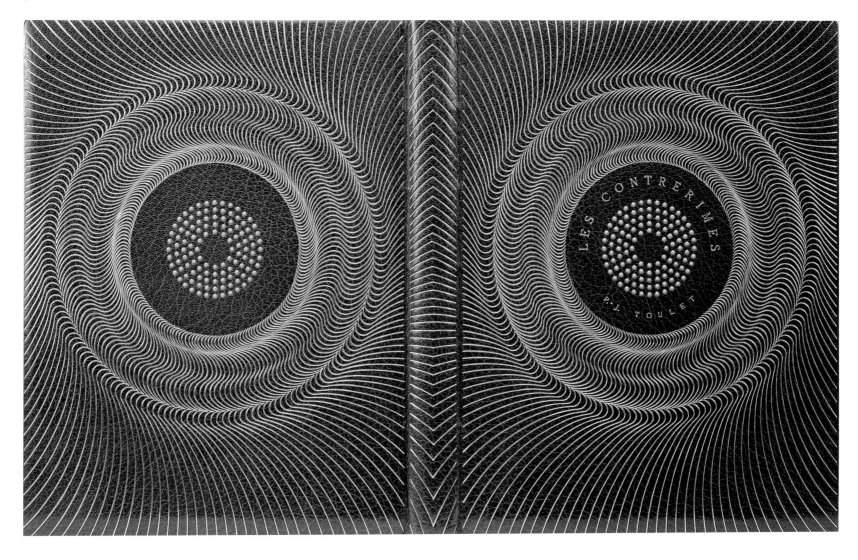

55 | **Paul Bonet**
Héroïdes (Ovid, translation by Marcel Prévost), 1941, leather with gold-tooling and palladium (bound by Clovis Lagadec, gilded by André Jeanne)

56 | **Paul Bonet**
Tartarin de Tarascon (Alphonse Daudet), 1942, pierced leather, with gold- and blind-tooling.
Photograph courtesy of the Sutton Place Foundation

Opposite
57 | **Paul Bonet**
La Treille Muscate (Colette), 1942, inlays of leather with gold-tooling.
Courtesy of Christie's, Geneva

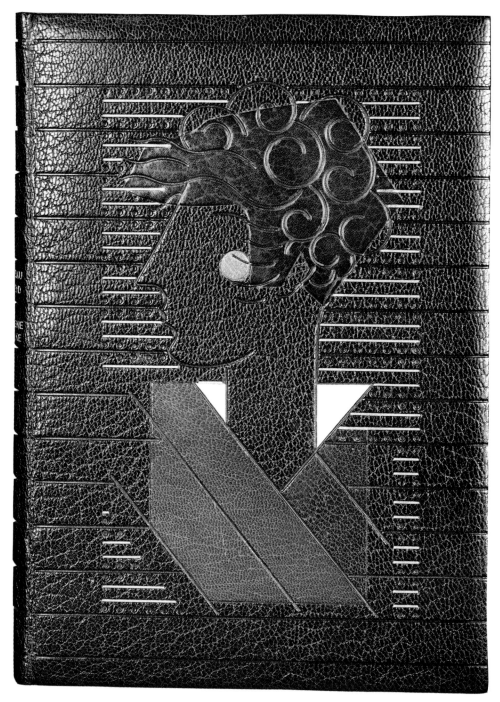

58 │ **Robert Bonfils**
Eugénie Grandet (Honoré de Balzac), 1920s,
inlays of leather with gold-tooling.
Collection Félix Marcilhac

59 │ **Robert Bonfils**
La Châtelaine de Vergy, 1920s, inlays of
leather with gold-tooling

60 │ **Robert Bonfils**
Le Chariot d'or (Albert Samain), 1920s,
inlays of leather

Robert Bonfils

1886-1971

Bonfils is known not only for his engaging bindings but also for his work as a painter, illustrator, engraver, and interior decorator. In 1919 he succeeded Henri de Waroquier as professor of design at the Ecole Estienne, passing to his students his belief that the design of a binding should merely suggest a book's contents, rather than define them. Bonfils's own covers were in leather or vellum (he preferred flat surfaces) and were applied with an enchanting Art Deco imagery of fashionable women, tribal African masks, musical instruments, etc., in a light and simple linear graphic style. *See also 69.*

61 | **Robert Bonfils**
Eugénie Grandet (Honoré de Balzac), 1920s, inlays of leather with gold-tooling.
Collection Félix Marcilhac

André Bruel

1895-?

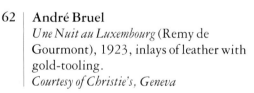

62 | **André Bruel**
Une Nuit au Luxembourg (Remy de
Gourmont), 1923, inlays of leather with
gold-tooling.
Courtesy of Christie's, Geneva

63 | **André Bruel**
La Leçon d'amour dans un parc (René
Boylesve), 1933, inlays of leather and calf,
with gold-tooling.
Courtesy of Christie's, Geneva

Bruel was the son-in-law of an Angers book
gilder, Légal, for whom he worked before
establishing his own bookbinding atelier in
1919. In the 1920s he exhibited his works at
the annual Paris Salons and was judged to be the
only provincial binder of note.

Bruel's designs were safe and harmonious,
composed of large, simple images executed in
the traditional materials – morocco or calf.
Additional detailing and color accents were
introduced by the use of inlays of leather in
preference to "foreign" incrustations of metal or
stones.

GEORGES CANAPE

1864-1940

Canape succeeded his father, J. Canape, in 1894. Like many of his contemporaries, he soon adopted a restrained version of the Art Nouveau esthetic popularized by Marius-Michel. Canape's own compositions often consisted of floral emblems within rather formal borders. At the annual Paris Salons, he offered the new style, blended with classical revival bindings, all executed with superb technical precision.

Canape depended on others, including François-Louis Schmied, Paul Jouve, and Robert Bonfils, to provide the designs for his most important bindings. During World War I he executed several of Legrain's covers for Doucet.

64 | **Georges Canape,** the panel painted by **Louis Legrand**
doublure, *Cours de danse – fin de siècle* (Louis Legrand), 1892, leather with gold-tooling, inlaid with a watercolor on silk panel.
Photograph courtesy of the Sutton Place Foundation

65 | **Georges Canape**
Les Erinnyes (Leconte de Lisle), 1909, inlays of leather with gold-tooling, inset with an engraved copper plate (used for one of the illustrations in the book).
Photograph courtesy of the Sutton Place Foundation

Overleaf

66 | **Canape & Corriez,** the panel designed by **François-Louis Schmied** and executed by **Jean Dunand**
Les Climats (Comtesse de Noailles), 1924, leather with gold-tooling, with lacquered eggshell panel.
Courtesy of Christie's, Geneva

67 | **Canape & Corriez**
Les Climats (Comtesse de Noailles), 1924, inlays of leather with gold-tooling.
Courtesy of Christie's, Geneva

68 | **Georges Canape**, designed by **Maurice Denis**
Fioretti (*The Little Flowers of St. Francis*: St. Francis of Assisi), 1919, inlays of leather

69 | **Georges Canape**, designed by **Robert Bonfils**
Le Chariot d'or (Albert Samain), 1920s, inlays of leather

70 | **Georges Canape**, the panel designed and executed by **Paul Jouve**
Le Livre de la jungle (*The Jungle Book*: Rudyard Kipling), 1920s

Emile Carayon

1843-1909

Carayon built his reputation on *cartonnage* (case binding), considered at the time an inferior and cheap form of binding and mainly confined to publishers' editions. In Carayon's hands a rather banal process became attractive and interesting. He used morocco, calf, vellum, brocade, and even simple paper, enhanced with romantic watercolor or oil sketches by the period's leading artists. Carayon's work reached the peak of its popularity at the 1894 Exposition du Livre, where his white vellum covers, decorated with delicate flower sprays, were particularly prized.

71 | **Emile Carayon**, the panel designed and executed by **Gustave Guétant**
Ballades dans Paris (Paul Eudel, Gausseron, and Adolphe Tette), 1906, inlays of leather with gold-tooling, and incised and tinted panel.
Photograph courtesy of the Sutton Place Foundation

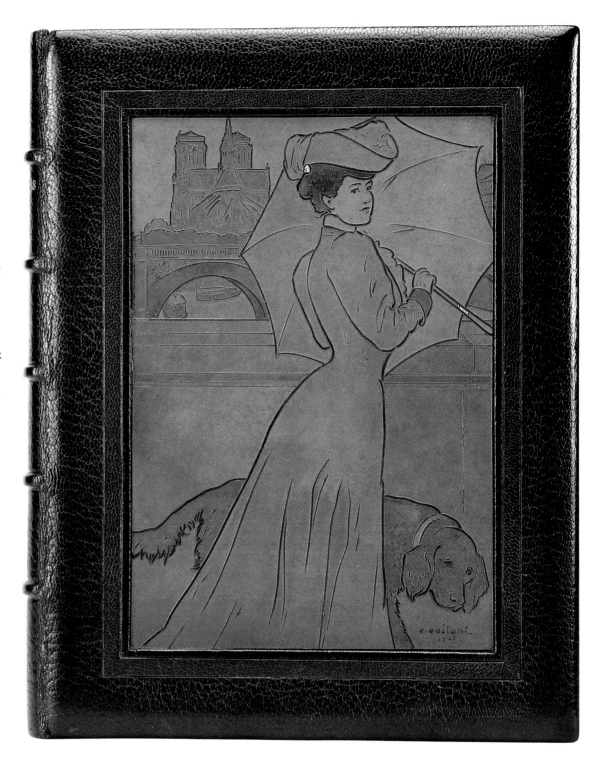

GEORGES CRETTÉ

1893-1969

Cretté was one of the Ecole Estienne's most brilliant pupils and after graduating he joined Marius-Michel's studio, eventually taking over a month before the master's death in 1925. In order to retain the studio's old clients, he continued the Art Nouveau floral esthetic, but gradually began to promote his own more traditional geometric style built around modernist compositions of gold- and blind-tooled fillets. His virtuosity as a gilder drew comparisons with the 19th-century master gilder Trautz, and earned him the title *maître des filets*.

Cretté's designs have been likened to those of Creuzevault: crisp and in harmony with the text.

72 **Georges Cretté**, from a design by **Marius-Michel**
A Rebours (Joris-Karl Huysmans), 1903, inlays of leather with gold-tooling.
Courtesy of Christie's, Geneva

74 | **Georges Cretté**
Ballade de la geôle de Reading (*The Ballad of Reading Gaol*: Oscar Wilde), *c.* 1918, inlays of leather, palladium, and silvered metal.
Courtesy of Habsburg-Feldman, S.A., Geneva

73 | **Georges Cretté**
Poèmes a l'eau-forte (Louis Legrand), 1914, inlays of leather with gold-tooling.
Courtesy of Christie's, Geneva

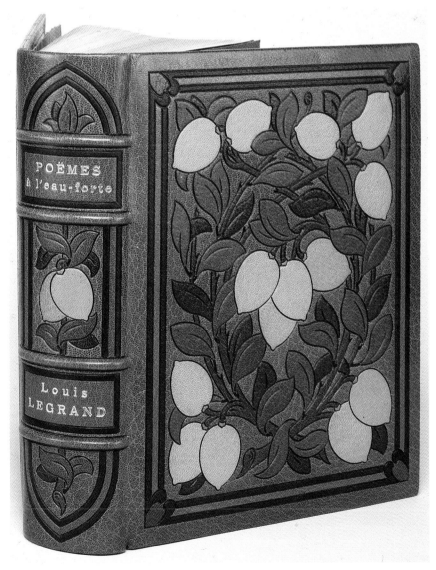

Overleaf

75 | **Georges Cretté**, the panel designed by **François-Louis Schmied** and executed by **Jean Dunand**
Les Climats (Comtesse de Noailles), 1924, lizard skin and palladium, inlaid with a lacquered panel.
Photograph courtesy of the Sutton Place Foundation

76 | **Georges Cretté**, the panel designed by **François-Louis Schmied** and executed by **Jean Dunand**
Le Cantique des cantiques (*The Song of Songs*), 1925, inlays of leather with gold-tooling and lacquered panel.
Courtesy of Habsburg-Feldman, S.A., Geneva

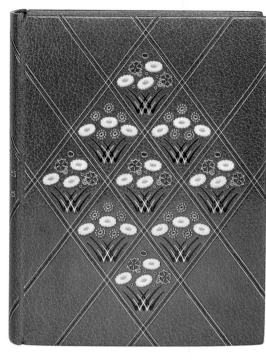

77 | **Georges Cretté**, the plaque designed by
François-Louis Schmied and executed by
Jean Dunand
Two Tales (Oscar Wilde), 1926, leather with
silver-tooling and lacquered and eggshell
panel.
*Photograph courtesy of the Sutton Place
Foundation*

78 | **Georges Cretté**
Les Ballades françaises (Paul Fort), 1927,
inlays of leather with gold- and blind-
tooling.
Courtesy of Christie's, Geneva

79 | **Georges Cretté**, the plaque executed by
Jean Dunand
Au Sujet d'Adonis (Paul Valéry), *c.*1927,
leather and gold-tooling, the plaque in
veneered woods

Opposite

80 | **Georges Cretté**, the plaque designed by
François-Louis Schmied, and executed by
Jean Dunand
Le Cantique des cantiques (The Song of Songs),
1930, leather and calf, with gold-tooling,
the plaque in lacquer and ivory.
Collection Félix Marcilhac

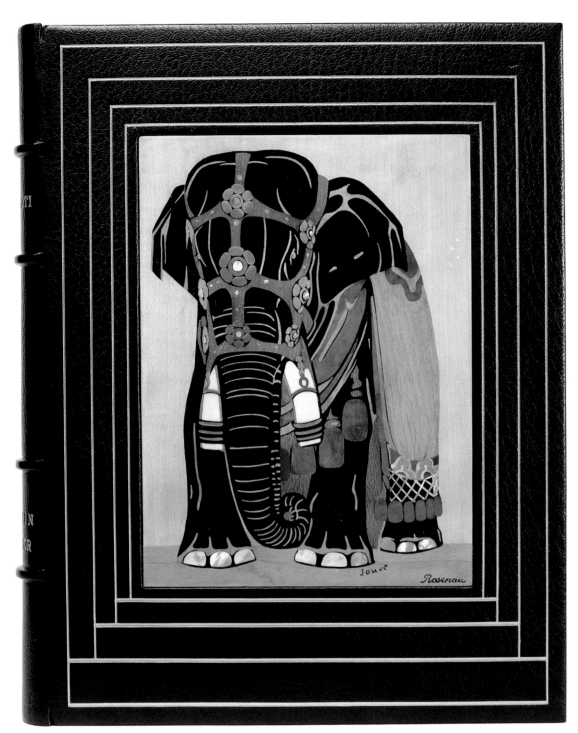

81 **Georges Cretté**, the plaque designed by
Paul Jouve and executed by **Rosenau**
Un Pélérin d'Angkor (Pierre Loti), 1930,
leather with gold-tooling, inset with a
plaque with wood veneers, ivory, mother-of-
pearl, and brass.
*Photograph courtesy of the Sutton Place
Foundation*

Opposite
82, 83 **Georges Cretté**, the panels designed by
François-Louis Schmied and executed by
Jean Dunand
doublures, *Peau-Brune, journal de bord*
(François-Louis Schmied), 1931, leather
with gold-tooling, inlaid with polychromed
mother-of-pearl panels.
Courtesy of Christie's, Geneva

NACRES DE JEAN DURAND

73

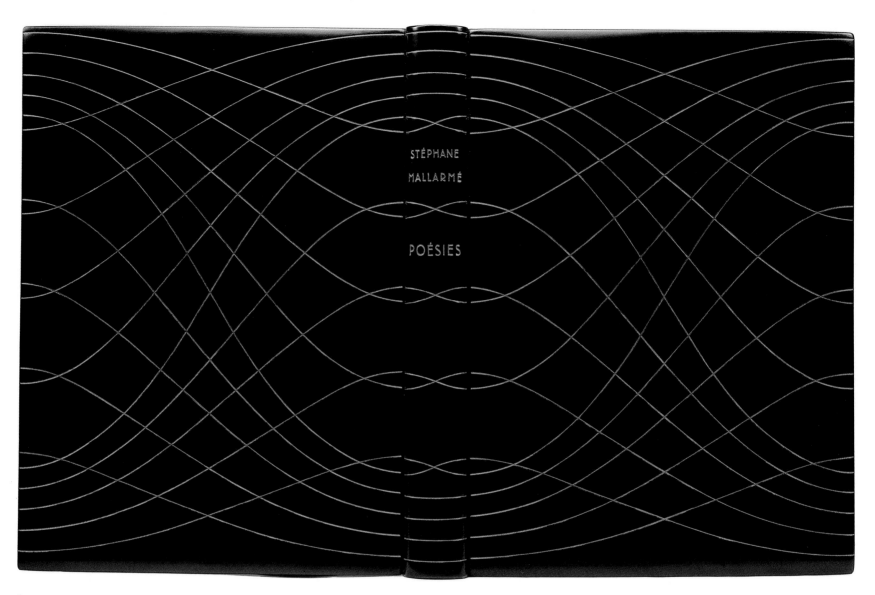

STÉPHANE
MALLARMÉ

POÉSIES

84 | **Georges Cretté**
Poésies (Stéphane Mallarmé), 1932, leather
with gold-tooling.
*Photograph courtesy of the Sutton Place
Foundation*

Opposite

85 | **Georges Cretté**, the panel designed by **Jean
Lambert-Rucki** and executed by **Jean
Dunand**
Paradis terrèstres (Colette), *c.* 1932, leather
with gold- and blind-tooling, and lacquered
and mother-of-pearl panel.
*Photograph courtesy of the Sutton Place
Foundation*

86 | **Georges Cretté**, the plaque designed by
François-Louis Schmied and executed by
Jean Dunand
Paysages Méditerranéens (Paul Morand), 1933,
inlays of leather with gold-tooling and
lacquered and eggshell panel.
*Photograph courtesy of the Sutton Place
Foundation*

87 | **Georges Cretté**
Histoires naturelles (Jules Renard), undated,
inlays of leather with gold- and blind-
tooling.
*Photograph courtesy of the Sutton Place
Foundation*

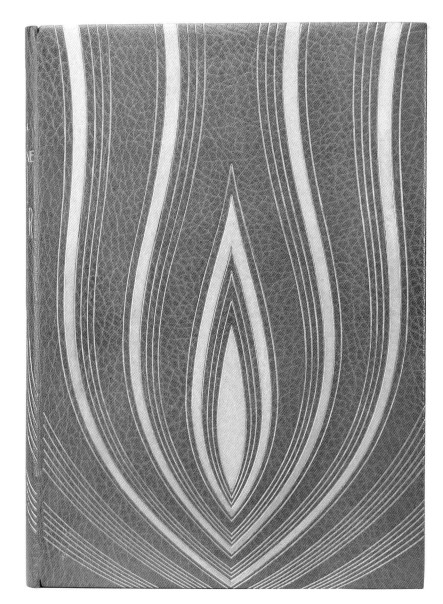

Georges Cretté
Fêtes galantes (Paul Verlaine), leather, gold-tooling, and palladium.
Photograph courtesy of the Sutton Place Foundation

89 | **Georges Cretté**
Chair (Paul Verlaine), 1939, inlays of leather with gold-tooling.
Photograph courtesy of the Sutton Place Foundation

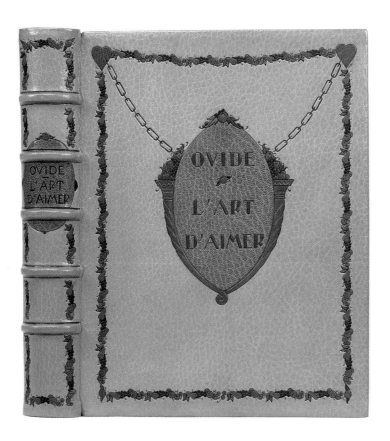

HENRI CREUZEVAULT

1905-71

Creuzevault was the son of Louis-Lazare Creuzevault (1879-1956). Creuzevault *père's* bindings always remained in the mainstream of the craft. Henri, however, who joined the family bindery in 1920, quickly took it into the front ranks of the avant-garde movement with a broad range of modernist designs executed in innovative techniques. From 1925 Creuzevault bindings began to incorporate Art Deco imagery, Henri's youthful and vigorous covers taking as their point of departure Legrain's revolutionary designs. By World War II, he was established as a major figure in the vanguard of the modernist movement.

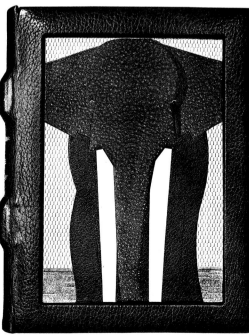

Opposite top

90 | **Henri Creuzevault**
L'Art d'aimer (*Ars Amatoria*: Ovid), 1923,
inlays of leather.
*Photograph courtesy of the Sutton Place
Foundation*

Opposite below

91 | **Louis-Lazare Creuzevault**
Le Bestiaire (Guillaume Apollinaire), 1911,
inlays of leather.
*Photograph courtesy of the Sutton Place
Foundation*

92 | **Henri Creuzevault**
L'Ile des pingouins (Anatole France), 2 vols.,
1926, inlays of leather, gold- and blind-
tooling, and palladium.
*Photograph courtesy of the Sutton Place
Foundation*

93 | **Henri Creuzevault**, the panel designed and
executed by **Paul Jouve**
Le Livre de la jungle (*The Jungle Book*: Rudyard
Kipling), 1919, inlays of leather, gold-
tooling, and ivory

Opposite

94 | **Henri Creuzevault**
Bubu du Montparnasse (Charles-Louis Philippe), 1929, inlays of leather, calf, and cork.
Collection Félix Marcilhac

95 | **Henri Creuzevault**
Carnets de voyage en Italie (Maurice Denis), 1920s, inlays of leather

96 | **Henri Creuzevault**
Assise (A. Pérate), 1920s, inlays of leather

97 | **Henri Creuzevault**
La Nuit Vénitienne (Alfred de Musset), 1929, inlays of leather, palladium, and blind-tooling.
Photograph courtesy of the Sutton Place Foundation

98 | **Henri Creuzevault**
La Chasse de Kaa ("Kaa's Hunting": Rudyard
Kipling), 1930, inlays of leather with gold-
and blind-tooling.
Courtesy of Christie's, Geneva

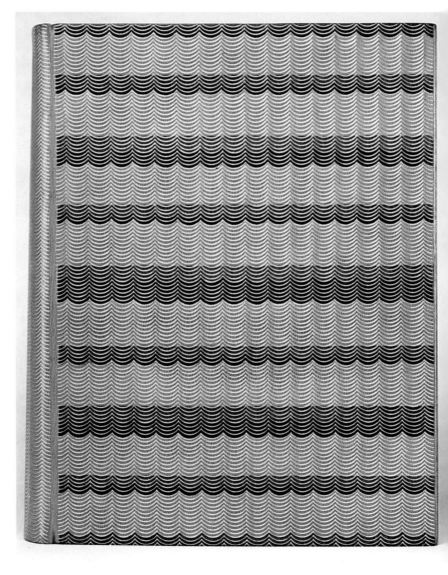

99 | **Henri Creuzevault**
Suzanne et le Pacifique (Jean Giraudoux),
1928, inlays of leather with gold-tooling.
Photograph courtesy of the Sutton Place
Foundation

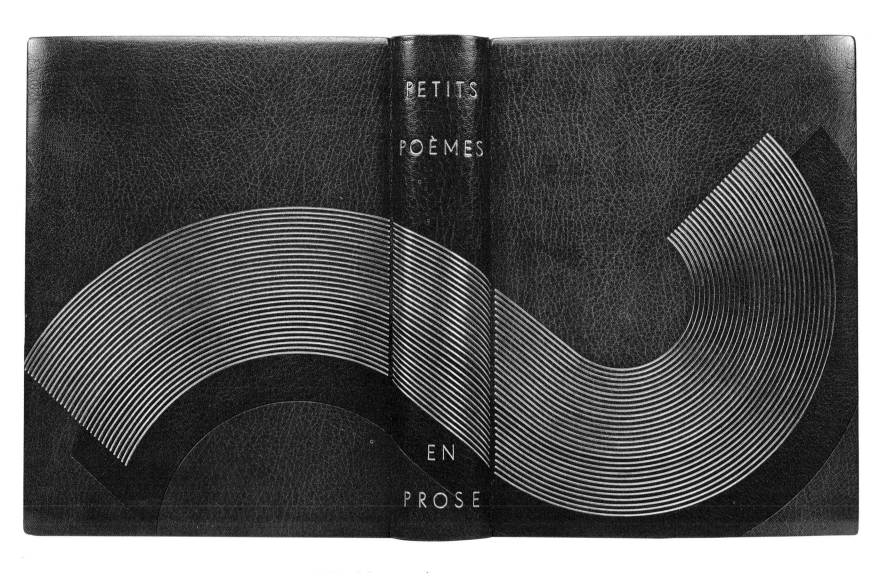

100 | **Henri Creuzevault**
Petits Poèmes en prose (Charles Baudelaire),
1948, inlays of leather with gold-tooling.
*Photograph courtesy of the Sutton Place
Foundation*

Geneviève de Léotard

1899-

The excitement of de Léotard's avant-garde covers lay in their fierce linearity and choice of modern materials. Leather bindings were often inlaid with tinted snakeskin or sharkskin in a refined and seductive manner. Her graphic style was particularly inspiring and varied, incorporating crisp combinations of diverging or overlapping lines interspersed with grids of *pointillé* gold or aluminum dots.

101 | **Geneviève de Léotard**
Thomas l'imposteur (Jean Cocteau), late
1920s, leather with gold- and silver-tooling.
Collection Bibliothèque Sainte-Geneviève, Paris

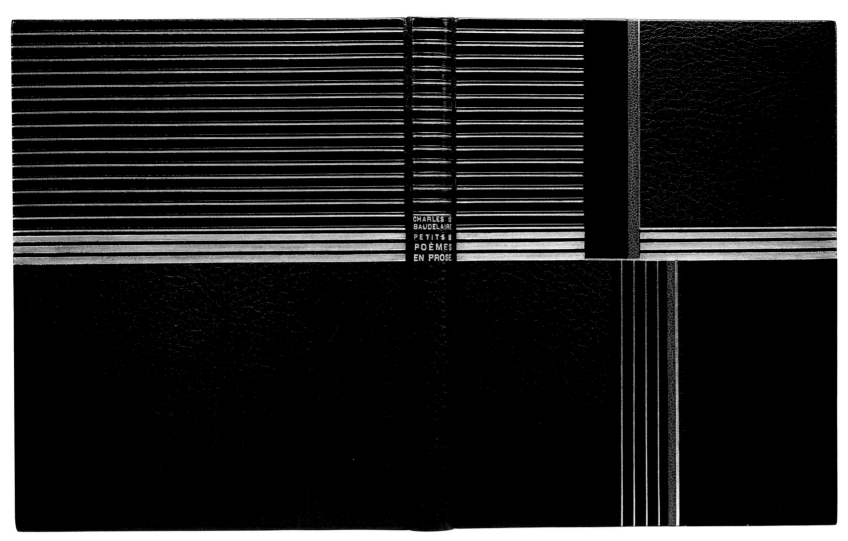

102 | **Geneviève de Léotard**
Petits Poèmes en prose (Charles Baudelaire),
1928, inlays of leather with gold-tooling and
palladium.
Spencer Collection, New York Public Library

103 | **Geneviève de Léotard**
La Maison de danses (Paul Reboux), 2 vols.,
1929, inlays of leather with gold-tooling and
palladium.
Courtesy of Christie's, Geneva

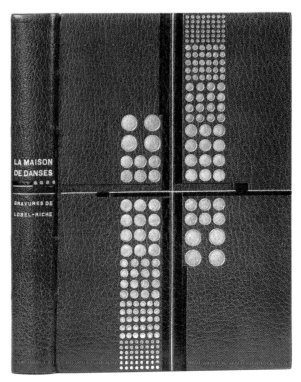 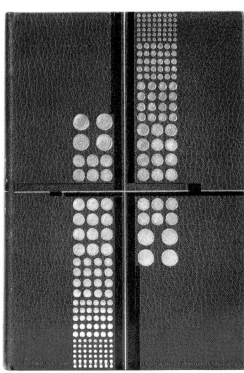

104 | **Geneviève de Léotard**
L'Ingénieux Hidalgo Don Quichotte de la Manche
(*Don Quixote de la Mancha*: Miguel de
Cervantes) 1931, 4 vols., leather with gold-
tooling and palladium.
*Photograph courtesy of the Sutton Place
Foundation*

105 | **Geneviève de Léotard**
Vers et prose (Paul Valéry), *c.* 1930, inlays of
leather with gold-tooling and palladium

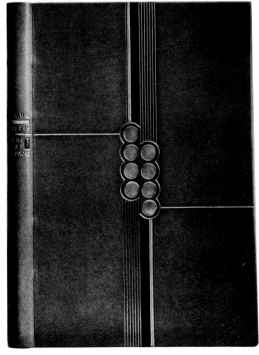

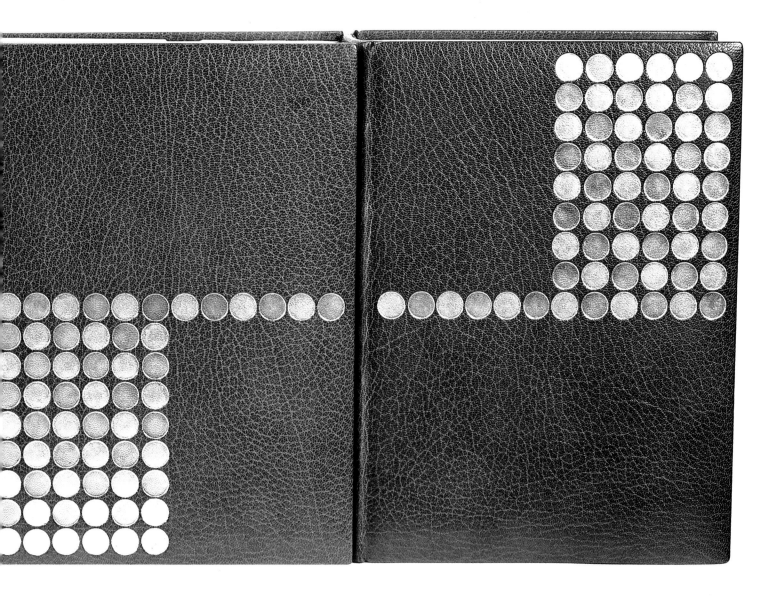

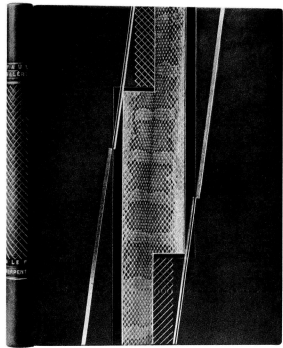

106 | **Geneviève de Léotard**
Le Serpent (Paul Valéry), *c*. 1930, inlays of
leather with snakeskin, and gold- and blind-
tooling

Jean Dunand

1877-1942

Dunand began as a sculptor, but is now best known for his furniture, metalwork, and lacquerwork. He is credited with the invention of crushed eggshell (*coquille d'oeuf*) as a dramatic substitute for the color white, which cannot be achieved successfully in lacquer. Accustomed to creating small *objets d'art*, such as jewelry, in lacquered metal, Dunand showed an equal facility for the lacquered panels which he executed for the bindings of his close friend François-Louis Schmied. In most cases Dunand simply translated Schmied's sketch into lacquer, although he did create several of his own designs in bold geometric or abstract compositions. The collaboration between the two led to many superb bindings, full of vibrant and exotic imagery. *See also 75-77, 79, 80, 82, 83, 85, 86, 117, 200, 202-204, 208, 210, 211, 214, 215.*

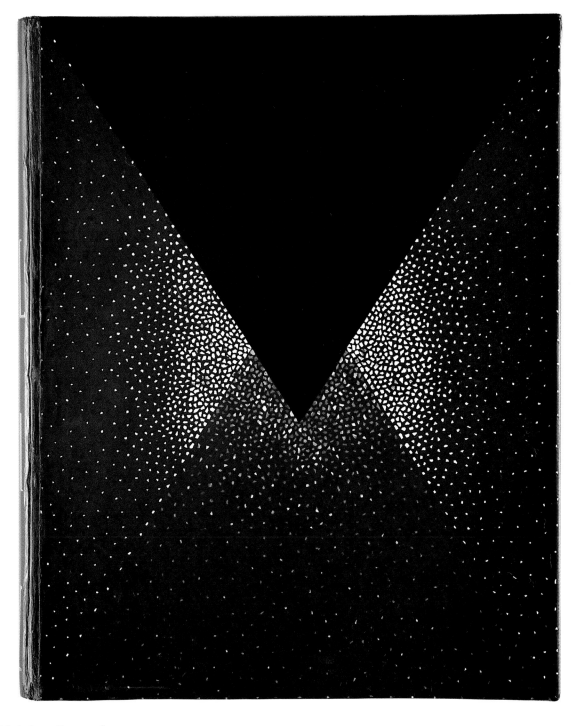

Opposite top

107 | **Jean Dunand**
Le Roi des Aulnes, Erlkönig (*The Erl-king*: Johann Wolfgang von Goethe), 1904, leather with etched and lacquered metal panels.
Photograph courtesy of the Sutton Place Foundation

Opposite below

108 | **Jean Dunand**
Daphné (Alfred de Vigny), 1924, leather with lacquered and eggshell panels.
Photograph courtesy of the Sutton Place Foundation

109 | **Jean Dunand**
Les Chansons de Bilitis (Pierre Louys), 1920s, leather with lacquered eggshell and mother-of-pearl panel.
Collection Félix Marcilhac

MAX FONSÈQUE

1891-1965

By 1930 the floral borders and architectural punches of Fonsèque's prewar covers had been replaced by a more assertive linear style which heralded his development into an accomplished modernist. Arresting calligraphic patterns were formed by the letters of a book's title, as, for example, in *Salammbô*, in which the letters stretch in a serpentine design across the entire back of the book.

110 | **Max Fonsèque**
Mitsou (Colette), 1920s, inlays of leather with gold-tooling.
Collection Félix Marcilhac

FRANZ

111 | **Franz**
doublures, *L'Homme traqué* (Francis Carco), 1929, inlays of leather with gold- and silver-tooling.
Photograph courtesy of the Sutton Place Foundation

90

Louise-Denise Germain

1870-1936

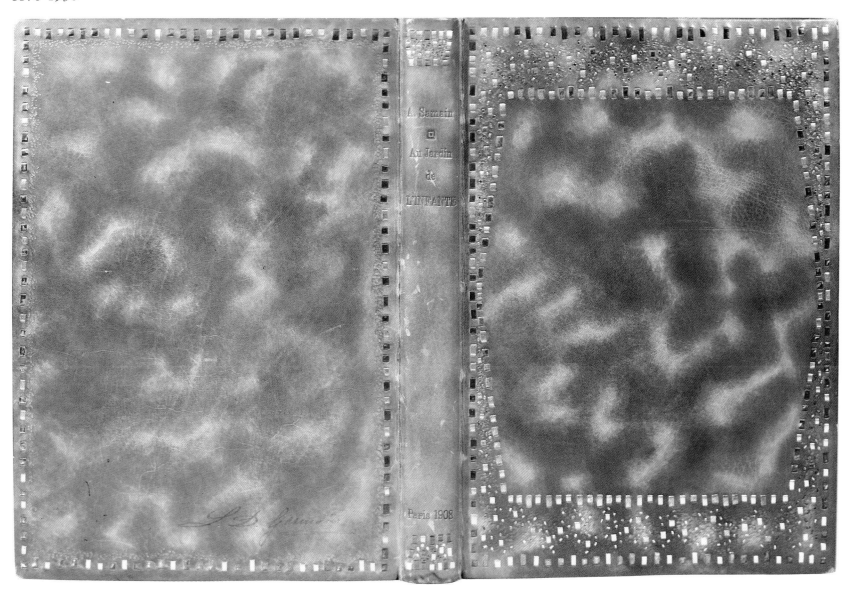

Germain began her career as a leatherworker and later applied the same tooled technique to the modeled and incised bindings she showed in her debut at the 1904 Salon of the Société des Artistes Décorateurs. In the 1920s her style evolved into one of great simplicity, the leather enhanced with tones of gray and silver. She occasionally substituted parchment or lizard skin for leather.

112 | **Louise-Denise Germain**
Au Jardin de l'Infante (Albert Samain), 1908, calf with metallic inlays.
Collection Bibliothèque Sainte-Geneviève, Paris

Jean Goulden

1878-1947

Goulden, a silversmith and enamelist, was instructed in *champlevé* enameling by Jean Dunand, and was to rejuvenate the technique, bringing to it in the late 1920s a highly distinctive and vigorous Cubist style. He designed several enameled silver plaques for incorporation into bindings by Georges Cretté and François-Louis Schmied. *See also 118.*

113 | **Jean Goulden** and **François-Louis Schmied**
Salonique. La Macedoine (Jean Goulden), 1922, leather with enameled silver panels and case.
Courtesy of Christie's, Geneva

Madeleine Gras

1891-1958

Gras did her best work in the 1930s. Influenced by Legrain, she developed a charming modernist style in which great attention was paid to detail both in the book's binding and in its doublures and endpapers. She eliminated ribs from her spines in order to provide an unbroken design across the cover's entire surface.

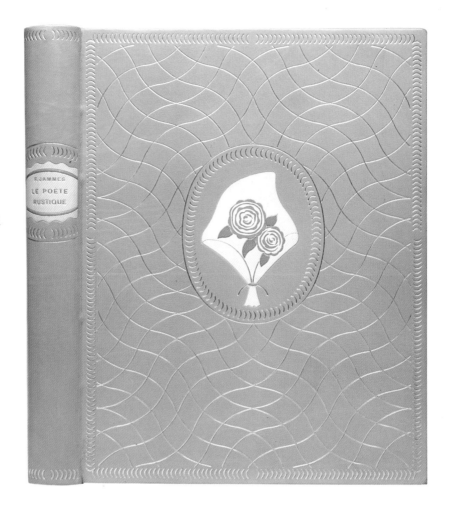

114 | **Madeleine Gras**
Le Poète rustique (Francis Jammes), 1930, inlays of leather with gold-tooling.
Photograph courtesy of the Sutton Place Foundation

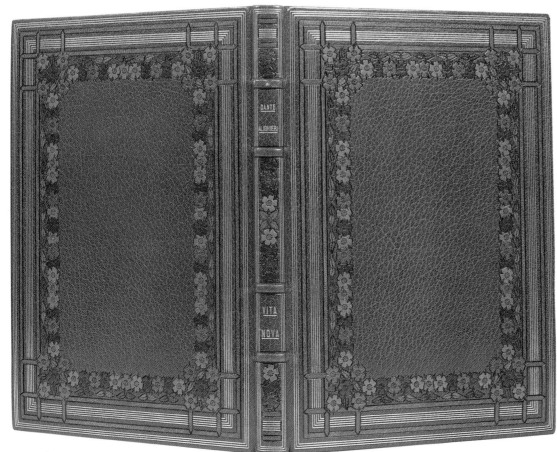

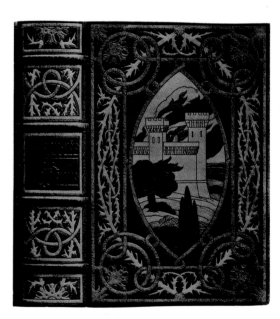

116 | **Paul Gruel**
designed by **Adolphe Giraldon**
La Jaquerie (Prosper Merimée), *c.* 1910, inlays of leather with blind-tooling

115 | **Léon Gruel**
Vita Nova (Dante Alighieri), 1907, inlays of leather with gold-tooling
Photograph courtesy of Priscilla Juvelis

94

Léon Gruel

1841-1923

Gruel was the author of *Manuel historique et bibliographique de l'amateur de reliure* (1887), in which he argued for the acceptance of non-traditional decoration for modern bindings. In practice, he matched this belief with a diverse range of emblematic and pictorial covers produced with his son Paul at the Gruel bindery, one of the oldest in Paris.

Gruel was accused of sacrificing good taste in his attempt to make his covers descriptive, and therefore commercial, by applying a mélange of inlaid ivory medallions, *repoussé* and incised leather panels, and garish colors. Despite his progressive viewpoint, he also created numerous conventional designs.

118 | **Léon Gruel**, the panel designed and executed by **Jean Goulden**
Le Roman de lièvre (Francis Jammes), 1929, inlays of leather with gold- and blind-tooling, and enameled silver panel.
Photograph courtesy of the Sutton Place Foundation

117 | **Léon Gruel**, the panel designed by **François-Louis Schmied** and executed by **Jean Dunand**
Histoire charmante de l'adolescente sucre d'amour (Dr. Joseph-Charles Mardrus), 1927, leather with lacquered panel.
Photograph courtesy of the Sutton Place Foundation

François Horclois Kauffmann

Little is known about François Horclois, except that he took over as head of the Kauffmann atelier in 1929, after the death of its founder. He subsequently signed his bindings Horclois-Kauffmann or H.-K.

119 | **François Horclois Kauffmann**
Le Feu (Gabriele D'Annunzio), undated, incised, modeled, and polychromed leather.
Courtesy of Christie's, Geneva

René Kieffer

1875-1964

Kieffer's earlier designs were safe rather than adventurous. A disciple of Marius-Michel, he employed Art Nouveau motifs but retained them within symmetrical borders that revealed his classical roots. At this time his preference for bright colors, such as vermilion and peacock, set him apart from the traditionalists more than his designs themselves.

After World War I Kieffer emerged as one of Paris's leading binders whose impeccable workmanship was now matched by a wide range of progressive designs inspired by Legrain. His style continued to evolve in the late 1920s and 1930s.

120 | **René Kieffer**
doublure, *Le Roman de la momie* (Théophile Gautier), 1901, inlays of leather with gold-tooling.
Photograph courtesy of the Sutton Place Foundation

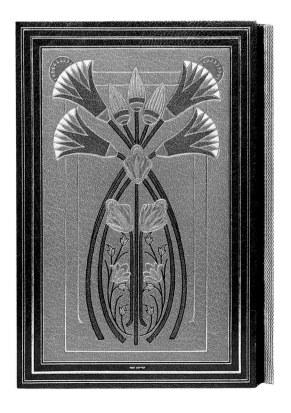

121 | **René Kieffer**, designed by **Léon Lebègue**
doublure, *Histoire de dona Maria d'Avalos et de don Fabricio, duc d'Andrea* (Anatole France), 1902, pen and watercolor on vellum.
Photograph courtesy of the Sutton Place Foundation

122 | **René Kieffer**
Faune parisienne (Erastene Ramira), 1901,
inlays of leather with gold-tooling.
*Photograph courtesy of the Sutton Place
Foundation*

123 | **René Kieffer**
Princesses de jade et de jadis (Jerome Doucet
and Lorant-Heilbronn), 1904, inlays of
leather with gold-tooling.
*Photograph courtesy of the Sutton Place
Foundation*

124 | **René Kieffer**
A Rebours (Joris-Karl Huysmans), 1903,
inlays of leather with gold-tooling.
Collection Bibliothèque Sainte-Geneviève, Paris

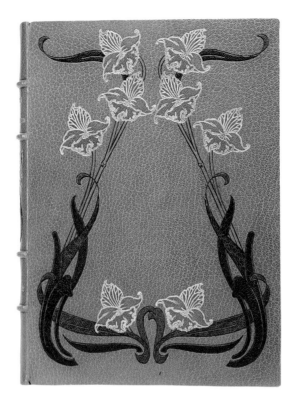
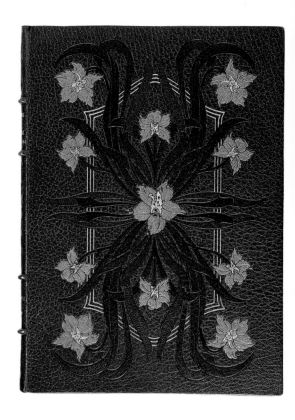
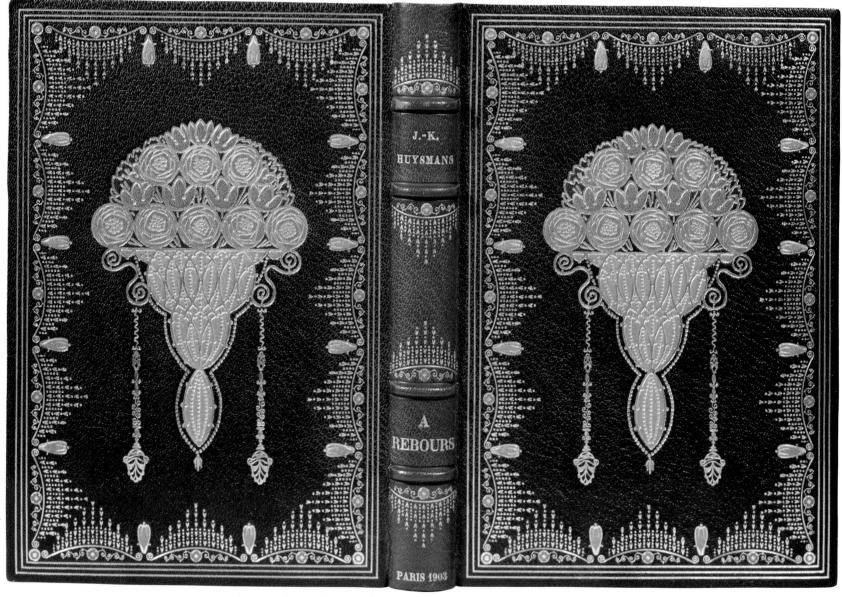

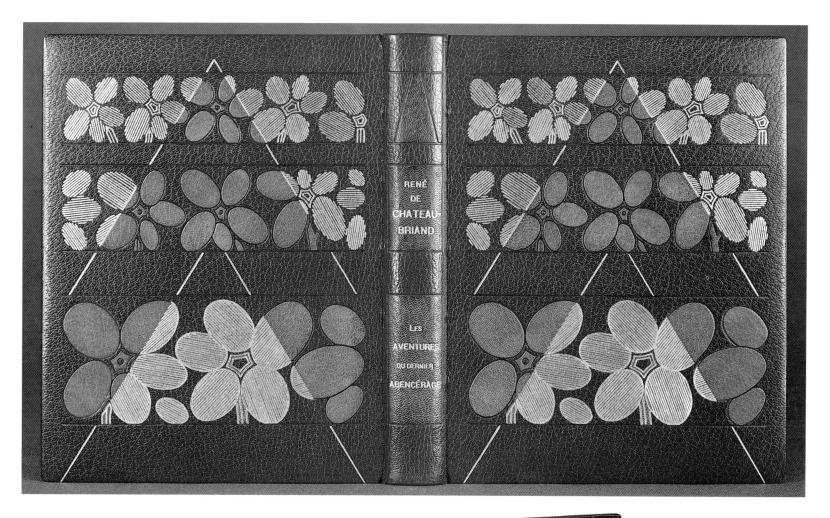

125 | **René Kieffer**
Les Aventures du dernier abencérage (René de Chateaubriand), *c.* 1910, inlays of leather with gold-tooling.
Collection Félix Marcilhac

126 | **René Kieffer**
La Vie des abeilles (Maurice Maeterlinck), 1908, inlays of leather with gold-tooling.
Courtesy of Christie's, Geneva

99

128 | **René Kieffer**
Simulacre, undated, inlays of leather and snakeskin.
Collection Bibliothèque Sainte-Geneviève, Paris

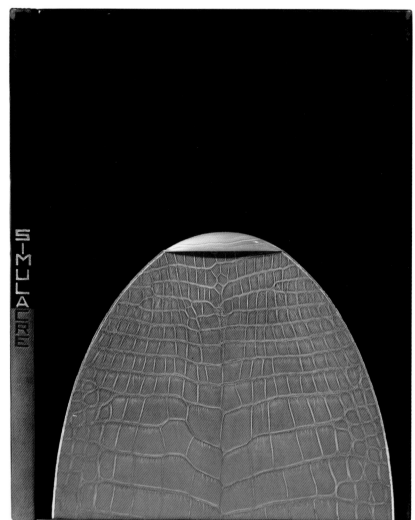

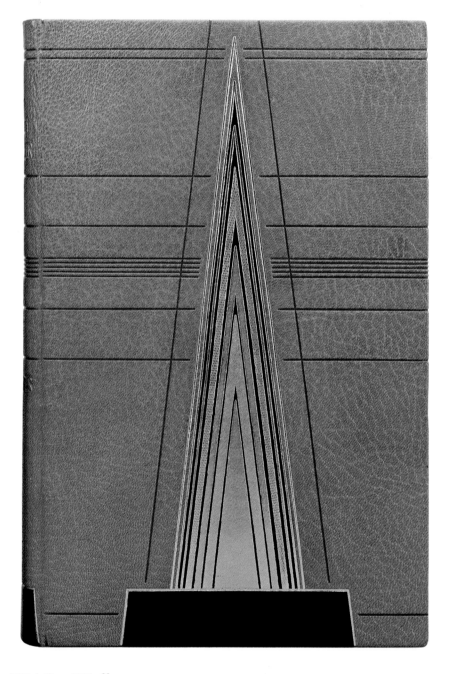

127 | **René Kieffer**
Contes (Albert Samain), 1926, inlays of leather with gold- and blind-tooling.
Courtesy of Christie's, Geneva

129 | **René Kieffer**
Trois Eglises (Joris-Karl Huysmans), 1920, inlays of leather with gold-tooling

Clovis Lagadec

One of Paul Bonet's specialist binders, Lagadec was in 1927 judged the finest binder in Paris. Between 1930 and 1933 he formed a partnership with Lahaye.

Lagadec was known for his development of a micro-mosaic form of ornamentation in which large numbers of minute pieces of leather were used in preference to the usual inlay technique to create naturalistic floral tableaux.

130 | **Clovis Lagadec**, designed by **Mos de H. Lehaye**
Candide (Voltaire), 1921, inlays of leather, gold-tooling, and marbleized paper.
Photograph courtesy of the Sutton Place Foundation

CHARLES LANOË

1881-1959

Lanoë was trained in the Classical style and his first bindings were predictably traditional, but he gradually introduced a range of floral motifs into the bands of gold fillets bordering his covers, sometimes including a small central *tableau* or bouquet to provide additional interest.

In the 1920s Lanoë appears to have embraced the Art Deco style, generating many charming covers of his own design in the modernist idiom.

131 | **Charles Lanoë**
detail of cover, *Personnages de comédie* (Albert Flament), 1920s, inlays of leather.
Collection Ralph Esmerian

Opposite
132 | **Charles Lanoë**
Méditations poétiques (Alphonse Marie-Louis de Lamartine), 1910, inlays of leather with gold-tooling.
Photograph courtesy of the Sutton Place Foundation

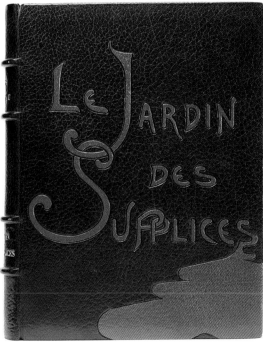

Opposite

133 | **Charles Lanoë**
doublure, *Personnages de comédie* (Albert Flament), 1920s, inlays of leather with gold-tooling and silk panel.
Collection Ralph Esmerian

134 | **Charles Lanoë**
Phili (Abel Hermant), 1921, inlays of leather with gold-tooling.
Photograph courtesy of the Sutton Place Foundation

135 | **Charles Lanoë**
Le Jardin des supplices (Octave Mirbeau), 1925, inlays of leather.
Photograph courtesy of the Sutton Place Foundation

Pierre Legrain

1889-1929

Legrain was as important to the Art Deco movement as Marius-Michel was to Art Nouveau. Like Michel before him, Legrain emerged with a completely new style that broke with all traditional influences. He not only produced bindings with purely geometric decoration, sometimes integrating the title or the author's name into the overall design, but also worked with new materials, such as ivory, sharkskin, wood, or metal. Thanks to his patron, the couturier Jacques Doucet, Legrain was able to work in complete freedom and without financial constraint.

136 | **Pierre Legrain**
Poèmes à l'eau-forte (Louis Legrand), undated, inlays of leather with gold- and blind-tooling.
Photograph courtesy of the Sutton Place Foundation

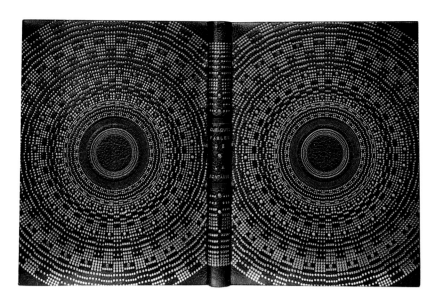

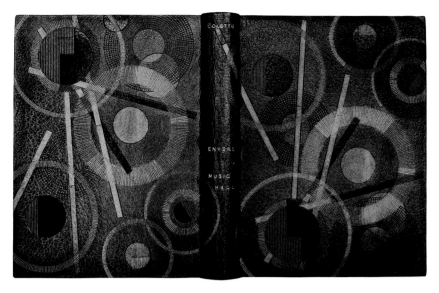

137 | **Pierre Legrain**
Quelques Fables de la Fontaine (La Fontaine),
undated, leather, gold-tooling, and
palladium

138 | **Pierre Legrain**
L'Envers du music hall (Colette), *c.* 1925,
inlays of leather with gold- and blind-
tooling

139 | **Pierre Legrain**
Théâtre complet (François de Curel), 6 vol. set,
1919, inlays of leather and palladium (bound
by René Kieffer).
Courtesy of Christie's, Geneva

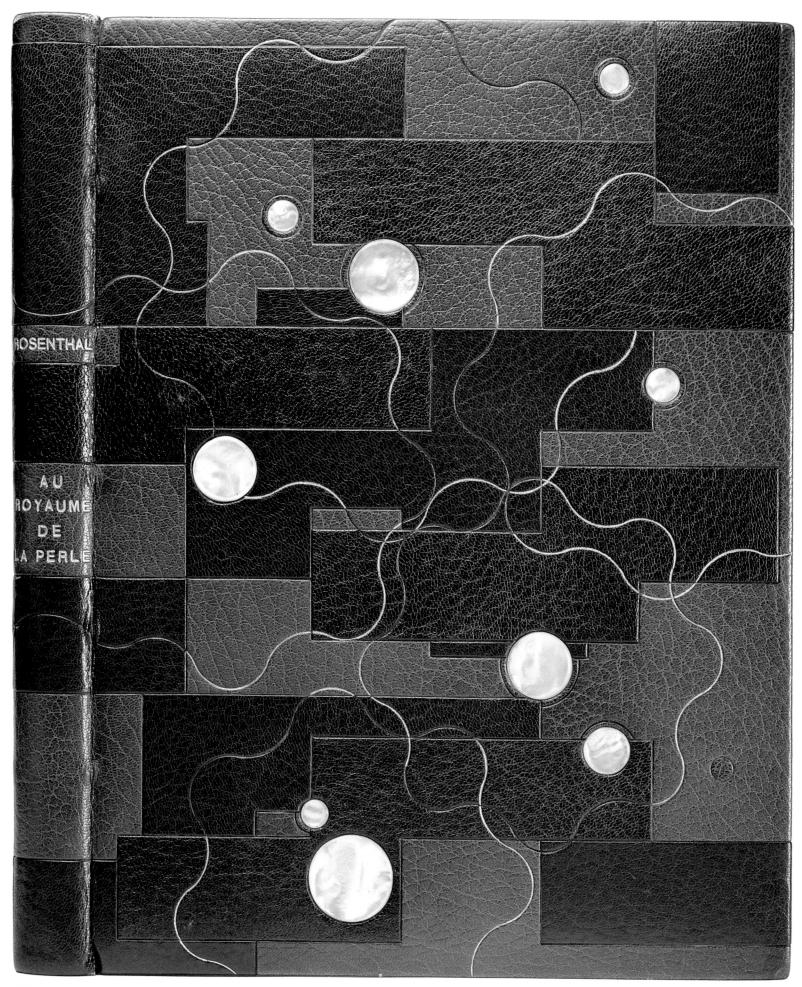

ROSENTHAL

AU
ROYAUME
DE
LA PERLE

108

Opposite

40 | **Pierre Legrain**
Au Royaume de la perle (Léonard Rosenthal),
1925, inlays of leather, gold- and blind-
tooling, and mother-of-pearl cabochons.
*Photograph courtesy of the Sutton Place
Foundation*

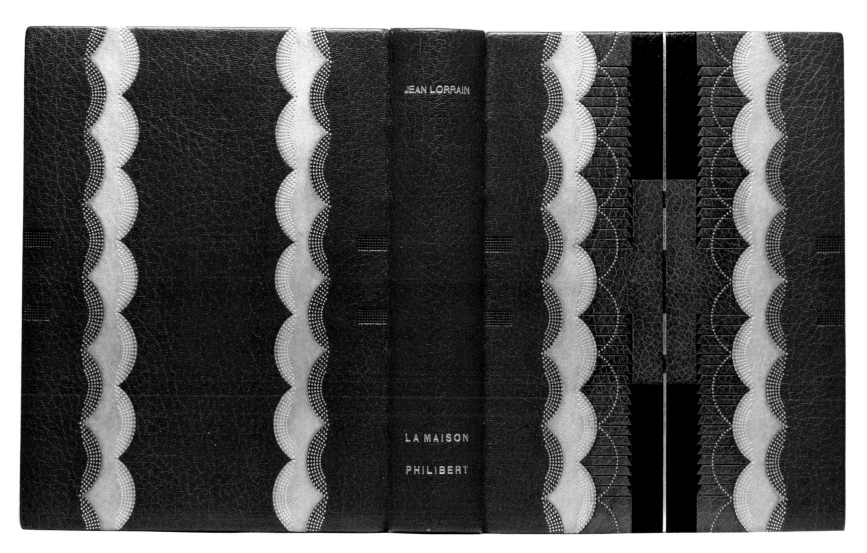

41 | **Pierre Legrain**
La Maison Philibert (Jean Lorrain), 1925,
inlays of leather with gold- and blind-
tooling.
*Photograph courtesy of the Sutton Place
Foundation*

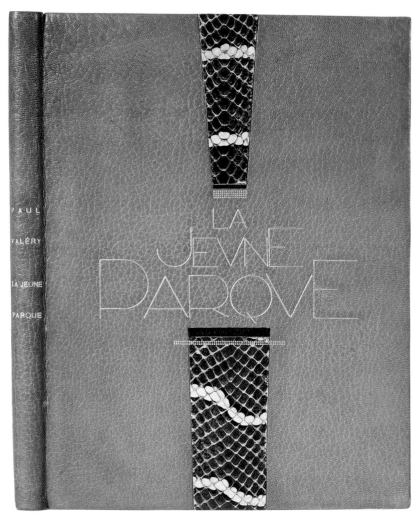

142 | **Pierre Legrain**
La Jeune Parque (Paul Valéry), 1925, leather
with gold-tooling, and applied snakeskin.
Courtesy of Christie's, New York

143 | **Pierre Legrain**
Trois Filles de leur mère (Pierre Louÿs), 1926,
inlays of leather and gold-tooling.
*Photograph courtesy of the Sutton Place
Foundation*

Opposite
144 | **Pierre Legrain**
Daphné (Alfred de Vigny), 1926, inlays of
leather, gold- and blind-tooling, and
palladium.
*Photograph courtesy of the Sutton Place
Foundation*

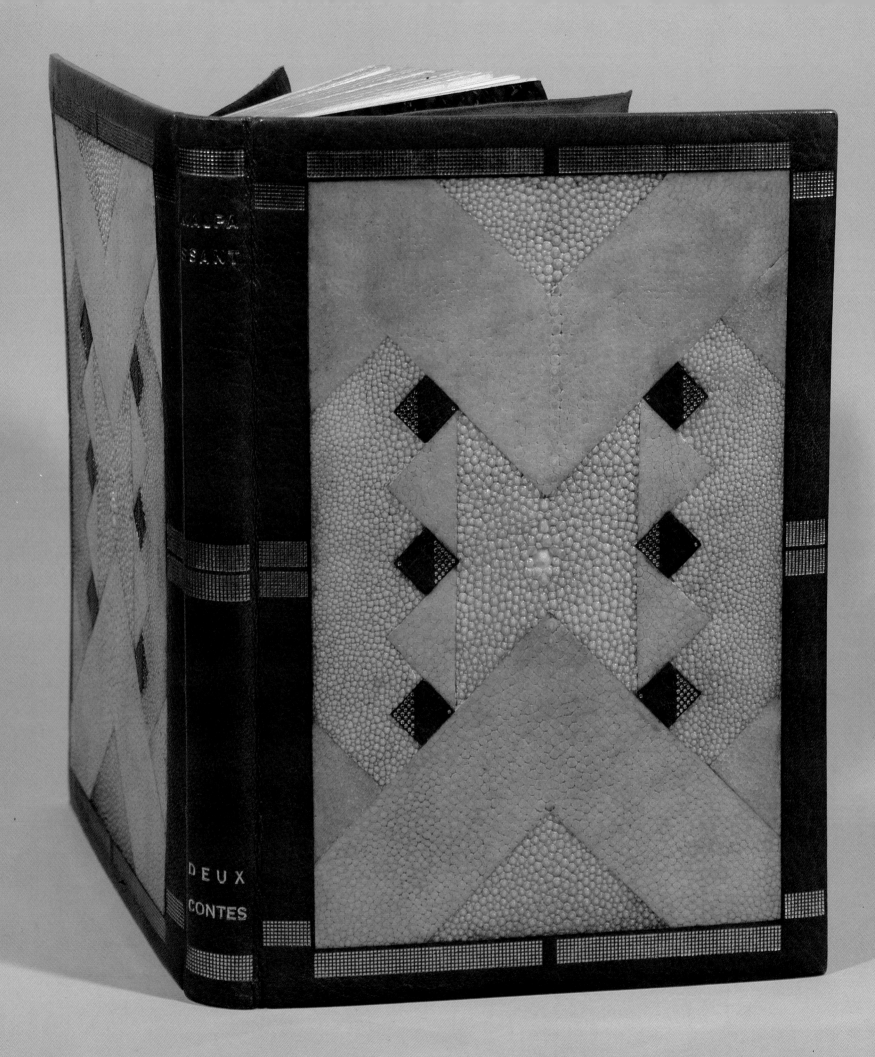

Opposite
145 | **Pierre Legrain**
Deux Contes (Guy de Maupassant), undated,
leather, gold-tooling, and sharkskin.
Courtesy of Christie's, Geneva

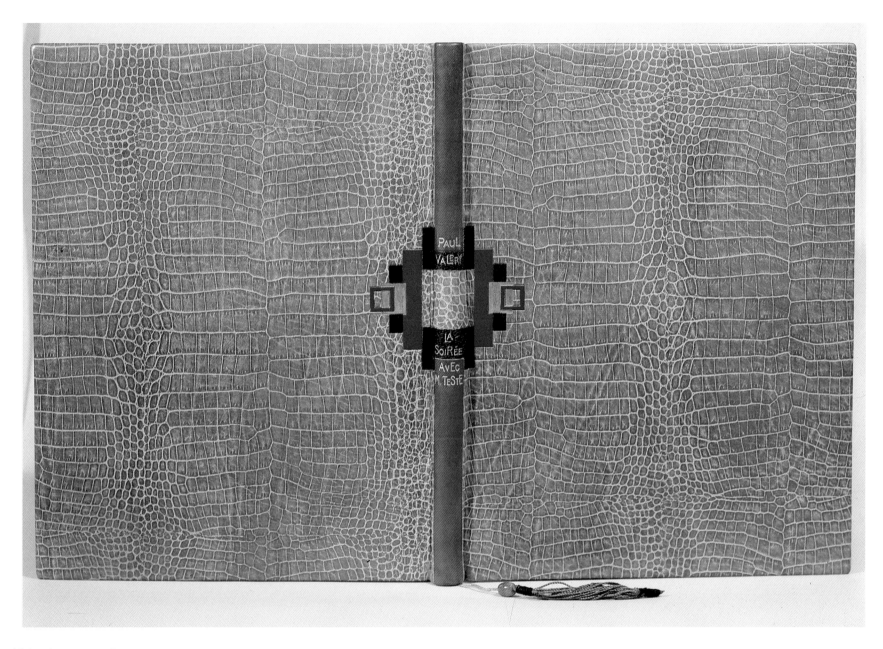

146 | **Pierre Legrain**
La Soirée avec M. Teste (Paul Valéry), 1922,
snakeskin, inlays of leather, and gold-
tooling.
Collection Bibliothèque Sainte-Geneviève, Paris

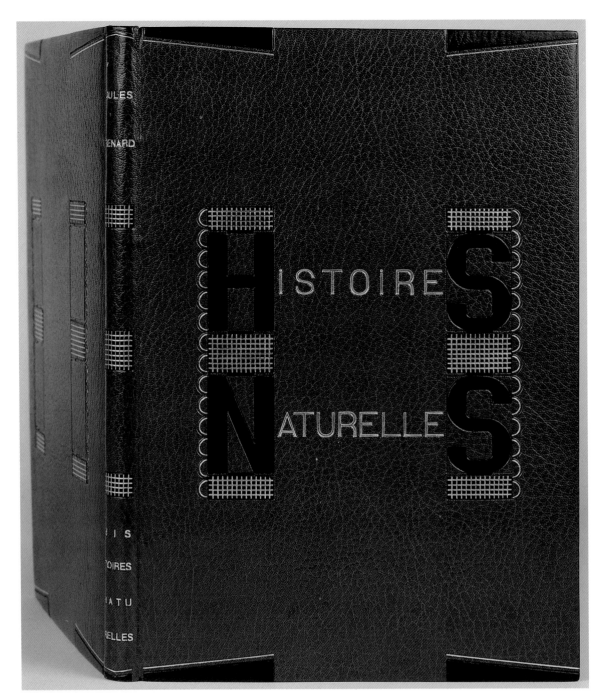

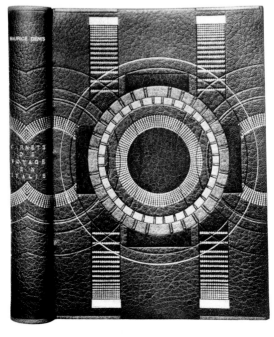

147 | **Pierre Legrain**
Histoires naturelles (Jules Renard), undated, inlays of leather with gold-tooling.
Courtesy of Christie's, Geneva

149 | **Pierre Legrain**
Carnets de voyage en Italie (Maurice Denis), *c.*1922, inlays of leather with gold- and blind-tooling

148 | **Pierre Legrain**
Daphné (Alfred de Vigny), 1924, inlays of leather with gold-tooling

Opposite

150 | **Pierre Legrain**
Madame Chrysanthème (Pierre Loti), undated, inlays of leather, gold-tooling, and palladium.
Photograph courtesy of the Sutton Place Foundation

Jacques Anthoine-Legrain

1907-?

Anthoine-Legrain made his début in 1929, the year his step-father, Pierre Legrain, died. Although in his early work he concentrated on continuing the Legrain tradition by applying a similar range of linear compositions and inlays of color to leather bindings, by the late 1930s he had achieved respect in his own right as both a designer and a technician.

Opposite
151 | **Jacques Anthoine-Legrain**, designed by **Pierre Legrain**
L'Art d'aimer (*Ars Amatoria*: Ovid), 1935, leather, gold- and blind-tooling, and mother-of-pearl.
Courtesy of Christie's, Geneva

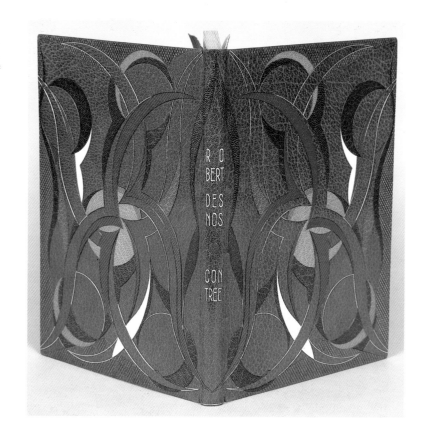

152 | **Jacques Anthoine-Legrain**
Contrée (Robert Desnos), 1944, inlays of leather with silver- and blind-tooling.
Photograph courtesy of the Sutton Place Foundation

153 | **Jacques Anthoine-Legrain**
Lespugue (Jean Fautrier and Robert Ganzo), 1942, inlays of leather, gold-tooling, and sharkskin.
Photograph courtesy of the Sutton Place Foundation

Leprêtre

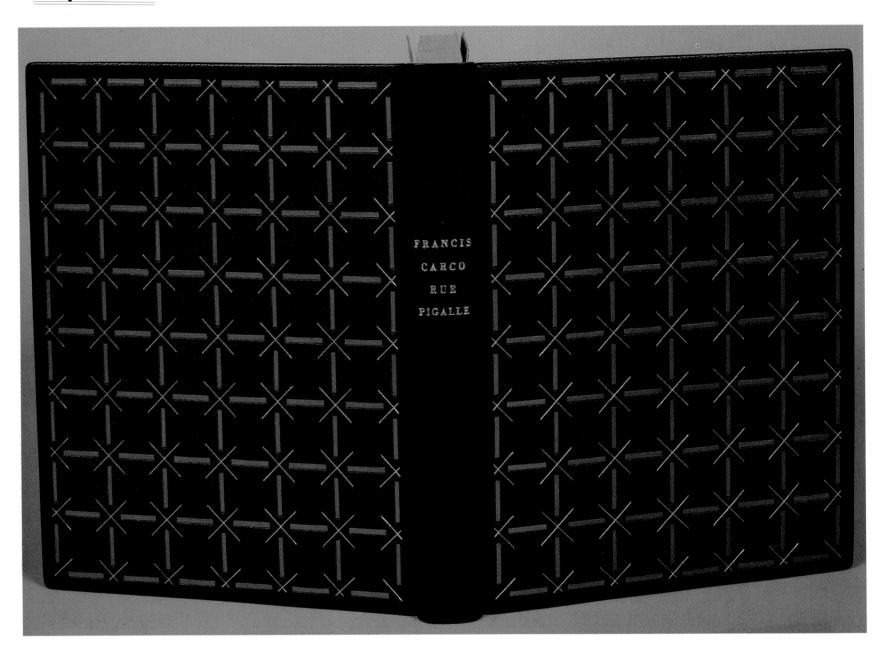

154 | **Leprêtre**
Rue Pigalle (Francis Carco), 1927, inlays of
leather with gold-tooling.
*Photograph courtesy of the Sutton Place
Foundation*

Georges Levitsky

1885-?

Well-known outside France, Levitsky applied a range of conventional designs to leather and parchment bindings for a clientele that included King Albert I of Belgium and Alexander I of Serbia. After World War I his style became increasingly dynamic and resourceful, including covers which incorporated ivory, gold, ebony, and mother-of-pearl.

155 | **Georges Levitsky**
Prière sur l'Acropolis (Ernest Renan), inlays of leather with gold-tooling, and polychromed mother-of-pearl panel.
Photograph courtesy of the Sutton Place Foundation

Overleaf
156, 157 | **Georges Levitsky**
Les Chansons de Bilitis (Pierre Louys), 1906, inlays of leather with gold-tooling; and *Les Sept Femmes de Barbe-Bleue* (Anatole France), 1921, inlays of leather with gold-tooling.
Courtesy of Christie's, Geneva

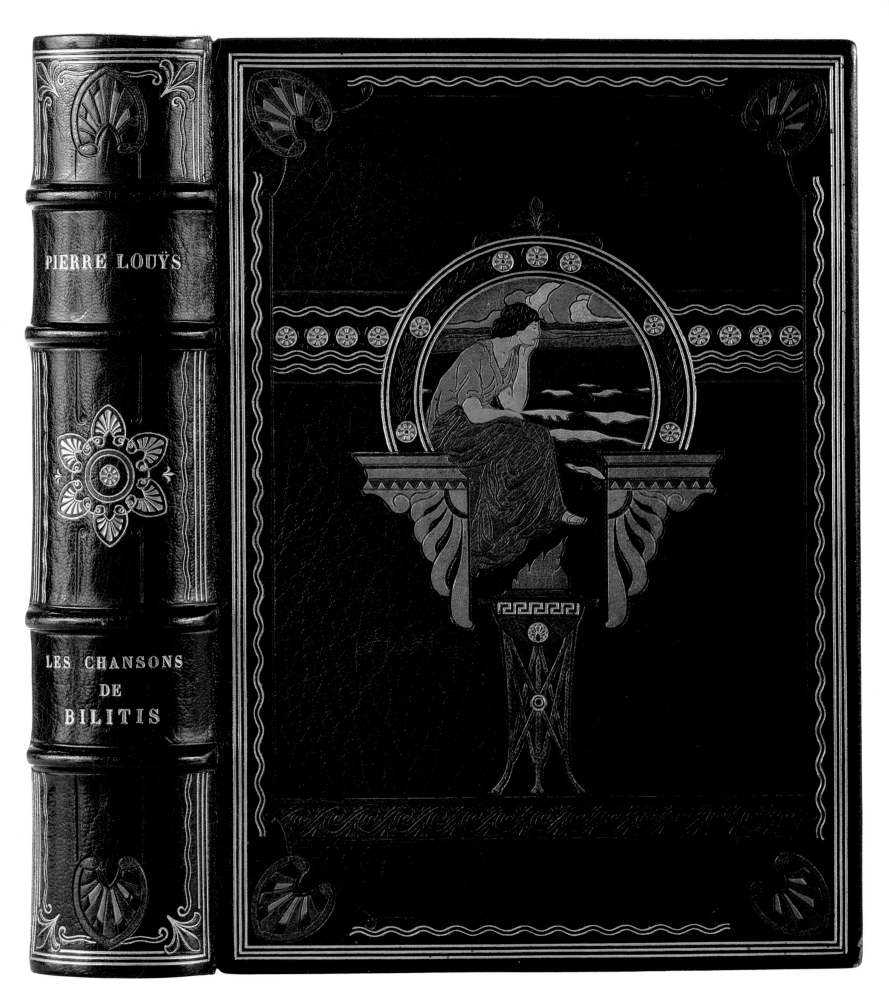

158 | **Georges Levitsky**
L'Île enchantée (Michel Rhune), 1920s, inlays
of leather with gold-tooling.
Photograph courtesy of the Sutton Place
Foundation

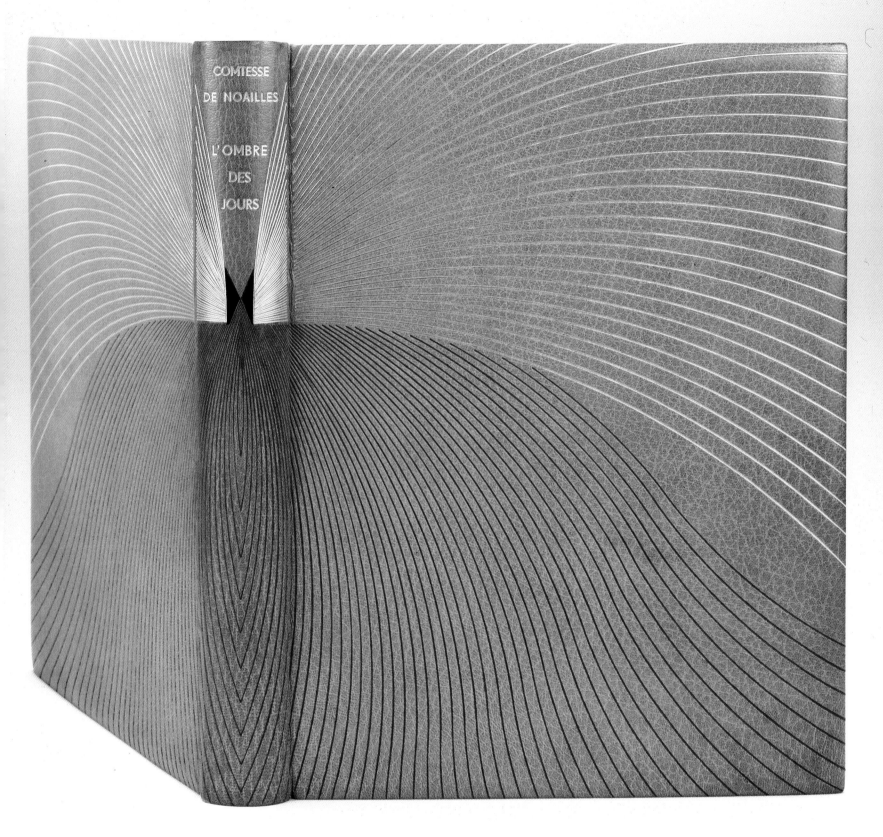

159 | **Georges Levitsky**
L'Ombre des jours (Comtesse de Noailles),
1938, inlays of leather with gold- and blind-
tooling.
Courtesy of Christie's, Geneva

MARIUS MAGNIN

Magnin was the son of Lucien Magnin, a little-known binder from Lyons who made his debut with designs incorporating curious inlaid patterns inspired by silk and upholstery designs. Magnin *fils* became a major exponent of emblematic bindings for volumes such as *L'Eventail*, *Ombrelle*, *Son Altesse* and *Française du Siècle*. He retained Albin Cabanes, a professor of design, to assist him in the ornamentation of his covers and also collaborated with other binders, such as René Chambolle, Salvador David, and Brétault.

160 | **Marius Magnin**, the panels designed by **Gustave Girrane**
L'Enseigne à Lyon (John Grand-Carteret and Gustave Girrane), 1918, inlays of leather with gold-tooling, and incised and polychromed panels.
Photograph courtesy of the Sutton Place Foundation

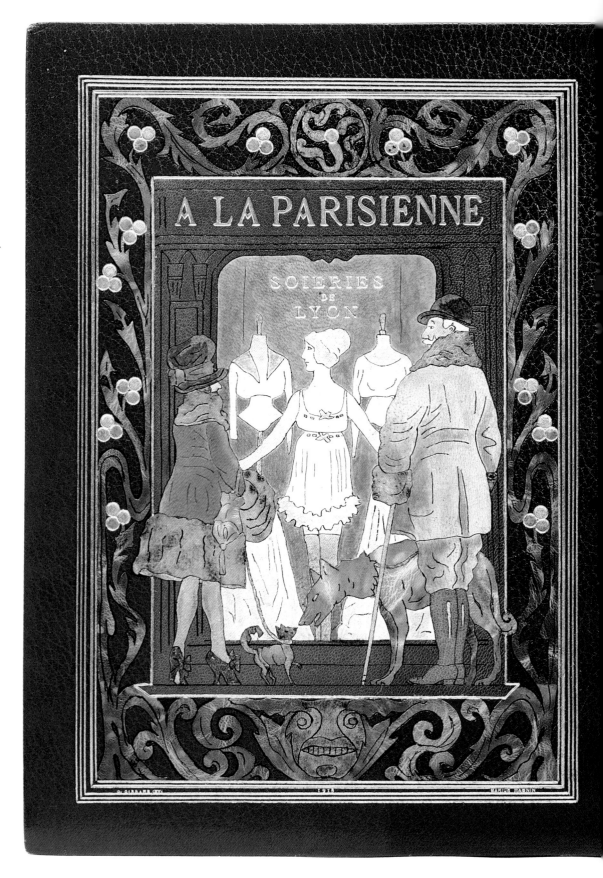

André Mare

1887-1932

A talented painter, designer, and *ensemblier*, Mare created highly distinctive bindings, in both their artistry and their technique. He preferred parchment and vellum to leather and, drawing on the same fanciful grammar of ornament that he applied to his furnishings — baskets, garlands of summer blooms and fruit, lovebirds, etc. — produced an appealing and lush effect. His palette was warm and refined, with an emphasis on red, blue, and green.

Mare's technique of engraving, followed by painting, followed by varnishing, gave the completed image a richly translucent and enameled appearance. Prized for its charm and high curiosity factor, his work was in great demand among Paris's foremost book collectors.

161 | **André Mare**
Les Pastorales de Longus, ou Daphnis et Chloë
(Longus), undated, painted vellum

162 | **André Mare**
Eloa (Alfred de Vigny), 1921, painted
parchment with gold-tooling.
*Photograph courtesy of the Sutton Place
Foundation*

MARIANNE

163 | **Marianne**, painted by **Grande**
endpapers and slipcase, *Romeo et Juliette* (Jean
Cocteau), 1926, watercolor on paper.
*Photograph courtesy of the Sutton Place
Foundation*

Mme Marot-Rodde

?-1935

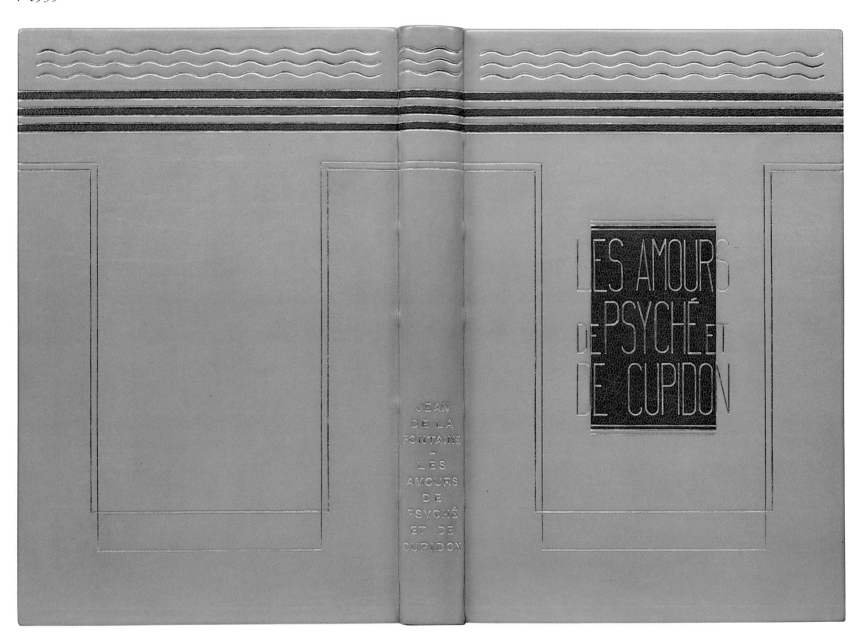

Marot-Rodde's style was highly distinctive and delicate. Her use of bright inlays of colors within compact geometric or floral compositions was most appealing and fresh in its respect for traditional materials blended with a modernist imagery.

164 | **Marot-Rodde**
Les Amours de Psyché et de Cupidon (Jean de la Fontaine), 1926, inlays of leather and calf, with gold- and silver-tooling.
Photograph courtesy of the Sutton Place Foundation

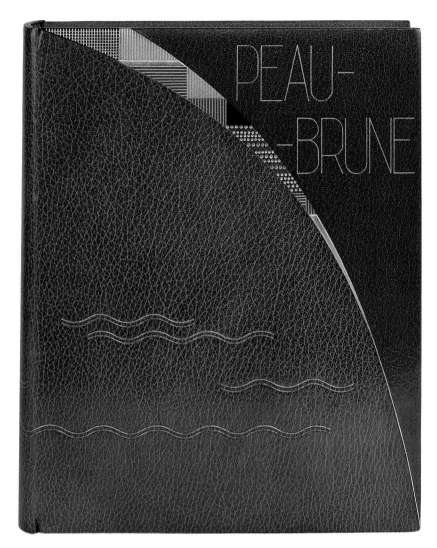

165 | **Marot-Rodde**
Tableau de l'au-delà (Frédéric Boutet), 1927,
inlays of leather, with gold- and silver-
tooling.
*Photograph courtesy of the Sutton Place
Foundation*

166 | **Marot-Rodde**
Peau-Brune (François-Louis Schmied), 1931,
inlays of leather with gold- and palladium-
tooling.
Courtesy of Christie's, Geneva

167 | **Marot-Rodde**
Eventail (*The Fan*: John Gay), late 1920s,
inlays of leather with gold-tooling

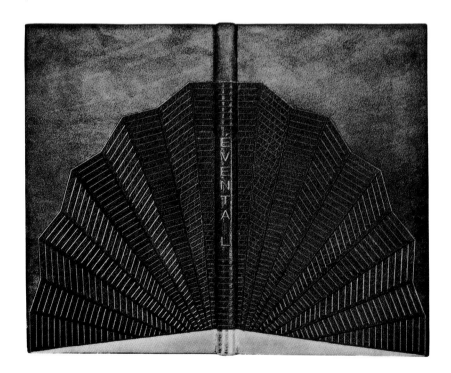

Overleaf
168, 169 | **Marot-Rodde**
Romances sans paroles (Paul Verlaine), 1935,
inlays of leather and calf, with gold-tooling,
and *Romances sans paroles* (Paul Verlaine),
1935, inlays of leather and calf, with gold-
and silver-tooling.
*Photographs courtesy of the Sutton Place
Foundation*

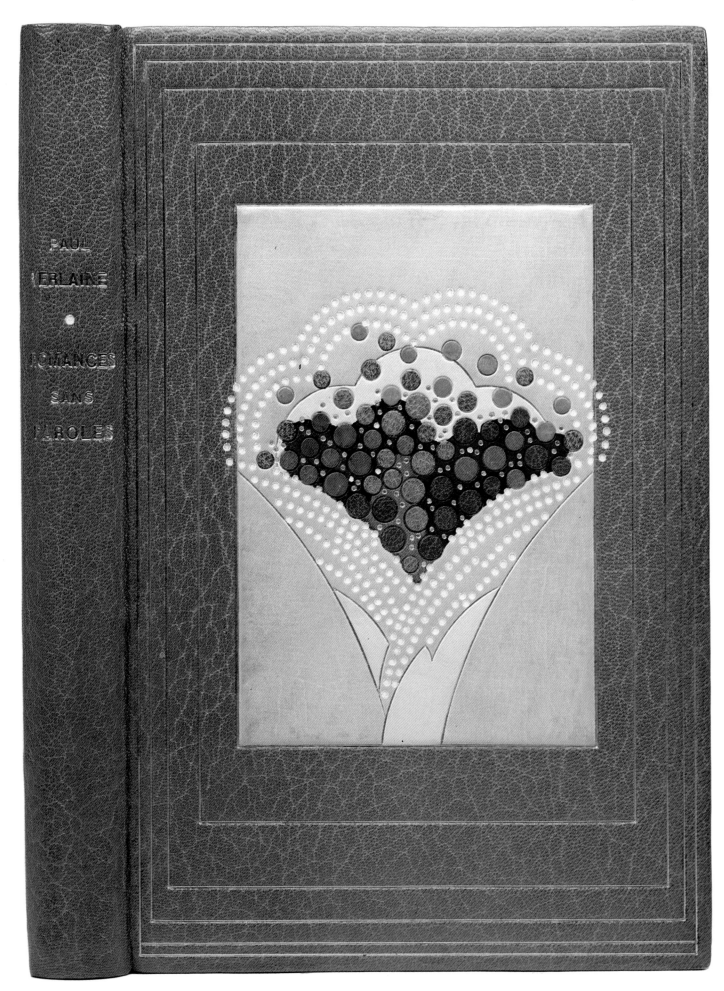

Emile Maylander

1867-1959

Maylander was primarily a gilder, but the reduction of book commissions during World War I forced him increasingly into bindings. He had a preference for classical designs, which he executed with a faultless technique. He was assisted by his two sons and from the 1920s they gradually replaced him. The Maylander *atelier* made the transition from the prewar *fin-de-siècle* floral esthetic to the later geometric style with restraint, incorporating understated variations of both, when appropriate, to its standard repertoire of gold- and blind-tooled fillets and punched ornamentation.

170 | **Emile Maylander**, the panel designed by **Théophile Steinlen**
La Chanson des gueux (Jean Richepin), 1910, leather with gold-tooling, the panel in incised and polychromed leather.
Courtesy of Habsburg, Feldman S.A.

Opposite
171 | **Emile Maylander**
Personnages de comédie (Albert Flament), 1922, inlays of leather with gold-tooling.
Photograph courtesy of the Sutton Place Foundation

GEORGES MERCIER

Mercier was the son of the binder and gilder Emile-Philippe Mercier. He joined his father's workshop in 1898 and took over as head on his father's death in 1910.

172 | **Georges Mercier**, the panel designed by **Gustave Guétant**
Le Livre de la jungle (*The Jungle Book*: Rudyard Kipling), 1928, inlays of leather with gold-tooling, with panel in incised and polychromed leather.
Photograph courtesy of the Sutton Place Foundation

Charles Meunier

1865-1940

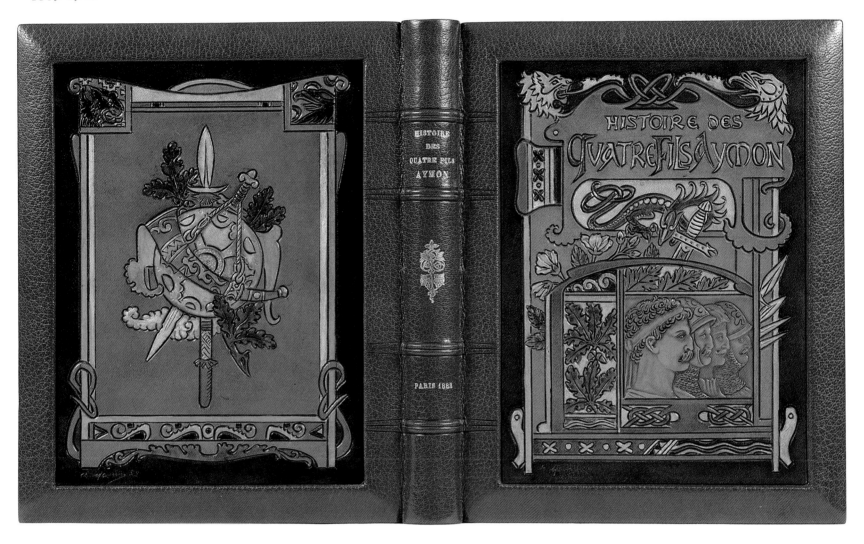

Contemporary criticism of Meunier was mixed. Although most observers found him talented, innovative, and instinctive, he offended contemporary bibliophiles by producing vast numbers of covers containing emblematic and pictorial themes, often thought to be gaudy and crudely executed commercial ventures pandering to the tastes of the period's bourgeoisie.

His output was prodigious and he moved with ease between styles and periods, a fact which further offended purists who felt that his talent lay primarily in the creation of half-bindings with decorative spines.

173 | **Charles Meunier**
Histoire des quatre fils Aymon (Joseph Bédier), 1883, leather with gold- and blind-tooling, and incised and polychromed panels.
Photograph courtesy of the Sutton Place Foundation

Overleaf

174 | **Charles Meunier**
doublure, *Contes choisis* (Guy de Maupassant), 1891-92, inlays of leather with gold-tooling.
Spencer Collection, New York Central Library

175 | **Charles Meunier**, the panels designed by **J. Masson**
Sapho (Alphonse Daudet), 1897, leather with blind-tooling, and incised and polychromed panels.
Photograph courtesy of the Sutton Place Foundation

139

176 | **Charles Meunier**
Le Rêve (Emile Zola), 1892, leather with
blind-tooling, and incised and polychromed
panels.
*Photograph courtesy of the Sutton Place
Foundation*

177 | **Charles Meunier**
Boule de suif (Guy'de Maupassant), 1897, inlays of leather with gold- and blind-tooling.
Photograph courtesy of the Sutton Place Foundation

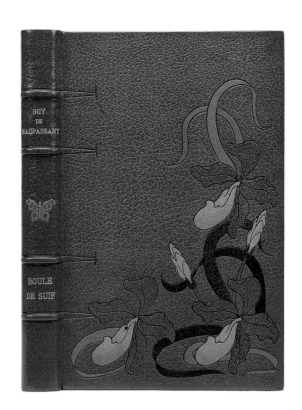

178 | **Charles Meunier**
Paroles d'un croyant (Félicité Lamennais), 1909, inlays of leather with gold- and blind-tooling, and incised and polychromed recessed panels.
Photograph courtesy of the Sutton Place Foundation

179 | **Charles Meunier**
La Belle Impéria (Honoré de Balzac), 1913,
inlays of leather with gold-tooling, with
incised and polychromed panels.
Courtesy of Christie's, Geneva

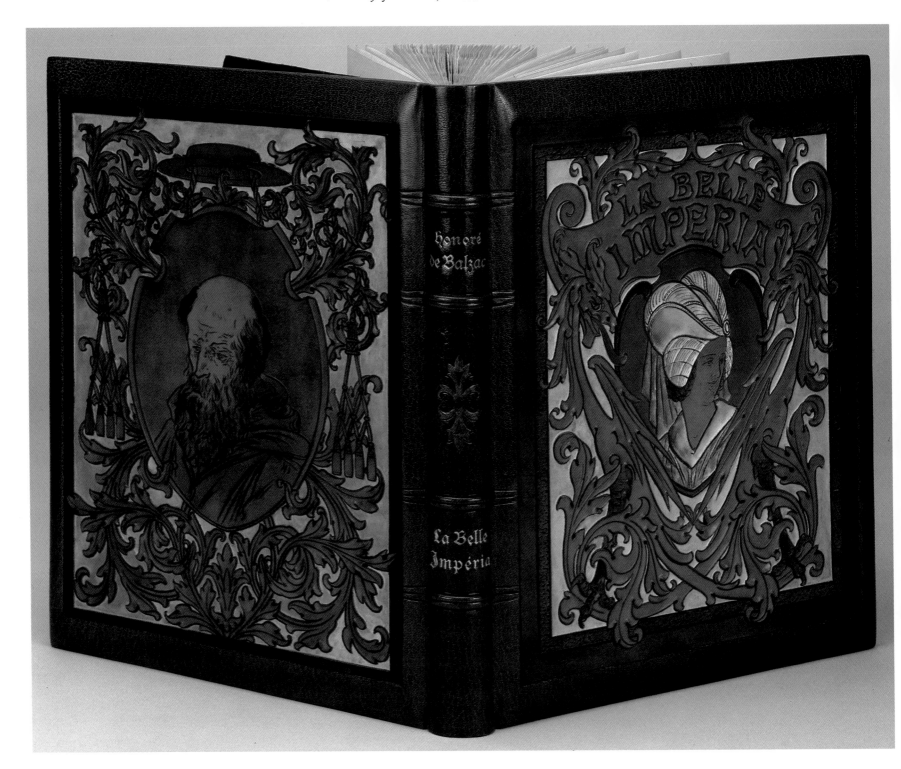

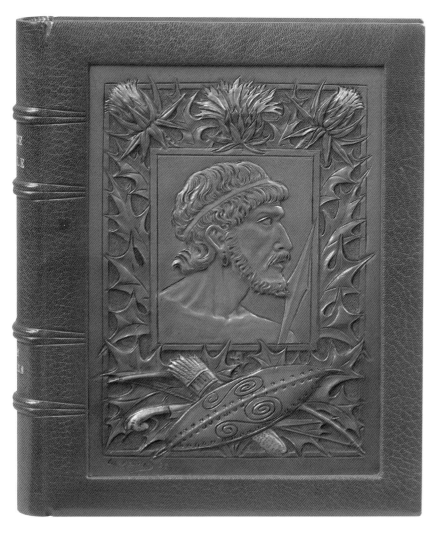
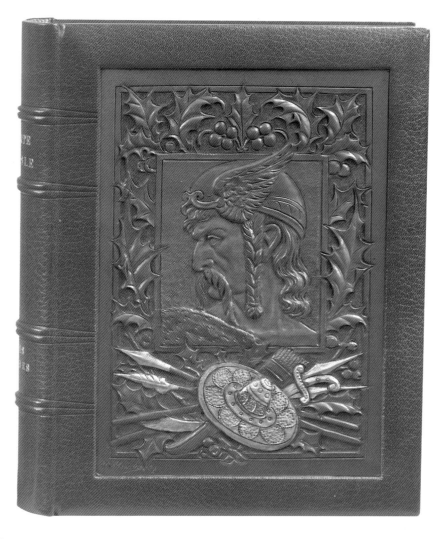

180 | **Charles Meunier**
Poèmes barbares (Leconte de Lisle), 2 vols.,
1925, leather with gold-tooling, and
incised, modeled and gilt panels.
*Photograph courtesy of the Sutton Place
Foundation*

Marius-Michel

1846-1925

Marius-Michel was the great pioneer of modern bookbinding. At first, his revolutionary belief that a book's cover should reflect its contents — that modern works demanded modern bindings — met with fierce resistance from his fellow binders and from collectors. His range of decorative ornaments derived from nature, "La Flore Ornamentale," were thought to fall into the category of "art" rather than bindings. But his passionate conviction and irreproachable technique soon won him followers and by 1885 his designs were seen as a viable alternative to traditional bindings. Awards at the 1900 Exposition saw him confirmed as France's supreme binder. *See also 72.*

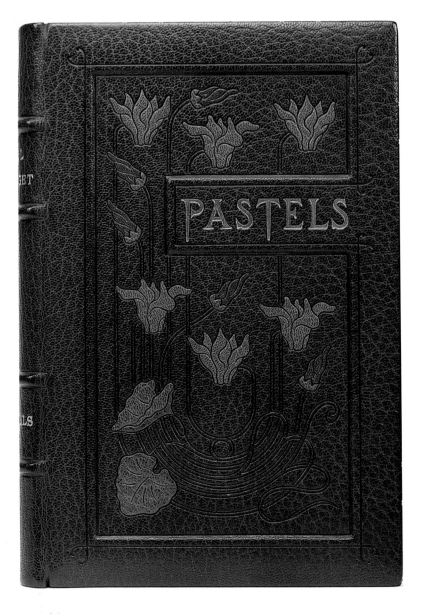

182 | **Marius-Michel**, the panel designed by **Pierre Vidal**
Les Affiches illustrées (Ernest Maindron), 1895, leather with incised and polychromed panel.
Photograph courtesy of the Sutton Place Foundation

181 | **Marius-Michel**
Les Pastels (Paul Bourget), 1895, inlays of leather with gold- and blind-tooling.
Photograph courtesy of the Sutton Place Foundation

Opposite
183 | **Marius-Michel**
Zadig (Voltaire), 1893, inlays of leather with gold-tooling.
Courtesy of Christie's, Geneva

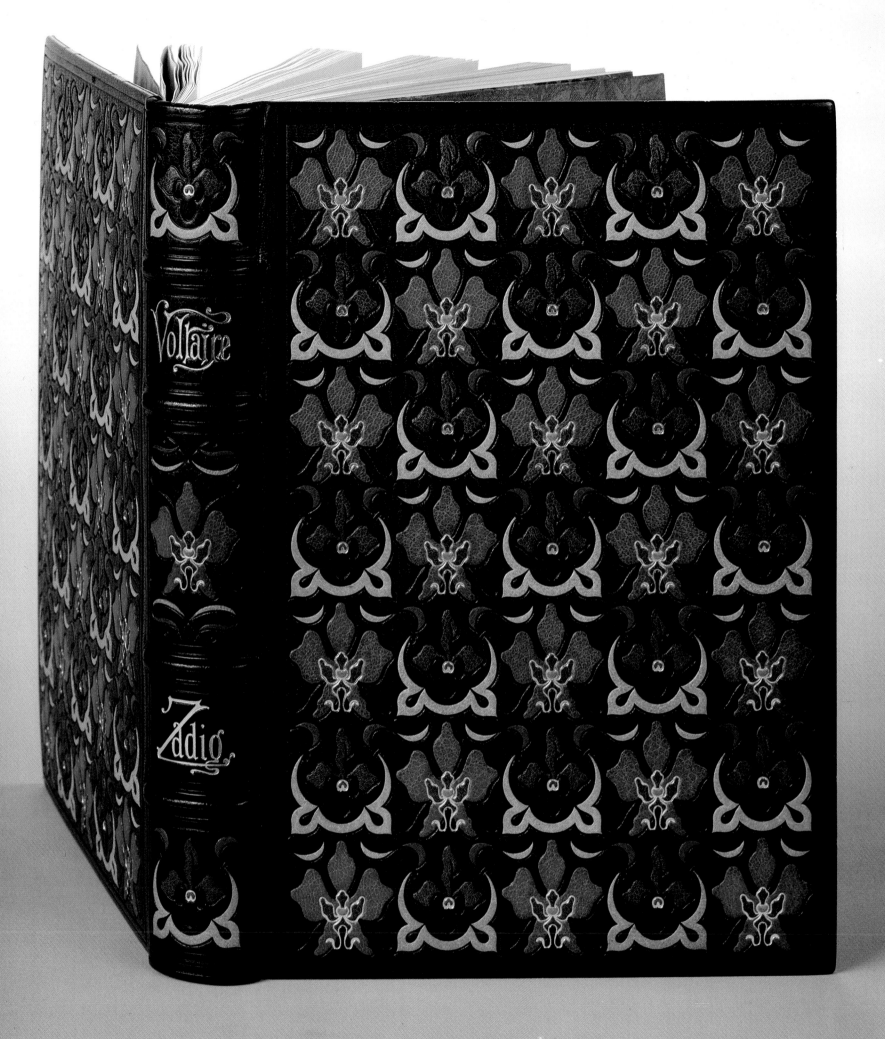

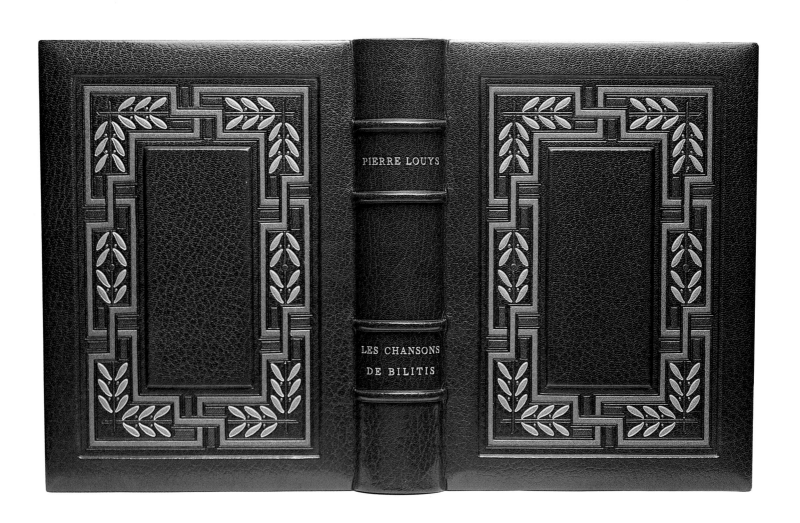

PIERRE LOUYS

LES CHANSONS
DE BILITIS

Prosper
Mérimée

La
Jaquerie

Luc-Olivier
Merson

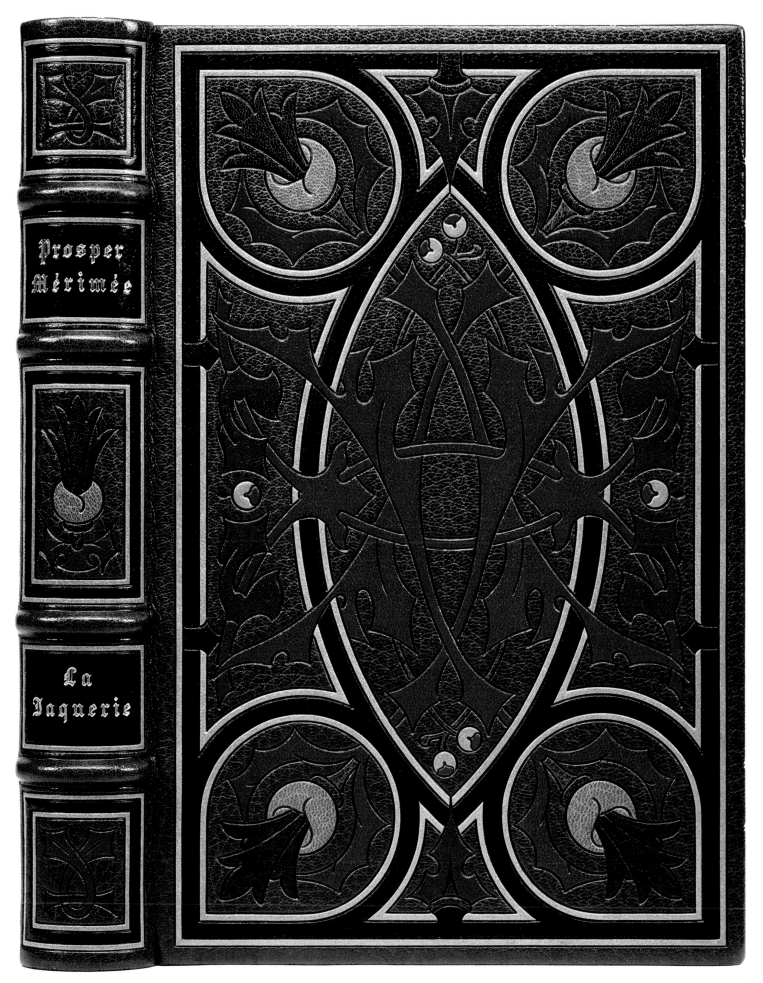

189 | **Thérèse Moncey**
La Brière (Chateaubriant), 1939, leather with gold- and blind-tooling.
Photograph courtesy of the Sutton Place Foundation

THÉRÈSE MONCEY

Moncey made her formal debut in 1946 and participated in expositions between 1947 and 1952. In 1950 she was awarded the Grand Prix de la Reliure Française. She initially executed her own designs, but later chose only to prepare the maquettes. Moncey's preference was for artist-illustrated books for which she would design covers that evoked the contents.

HENRI NOULHAC

1866-1931

A superlative craftsman, Noulhac specialized initially in plain leather bindings (*reliures jansénistes*) and copies of 18th-century bindings. By 1900 he had begun to incorporate modest floral emblems into the dentilled fillet borders on his covers. Noulhac never attempted to create a reputation for himself as a book designer *per se*, though he did achieve respect as an instructor, numbering Rose Adler and Madeleine Gras among his students.

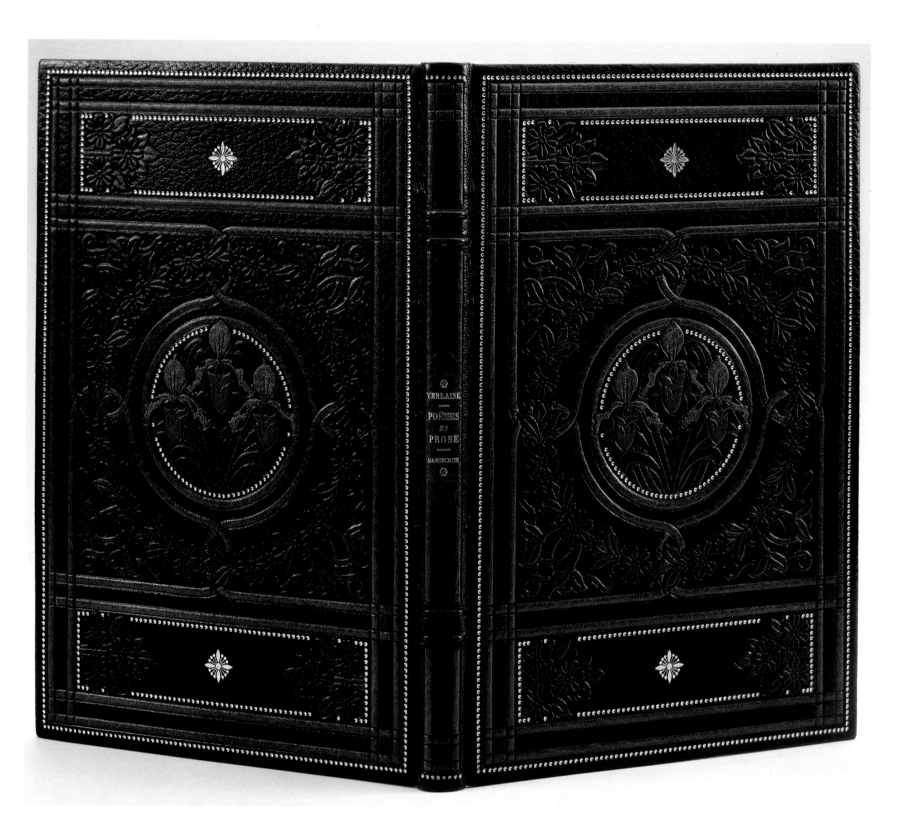

190 | **Henri Noulhac**
Poèmes et proses (Paul Verlaine), undated,
inlays of leather with gold-tooling.
Courtesy of Christie's, Geneva

191 **Henri Noulhac**
Lysistrata (Aristophanes), 1921, inlays of
leather with gold- and blind-tooling.
*Photograph courtesy of the Sutton Place
Foundation*

192 **Henri Noulhac**, designed by **Adolphe
Giraldon**
Daphnis et Chloë (Longus), undated, inlays of
leather with gold-tooling with painted panel

193 | **Henri Noulhac**
Madame Bovary (Gustave Flaubert), 1922,
inlays of leather with gold-tooling.
*Photograph courtesy of the Sutton Place
Foundation*

Louise Pinard

Little has so far been discovered about Louise Pinard, except that she was the daughter of Durvand (1852-1924), a noted late 19th century and early 20th century binder.

194 | **Louise Pinard**
Vie amoureuse de Casanova (Maurice Rostrand), 1930, inlays of calf with gold- and blind-tooling.
Photograph courtesy of the Sutton Place Foundation

A. Pinard-Lefort

Opposite
195 | **A. Pinard-Lefort**
La Création (Dr. Joseph-Charles Mardrus), 1928, inlays of leather with gold-tooling.
Courtesy of Christie's, Geneva

Victor Prouvé

1858-1943

Prouvé was the inspiration behind the Ecole de Nancy, assuming leadership after the death of Emile Gallé in 1904. A man of many talents— watercolorist, decorative artist, sculptor, and leatherworker—he created bindings in tooled and polychromed leather decorated in the Art Nouveau spirit with the flora and fauna of his native Alsace-Lorraine. His most noteworthy binding, *Salammbô*, depicts in broad panorama the splendors and cruelty of Carthage as imagined by Flaubert. Prouvé received, with René Wiener, an equal share of the criticism heaped on the Nanceiens for their revolutionary figurative and pictorial work. *See also 222.*

Camille Martin

1861-98

In addition to those bindings which René Wiener executed for him, Martin also created some on his own and others in collaboration with Victor Prouvé. All are distinctly painterly: transferals on to leather of his paintings on canvas. Several convey a delightful *fin-de-siècle* mood mixed with a predictable Japanesque influence. Martin was one of the most gifted and versatile artists of the Nancy movement. *See also 223.*

196 | **Victor Prouvé** and **Camille Martin**
Salammbô (Gustave Flaubert), 1893, inlays of leather with gold-tooling.
Collection Musée de l'Ecole de Nancy, photograph courtesy of Studio Image-Nancy

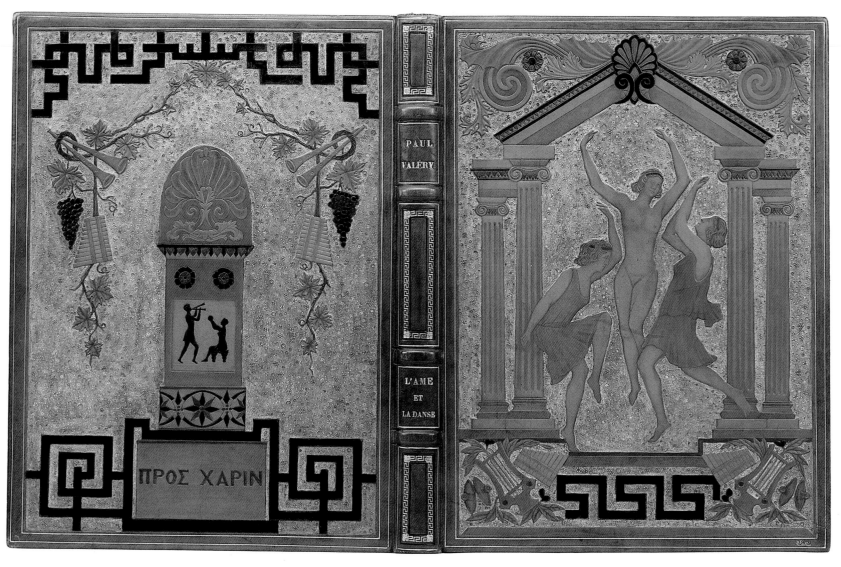

Ralli

Petrus Ruban

1851-1929

In his early work Ruban vacillated between traditionalism and the fashionable pursuit of the new esthetic typified by Marius-Michel. At this time his most innovative and charming covers comprised striking Art Nouveau floral compositions in inlays of color that used the binding's entire surface, but by around 1905 he had aligned himself with the conservative, neo-classicist binders and gilders, a group headed by Emile-Philippe Mercier. An important aspect of Ruban's work was his irreproachable technique.

198 | **Petrus Ruban**
| *L'Effort* (Edmond Haraucourt), 1894, inlays
| of leather and gold-tooling.
| *Spencer Collection, New York Public Library*

199 | **Petrus Ruban**
| *La Vie des boulevards* (G. Montegueil), 1896,
| inlays of leather with gold-tooling.
| *Photograph courtesy of the Sutton Place
| Foundation*

Fʀᴀɴçᴏɪꜱ-Lᴏᴜɪꜱ Sᴄʜᴍɪᴇᴅ

1873-1941

Painter, illustrator, engraver, and binder, Schmied created some of the most dramatic and lavish bindings of the era. His versatility is apparent in the painted panels that embellish many of his works, executed in lacquer and *coquille d'oeuf* by his friend and collaborator Jean Dunand.

After World War I Schmied turned increasingly to the total production of *éditions de luxe*: their illustration, typography, typesetting, page design, and printing. Though he executed many of the bindings himself, some he commissioned from others, such as Georges Cretté. Cretté and Dunand both worked with Schmied on *Le Cantique des cantiques*. The sumptuousness of Schmied's work has often obscured the fact that he was a highly gifted modernist designer. *See also 75-77, 80, 82, 83, 86, 113, 117.*

200 | **François-Louis Schmied**, the panels executed by **Jean Dunand**
Daphné (Alfred de Vigny), 1924, leather with lacquered and eggshell panels.
Photograph courtesy of the Sutton Place Foundation

Opposite
201 | **François-Louis Schmied**
La Campagne romaine (René de Chateaubriand), late 1920s, inlays of leather with gold- and silver-tooling.
Collection Félix Marcilhac

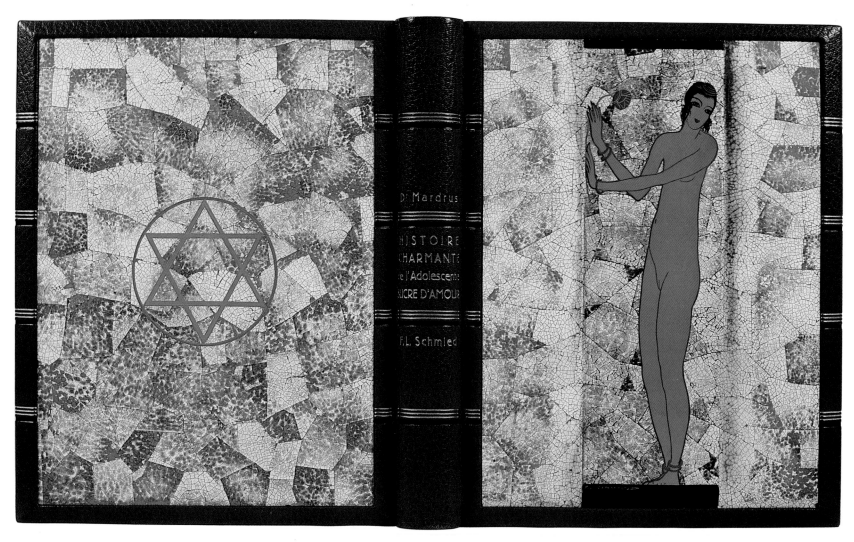

202 | **François-Louis Schmied**, the panels
executed by **Jean Dunand**
Histoire charmante de l'adolescente sucre d'amour,
(Dr. Joseph-Charles Mardrus), leather, gold-
tooling, and lacquered eggshell panels.
*Photograph courtesy of the Sutton Place
Foundation*

Opposite

203 | **François-Louis Schmied**, the panel
executed by **Jean Dunand**
Le Cantique des cantiques (*The Song of Songs*),
1925, leather with lacquered and eggshell
panel (bound by Georges Cretté).
*Photograph courtesy of the Sutton Place
Foundation*

Opposite

204 | **François-Louis Schmied**, the panel
executed by **Jean Dunand**
Le Cantique des cantiques (*The Song of Songs*),
1925, leather with lacquered and eggshell
panel (bound by Georges Cretté).
*Photograph courtesy of the Sutton Place
Foundation*

205 | **François-Louis Schmied**
Le Cantique des cantiques (*The Song of Songs*),
1925, leather with gold-tooling (bound by
Georges Cretté).
*Photograph courtesy of the Sutton Place
Foundation*

Overleaf

206, 207 | **François-Louis Schmied**
doublures, *Le Livre de la jungle* (*The Jungle
Book*: Rudyard Kipling), 1928, inlays of
leather with gold-tooling, inset with paper
panels in watercolor and ink.
*Photograph courtesy of the Sutton Place
Foundation*

209 | François-Louis Schmied
Deux Contes (*Two Tales*: Oscar Wilde), 1920s, inlays of leather

208 | **François-Louis Schmied**, the panel executed by **Jean Dunand**
Les Ballades françaises (Paul Fort), 1927, inlays of leather with gold-tooling, the panel in lacquered eggshell.
Courtesy of Habsburg, Feldman S.A.

Opposite

210 | **François-Louis Schmied**, executed by **Jean Dunand**
doublure, *Le Livre de la vérité de parole* (Dr. Joseph-Charles Mardrus), 1929, lacquered metal.
Photograph courtesy of the Sutton Place Foundation

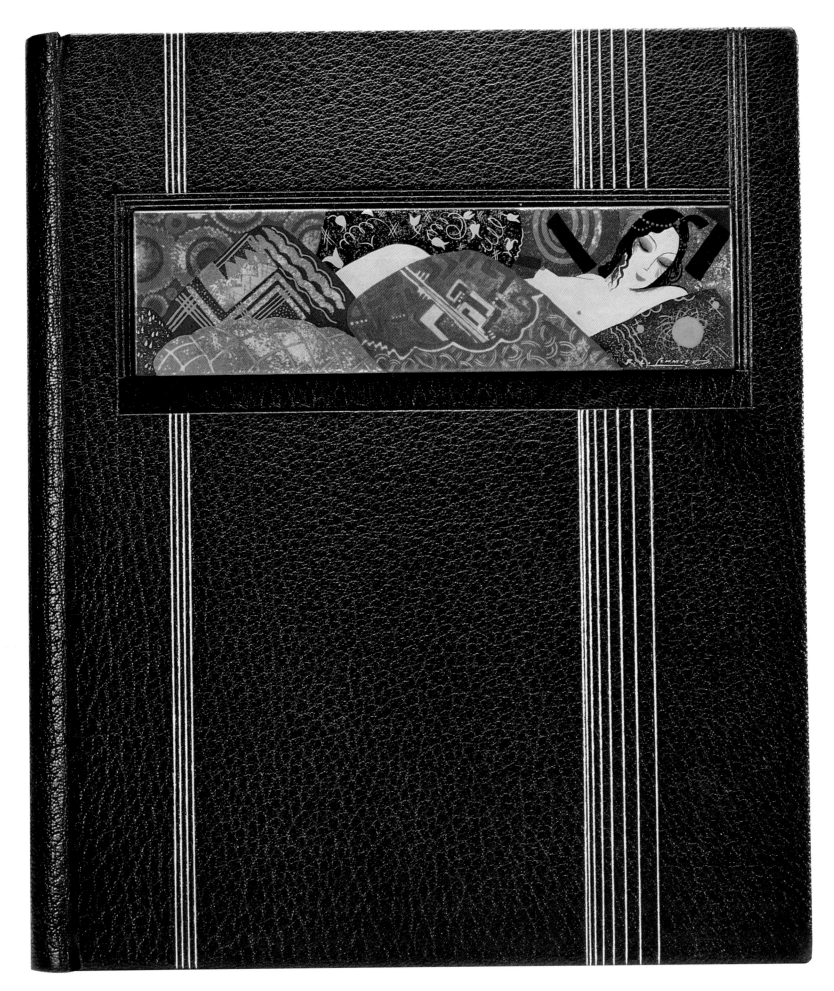

Opposite

211 | **François-Louis Schmied**, the panel
executed by **Jean Dunand**
Histoire de la Princesse Boudour (Dr. Joseph-
Charles Mardrus), 1926, inlays of leather,
gold- and blind-tooling, and lacquered
panel.
*Photograph courtesy of the Sutton Place
Foundation*

213 | **François-Louis Schmied**
Le Livre de la vérité de parole (Dr. Joseph-
Charles Mardrus), 1929, inlays of leather
with gold- and blind-tooling.
*Photograph courtesy of the Sutton Place
Foundation*

212 | **François-Louis Schmied** and **Gonin et Cie**
La Création (Dr. Joseph-Charles Mardrus),
2 vols., 1928; inlays of leather, gold-
tooling, and palladium (vol. 1); leather with
palladium, blind-tooling, and inlaid
lacquered panel (vol. 2).
*Photograph courtesy of the Sutton Place
Foundation*

171

Opposite
214 | **François-Louis Schmied**, the panel
executed by **Jean Dunand**
Ruth et Booz (Dr. Joseph-Charles Mardrus),
1930, leather with gold-tooling, and
polychromed lacquered panel.
Courtesy of Christie's, New York

215 | **François-Louis Schmied**, the panel
executed by **Jean Dunand**
Le Paradis musulman (Dr. Joseph-Charles
Mardrus), 1930, leather with lacquered and
eggshell panel.
Collection Félix Marcilhac

Overleaf
216, 217 | **François-Louis Schmied**
doublures, *Histoire charmante de l'adolescente
sucre d'amour* (Dr. Joseph-Charles Mardrus),
c. 1930, inlays of leather.
Collection George Matheson Gerst

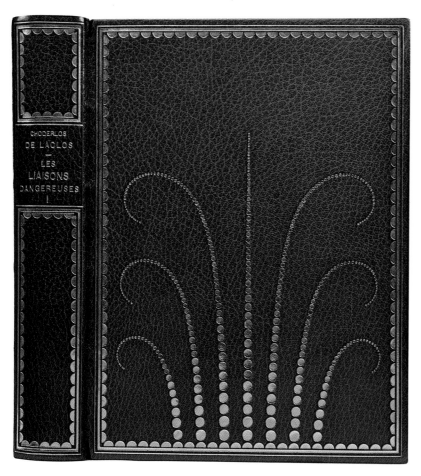

Marcellin Semet

1894–?

Georges Plumelle

1902–?

Semet and Plumelle had a reputation for blending impeccable binding techniques with a fresh modernist vocabulary of design. At their finest, their bindings consist of flowing lines or arabesques on subtle two- or three-color grounds. Their style remained remarkably consistent for many years.

218 | **Semet et Plumelle**
Les Liaisons dangereuses (Pierre Choderlos de Laclos), vol. 1, 1930, leather with gold-tooling.
Photograph courtesy of the Sutton Place Foundation

219 | **Semet et Plumelle**
Poésies (Stéphane Mallarmé), 1932, inlays of leather with gold-tooling
Photograph courtesy of Priscilla Juvelis

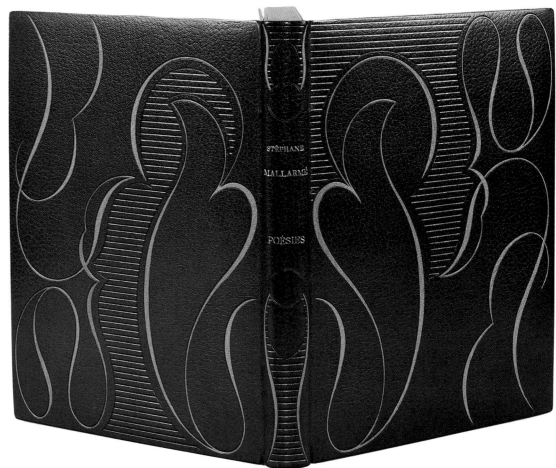

220 | **Semet et Plumelle**, the panel designed and
executed by **Paul Jouve**
La Chasse de Kaa ("Kaa's Hunting": Rudyard
Kipling), 1930, inlays of leather with
lacquered and eggshell panel.
*Collection Priscilla Juvelis, photograph courtesy of
Sotheby's, New York*

J. K. Van West

Jules Karel Van West was born in Belgium and studied at the Ecole de la Cambre in Brussels. He worked in Paris, where he retained several top bibliophile clients.

221 | **J. K. Van West**
La Mort de Venise (Maurice Barrès), 1936, inlays of leather, gold-tooling, and palladium.
Photograph courtesy of the Sutton Place Foundation

VERMOREL

?-1925

Vermorel's initial specialty was liturgical books, to which he later added half- and full-bindings. After World War I, following Legrain's example, he turned to modern compositions, introducing linear designs into his works at the Salons. His new style was pleasing and fresh, though it lacked the verve and impetuosity of the younger generation of binders with whom he exhibited.

222 | **Vermorel,** the panel designed and painted by **Georges Baudin**
doublure, *Le Chevrier* (author unknown), 1918, inlays of leather with gold-tooling, inlaid with a panel with gouache and opal cabochons on paper.
Collection Ralph Esmerian

223 | René Wiener, designed by **Camille Martin**
L'Estampe originale (Roger Marx), 1894,
inlays of leather.
*Collection Musée de l'Ecole de Nancy, photograph
courtesy of Studio Image-Nancy*

RENÉ WIENER

1855-1940

Although not a bookbinder *per se*, Wiener
achieved enormous notoriety in the 1890s when
his bindings for Nancy and Art Nouveau artists
were first shown at the Salons. "Wienerism"
became the term used to describe the most
commercial and shoddy aspects of book cover
design. In fact, his crime was primarily to have
introduced the Art Nouveau esthetic, a new and
immensely appealing pictorial style, into the
bastions of conservatism.

224 | René Wiener, designed by **Victor Prouvé**
La Chanson des gueux (Jean Richepin), 1890s,
inlays of leather.
Courtesy Musée des Arts Décoratifs, Paris

179

YSEUX

?-1951

From his small family bindery, Yseux created Jansenist and half-bindings ornamented with turn-of-the-century punches. After World War I he specialized in inlaid leather and white vellum romantic bindings, some enhanced with oils by Théophile Gautier.

225 | **Yseux**, painted by **Louis Legrand**
Cours de danse – fin de siècle (Louis Legrand), 1892, painted parchment.
Photograph courtesy of the Sutton Place Foundation

unidentified binders

226 | **Unidentified binder**
La Walkyrie and *Siegfried* (Richard Wagner, French translation by Alfred Ernst), 1895, incised and polychromed calf.
Photograph courtesy of the Sutton Place Foundation

227 | **Unidentified binder**, designed by
A. Vanteyne
Les Cafés-concerts (Gustave Coquiot), *c.* 1901-
02, inlays of leather with gold- and blind-
tooling, and incised and polychromed panel.
Photograph courtesy of the Sutton Place
Foundation

229 | **Unidentified binder**
Daphnis et Chloé (Longus), inlays of leather,
with gold- and blind-tooling.
*Photograph courtesy of the Sutton Place
Foundation*

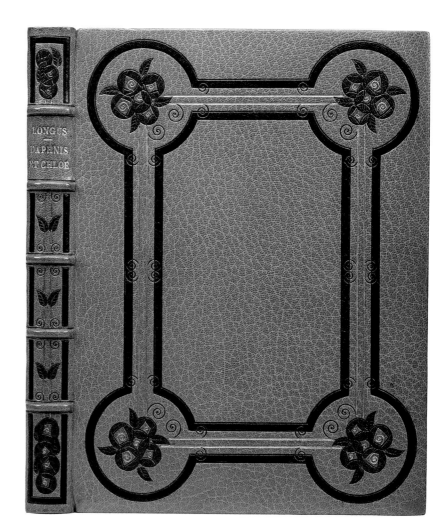

228 | **Unidentified binder**
L'Oiseau bleu (Maurice Maeterlinck), 1925,
inlays of leather with gold- and silver-
tooling.
*Photograph courtesy of the Sutton Place
Foundation*

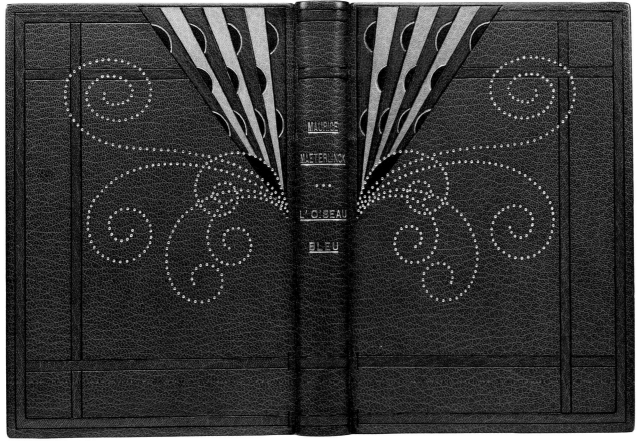

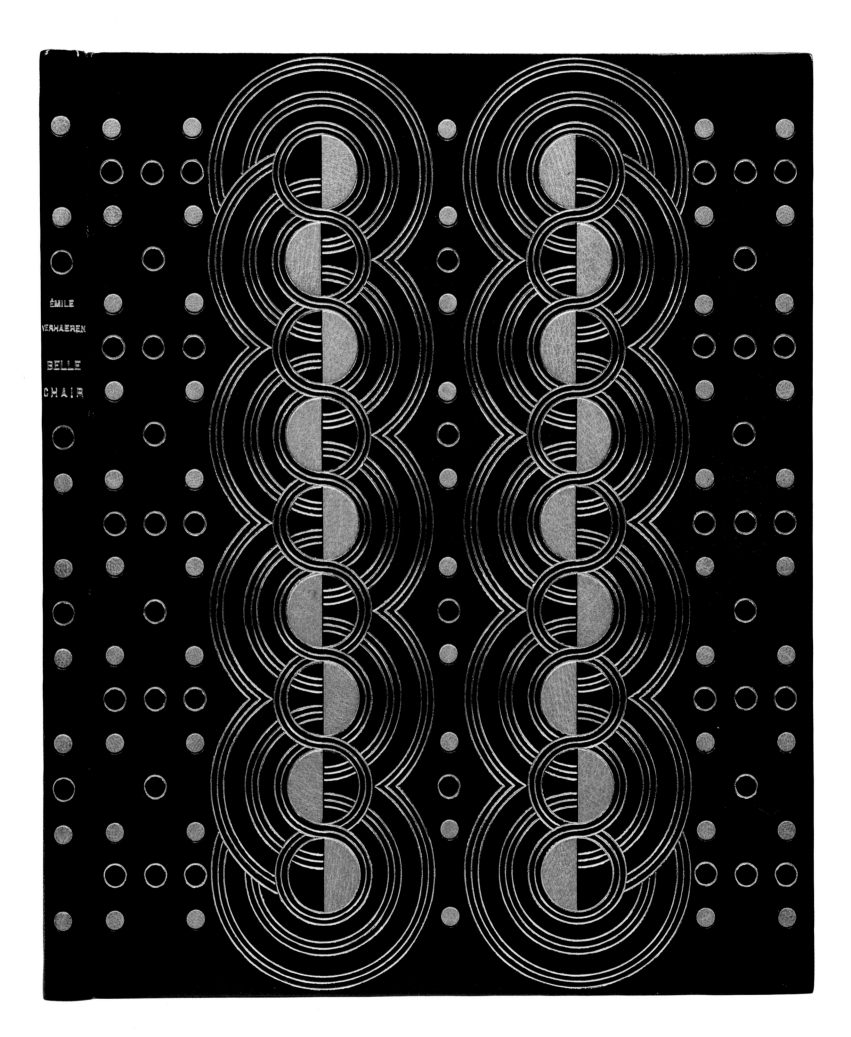

NOTES

1. Binding is by tradition a family business in which skills pass from generation to generation. It has also, for de luxe editions, been an arcane profession in which business has been conducted in private. In Paris, binders at the beginning of the period under discussion in this book (1880–1940) were congregated on the Left Bank in the parish of Saint-André-des-Arts (now the university quarter), where the craft had long since established its guild and church. To this obscure working-class district came the city's wealthiest bibliophiles.

Most ateliers consisted of the owner (himself a master binder), two or three "forwarders" (who prepared the leather, cut punches, etc.), and two or three "finishers" (master binders and gilders).

For comprehensive histories of French bookbinding, *see* Roger Devauchelle, *La Reliure en France de ses origines à nos jours* (vol. 1: up to the late 1600s, and vol. 2: Louis XV up to the mid-1850s), Paris, 1961; Etienne Deville, *La Reliure française* (vols. 1 and 2), Paris, 1930–31; Paul Elek, *The Art of the French Book*, Paris, 1947, pp. 141–45; and Marie Michon, *La Reliure française*, Paris, 1951.

2. Bookbinding's preferred material is goatskin from Morocco, known as morocco, or morrocan leather. It is highly prized for its durability and rich texture.

3. Imperial emblems returned to favor after the 1791 revolution. For typical examples, *see* Marius-Michel, *La Reliure française commerciale et industrielle depuis l'invention de l'imprimérie jusqu'à nos jours.* . ., Paris, 1881, p. 65*ff*. For examples of Louis Philippe motifs, *see* pp. 82–87, and for examples of Second Empire motifs, *see* p. 91*ff*.

4. For a wide selection of Second Empire motifs, *see* Devauchelle (note 1), vol. 2, pp. 94–95.

5. *See* S.T. Prideaux, *Modern Bookbindings: Their Design and Decoration*, New York, 1906, p. 78.

6. For a discussion of Trautz and the popularity of his bindings, *see* Elek (note 1), p. 145.

7. Les Bibliophiles Contemporains had an initial membership of 160. After some years it was disbanded and re-created as the Société des Cent Bibliophiles, presided over by Eugène Roderigues. *See* Prideaux (note 5) p. 74.

8. For a discussion of Amand's impact on traditional bindings, *see* Octave Uzanne, *L'Art dans la décoration extérieure des livres en France et à l'étranger*, Paris, 1898, pp. 194–95; and Devauchelle (note 1), pp. 88–89.

9. In *La Décoration de la reliure moderne*, Marius-Michel discussed the extent to which he felt the outside decoration of a book should harmonize with the text. He cautioned against the trap of direct representation, and scolded binders who claimed to be his disciples and then proceeded to design a fan for the cover of *The Fan*, a violin for *The China Violin*, and a nose for *The Notary's Nose*.

10. The French master *verrier*, Emile Gallé, later developed a similar floral vernacular to convey the symbolism in his glassware. The orchid, for example, imparted to Gallé "an unimaginable richness and strangeness of forms, substances, perfumes, colors, caprices, sensual pleasures and disturbing mysteries" (included in a speech entitled "Le Décor symbolique," presented by Emile Gallé to the Académie de Stanislas on 17 May 1900).

11. "The book of its time in the original binding of its time" (quoted in Prideaux [note 5], p. 75).

12. The status of the binding craft in the late 1900s was the subject of several books at the time; *see*, for example, Octave Uzanne, *L'Art dans la décoration extérieure des livres*. Paris, 1898, and *La Reliure moderne et artistique*. Paris, 1887; Marius-Michel, *L'Ornamentation des reliures modernes*, Paris; Henri Béraldi, *La Reliure de XIX siècle* (4 vols.), Paris, 1895–97; L. Derome, *La Reliure de luxe*, Paris, 1888; S.T. Prideaux, *An Historical Sketch of Bookbindings*, New York, 1893; Léon Gruel, *Manuel historique et bibliographique de l'amateur de reliures*. 2 vols., Paris, 1887; and Emile Bosquet, *L'Art du relieur*, Paris, 1890.

13. Béraldi was among the most outspoken critics of the use of incising and modeling to decorate leather bindings. He wrote, "Everything that stands in the way of that caress is unnatural and wrong. Modeling conflicts with the inlays of moroccan leather that make up the very attractive hide covering the book. The hide is perfect just as it is. Yet they persist in modeling it, they spoil the natural shape and substance of this wonderful object: the bound book. Modeling creates actual bumps which are insidious and questionable on the book's cover. First and foremost it is a terrible mistake, the carving is offensive and irritating to the hand that holds the book, that moves over it and caresses it. . ." (quoted in Ernest de Crauzat, *La Reliure française de 1900 à nos jours* (vol. 1), Paris, 1932, pp. 94–95).

14. For illustrations of the leatherwork exhibited by members of the Ecole de Nancy at the turn of the century, *see Exposition de l'Alliance Provinciale des Industries d'Art Ecole de Nancy*, exhibition catalogue, Pavillon de Marsan, Paris, March, 1903; and *Société Lorraine des Amis des Arts Catalogue Exposition XLI*, exhibition catalogue, Nancy, 1904.

15. For an example of a binding designed by Georges de Feure, *see* Uzanne (note 8), p. 65.

16. Uzanne (note 8), p. 58.

17. Elek (note 1), p. 146.

18. An artist-decorator, Séguy used a vigorous Art Nouveau imagery, including crickets, cicadas, and fruit, on his covers, which were executed by Durvand. He combined incising and modeling with mother-of-pearl, metal, and hardstone cabochons to achieve a bright and colorful effect.

19. For a discussion of the foremost artist-decorators of the period, *see* Uzanne (note 8), p. 203*ff*.

20. *See* Devauchelle (note 1), vol. 2, pp. 112–16, for a discussion of industrial bindings.

21. Uzanne (note 8), pp. 58, 60.

22. For illustrations of Giraldon's designs, *see* Gaston Quénioux, *Les Arts décoratifs modernes*, Paris, 1925, p. 334. Other Giraldon bindings are listed in de Crauzat (note 13), vol. 1, pp. 91–92. In the preface to the auction catalogue of the Couderc sale, Henri Vever wrote of Giraldon "His bindings have the rare quality of being completely in harmony with the nature of the work that they cover."

23. Four Grand Prix were awarded to binders at the 1900 Exposition Universelle: two for industrial bindings (Magnier and Engel), and two for artistic bindings (Marius-Michel and Mercier *père*).

24. Meunier's criticism of the binding display at the exposition revealed, in part, his refusal to participate, "Why do you want me to pay seven hundred and fifty francs a metre to exhibit bindings in display cases lost in the middle of the paper-bound section, killed off by these icy black and white surroundings which drive away the visitors! On days when there are four hundred thousand people at the Exposition, one finds two in front of the bindings, and they are the bookbinders themselves!" (quoted in de Crauzat [note 13], vol. 1, p. 19).

25. *See* Henri Nicolle, "La Reliure moderne," in *Les Arts français: la reliure d'art*, Paris, 1919, p. 190; and E.A.

Taylor, *The Art of the French Book*, London, 1914, p. 179.

26. Several French publishing houses produced *éditions de luxe* between the 1890s and the early 1920s; for example, Auguste Blaizot, L. Carteret, H. Floury, F. Ferroud, Jules Meynial, E. Ray, Larousse, Hachette et Cie., E. Flammarion, and Ollendorff.

27. Spencer lived in Paris, where he formed his book collection between 1880 and 1910. On his death in 1912, he bequeathed the collection to the New York Public Library with an endowment to purchase further books bound in "handsome bindings representative of the arts of illustration and bookbinding throughout the centuries." The collection today houses over 6,000 titles and printed books. For further information, *see The Dictionary Catalog and Shelf List of the Spencer Collection of Illustrated Books and Manuscripts and Fine Bindings*, information brochure, The New York Public Library, The Research Libraries, Boston, Mass., 1971.

28. The school continues today, on its one hundredth anniversary, to serve this generation of French book designers, printers, binders, and artists. Initially for boys only, registration is now coeducational. Examples of bindings designed and executed by students at the Ecole Estienne are illustrated in Quénioux (note 22), p. 344.

29. *See* Edith Diehl, *Bookbinding: Its Background and Technique* (vol. 1), New York, 1946, p. 106.

30. Two Paris trade newspapers provided binders – both the employers and their artisans – with information on new developments within the medium: *La Reliure*, the organ of the Chambre Syndicale, an association of master binders founded by Léon Gruel; and *Le Relieur*, the organ of the Chambre Syndicale Ouvrière, the corresponding association for workers.

31. Chadel joined the Maison Vever in 1904 as a jewelry designer.

32. Among Chadel's other clients were Barthou, Bellanger, the Comte de Laroche-Foucauld, Prost, Rousset, and Miguet.

33. Doucet's original collection of books was donated to the City of Paris in 1918.

34. "I have been in turn my grandfather, my father, my son, and my grandson" (quoted in *Pierre Legrain, relieur: répertoire descriptif et bibliographique de mille deux cent trente-six reliures*, Paris, 1965, p. xxvii).

35. Marie Dormoy collaborated with Doucet for ten years on his book collection. On his death she published an article describing the collection's growth, which was published in both the *Bulletin de la Société des Amis de la Bibliothèque d'Art et d'Archéologie de l'Université de Paris* (2nd semester, 1929) and the *Bulletin du bibliophile*, December 1929.

36. *Pierre Legrain, relieur* (note 34), p. xxx.

37. For illustrations of the use of a book's title as design, *see* Ph. Dally, "Les Téchniques modernes da la reliure," *Art et décoration*, January 1927, in which works by Legrain, Schroeder, Gras, de Léotard, Langrand, and Adler, are represented.

38. Quoted in de Crauzat (note 13), vol. 2, p. 69.

39. *Pierre Legrain, relieur* (note 34), p. xx.

40. Quoted in de Crauzat (note 13), vol. 2, p. 29.

41. *Pierre Legrain, relieur* (note 34), p. xxiii.

42. *Ibid*.

43. Legrain's version of *Le Neveu de rameau* is illustrated in color in Devauchelle (note 1), vol. 3, frontispiece.

44. After the 1925 Exposition Universelle, Legrain continued to display his bindings at the annual Salons and through Les Cinq, which exhibited initially at the Galérie Barbazanges, and then at the Galérie de la Renaissance.

45. For a contemporary criticism of women binders, see de Crauzat (note 13), vol. 2, p. 129*ff*.

230 | **Unidentified binder**
Belle Chair (Emile Verhaeren), 1931, inlays of leather with gold-tooling.
Photograph courtesy of the Sutton Place Foundation

46. For a discussion of the Ecole and the role played in it by women, both as instructors and students, *see* de Crauzat (note 13), vol. 2, pp. 143–44.

47. Georges Cretté, "Distinctive Designs in Hand Tooled Book Bindings," *Creative Art*, no. 7 (1930): 279.

48. After Marius-Michel's death, Cretté introduced a range of stylized Art Deco floral motifs for his bindings, in part perhaps as a form of respect for his previous employer, but also probably to show his affinity with the modern movement.

49. For a comprehensive list of the major collaborative bindings by Schmied and Dunand, *see* de Crauzat (note 13), vol. 2, pp. 104–8.

50. *See* de Crauzat (note 13), vol. 1, p. 135*ff*.

51. By 1930 it even appeared threatened by its own success, as Cretté explained, "Book collecting, which used to be the privilege of but a select few, for whom certain publishers, artists, printers and binders worked in obscurity and silence, has since the war become so violently fashionable that one wonders how long it will last. . . . *Editions de luxe* are innumerable, and new ones are continually appearing" (quoted in Cretté [note 47], p. 378).

52. The next major auction of bookbindings after the Marty sale was that of Louis Barthou, conducted by Auguste Blaizot on 25/26/27 March 1935.

53. "Sans Pierre Legrain, je n'aurais sans doute eu l'idée de dessiner des reliures" (quoted in Georges Blaizot, *Masterpieces of Modern French Bindings*, New York, 1947).

54. At the advent of World War II, Scherrer returned to the Argentine, taking his books with him. After his death years later, the Parisian book dealer, Marcel Sautier, acquired some of his collection, which he sold in Paris in 1963. Included were 180 of Bonet's most spectacular works, many seen by the public for the first time since their creation.

55. Bonet was excited at the prospect of binding the works of the Surrealists André Breton and Paul Eluard. As he noted, "How can one neglect to be grateful for this door opened to spiritual infinity, to the right which it has given to evasion?" (quoted in Blaizot [note 53], p. 96).

56. Georges Blaizot (note 53), pp. xiv–xv.

57. *La Reliure originale*, exhibition catalogue, Bibliothèque Nationale, Paris, 1947, p. 166; quoted in *Cent Ans de reliures d'art 1880–1980*, exhibition catalogue, Bibliothèque Municipale de Toulouse, 1981, p. 74.

58. Bonet's all-metal bindings generated new challenges for the medium. As Georges Blaizot noted, "The years 1931 and 1932 produced bindings entirely of metal. They put before the designer and his collaborator, the jeweler Pierre Boit, [demands] which made profound alterations of the book itself necessary. To mention only the most noticeable one: it was found necessary to use hinges to connect sides and sides. Carried out in dural and nickel. these bindings . . . prove the thorough contemporaneousness of their maker, and his entire lack of prejudice" (quoted in Blaizot [note 53], p. 104).

59. Other titles which Bonet reproduced in multiple variations included *Alcools. Le Poète assassiné. Daphnis et Chloé. La Belle Enfant*, and *Parallèlement*.

60. Georges Blaizot (note 53), pp. xv–xvi.

61. For an example of Adler's helix design, *see Peau d'âne* (1936) illustrated in Devauchelle (note 1), vol. 3, p. 173.

62. For a discussion on the saturation of de luxe bindings in 1935, *see* Georges Pascal, *La Reliure. le livre et l'illustration*, exhibition catalogue, May-October 1935.

63. The display generated a full complement of participants which, in addition to those listed above, included Lucie Weill, Georges Levitsky, Martita Garcia, Odette Pilon, and Gilberte Givel.

64. Edith Diehl (note 29), vol. 1, 1946, pp. 108–9.

65. The shortage of leather during World War II forced binders to use inferior goat and sheep skins and even cow's bladder.

BIOGRAPHIES AND BIBLIOGRAPHIES

Information on binders is given wherever it is available, but in certain cases no records have come to light so far.

Rose Adler (1890–1959)
Bookbinder and leather worker

Born in Paris, Adler entered the Villa Malesherbes division of the city's Ecole de l'Union Centrale des Arts Décoratifs in 1917 and studied under Andrée Langrand. She remained at the school until 1925, and from 1923 took extra-curricular instruction in binding and gilding from Henri Noulhac at his atelier. Throughout her career, Adler created a wide range of decorative objects, including jewelry, small toiletry items, clothes, and furniture, but today she is almost exclusively known for her bindings. A rare ebony table, commissioned by Jacques Doucet in the 1920s for his studio in Neuilly and now in the collection of the Virginia Museum of Fine Arts, Richmond, Virginia, shows the same inspired use of exotic and precious materials – sharkskin, metal, and enamel, in this case – that is found in her bindings.

A selection of Adler's earliest bindings was included in an exhibit of work from students at the Ecole des Arts Décoratifs shown at the 1923 Salon of the Société des Artistes Décorateurs. These impressed Doucet, who purchased three examples, thereby beginning an association that was to continue until his death six years later. Doucet also introduced Adler to Pierre Legrain, whose work she greatly admired.

In the 1920s, Adler's bindings for Doucet showed a similar range of materials and designs to those used at the time by Legrain. Her covers for *Calligrammes. Poèmes. Le Paysan de Paris*. and *A. O. Barnabooth*, for example, consisted largely of nonfigurative, geometric compositions executed in brilliant inlays of color embellished with incrustations of mother-of-pearl, metal strips, hardstones, and animal skins. Like Legrain, also, she made full use of the letters in the book's title by combining them in complex overlapping configurations. Often the sizes, colors, and typefaces of each letter were different, as in her cover design for *Beauté. mon beau souci*.

After Doucet's death in 1929, Adler began to concentrate on other major commissions, both for private book collectors and for libraries and institutions such as the Bibliothèque Nationale, the Fondation Littéraire Jacques Doucet, the Victoria & Albert Museum, and the New York Public Library. Her style underwent a distinct change. The arresting colors and imagery of the earlier designs were replaced by a more refined and simplified range of covers executed in combinations of leather, often without incrustations of other materials. By this time she had identified herself fully with the avant-garde movement in architecture, painting, and the decorative arts headed by Pierre Robert, Pierre Chareau, Robert Mallet-Stevens, Etienne Cournault, Jean Puiforcat, and others, an evolution that can be clearly traced in her binding designs.

Adler showed her work at salons and expositions throughout her career. She exhibited independently at the Salon of the Société des Artistes Décorateurs from 1924 until 1929, when she transferred to the newly formed Union des Artistes Modernes (U.A.M.). She also participated in the 1925 Exposition Universelle, the 1931 Exposition Internationale du Livre, the 1937 Exposition Internationale, and the 1939 Golden Gate Exposition in San Francisco.

Adler strongly believed that the cover's design should be at the service of the text, and that a binding should be judged on how successfully it persuaded the reader to open the book. In 1960, a year after her death, a retrospective exhibition of her work was held at the Bibliothèque Jacques Doucet.

Bibliography

Adler, Rose, *Reliures. présenté par Rose Adler*, Paris, 1929

Brunhammer, Yvonne, *The Nineteen Twenties Style*, London, 1966

Catalogue de l'exposition de la reliure originale, Société de la Reliure Originale, Bibliothèque Nationale, Paris, 1947

Chapon, François, "Rose Adler," *Le Jardin des arts*, April 1961, pp. 53–55

Dally, Ph., "Les Téchniques modernes de la reliure," *Art et décoration*. January 1927, pp. 22–24

de Crauzat, Ernest, *La Reliure française de 1900 à 1925* (vol. 2), Paris, 1932, pp. 147–53

Devauchelle, Roger, *La Reliure en France de ses origines à nos jours* (vol. 3), Paris, 1961, pp. 241–42, 171, 202, 207, 210, 212, 217, 228

Exposition de la Société de la Reliure Originale, exhibition catalogue, Bibliothèque Nationale, Paris, 1959, p. 65ff

Farnoux-Reynaud, Lucien, "La Reliure d'art: Triomphe du goût français," *Mobilier et décoration*, February 1938, pp. 58–78

Fleming, John F., and Juvelis, Priscilla, *The Book Beautiful and the Binding as Art*, New York, 1983 and 1985; (vol. 1), p. 89; (vol. 2), p. 6

Guignard, Jacques, "Aspects de la reliure française reliures modernes," *Art et décoration*, April 1947, pp. 22–29

Lecomte, Georges, "Reliures modernes," *Plaisir de France*, December 1937, pp. 65–73

Quénioux, Gaston, *Les Arts décoratifs modernes 1918–1925*, Paris, 1925, p. 186

Sickles, Daniel, *Masterpieces of French Bindings*, New York, 1947, p. 125

Laura Albin-Guyot
Bookbinding designer

In a style strikingly different from any other binder of the late 1920s, Albin-Guyot applied treated photographs of micro-organisms to the covers and endpapers of her books. These introduced new possibilities for the medium and were adapted by Bonet in the series of Surrealist bindings which he designed around 1933 for works by André Breton and Paul Eluard. Albin-Guyot's subjects included unicellular marine life, such as plankton and algae, or bacteria photographed under a microscope and reproduced in somber tones of brown and gold or black and silver. Some of these, such as *Les Chansons de Bilitis* and *Le Trèfle noir*, were bound by Kieffer. Others, *L'Ombre de la croix*, for example, were bound by Adler.

Bibliography

Adler, Rose, *Reliures, présenté par Rose Adler*, Paris, 1929, pls. 5, 7, 24, 33, 43

Michon, Marie, *La Reliure française*, Paris, 1951, pp. 133–34

René Aussourd (?–1968)
Bookbinder and gilder

Aussourd studied under his uncle, Charles Meunier, and also worked as a gilder for Chambolle-Duru before establishing his own studio at 8 rue du Fouarre in 1912. His bindings were mostly classical, incorporating borders of Greek key motifs (for example, *La Prière sur l'Acropole*) and ivy leaves. Several elegant examples have survived, such as his cover for *Les Chansons de Bilitis*, which included a colorful floral composition in inlays of leather enhanced with crisply tooled gold fillets. He retired in 1960.

Bibliography

de Crauzat, Ernest, *La Reliure française de 1900 à 1925* (vol. 2), Paris, 1932, pp. 48–49

Henri Blanchetière (1881–1933)
Bookbinder and publisher

A graduate of the Ecole Estienne, Blanchetière worked for both Lortic *fils* and René Kieffer before establishing himself first on the boulevard Saint-Germain and then in the rue de l'Epéron. In 1906 he took over Joseph Brétault's workshop, where he aligned himself with Marius-Michel in the pursuit of a modern binding style inspired by nature. His designs incorporated a cautious blend of Art Nouveau flowers interspersed with curved gold fillets, similar to the many Michel-inspired covers which appeared at the Paris Salons after 1900. After World War I, he gradually cut his remaining ties to traditionalism and introduced modern covers consisting of symmetrical linear patterns, of which *Les Climats*, *La Canne de Jaspe*, and *L'Age d'or* provide fine examples.

From 1923, like Meunier and Kieffer, Blanchetière began to publish editions of de luxe art books, such as *Les Chansons de Miarka*, with wood-block engravings by Gabriel Belot and water colour illustrations by Alméry Lobel-Riche.

Bibliography

de Crauzat, Ernest, *La Reliure française de 1900 à 1925*, Paris, 1932; (vol. 1), pp. 50–51; (vol. 2), p. 58

Devauchelle, Roger, *La Reliure en France de ses origines à nos jours* (vol. 3), Paris, 1961, pp. 127, 136, 244

Fleming, John F., and Juvelis, Priscilla, *The Book Beautiful and the Binding as Art* (vol. 1), New York, 1983, pp. 61, 108, 178

Paul Bonet (1889–1971)
Bookbinding designer

Born in Paris to Belgian parents from Namur, Bonet attended the Ecole Communale de la Rue des Blancs-Manteaux from 1895 to 1903, before taking up an apprenticeship in an electrical shop from 1904 to 1906. At this time he discovered that his real interest lay in painting and, on the advice of Jean-Paul Laurens, he asked his father if he could enrol at the Académie-Julian, a request that was denied. Three years later, still determined to pursue a career in the arts, he became a modeler of wooden fashion mannequins, employment that was interrupted by military service from 1910 to 1912. In 1914 his father died and Bonet volunteered for action. Wounded near the Belgian border, he was sent to hospital in Montpellier and then demobilized. He returned to Paris to take up his old job.

Bonet first turned to bookbinding in 1920, when an acquaintance invited him to design simple covers for his modest collection. Bonet proposed half-bindings in shagreen, which were executed by a local binder. Bookbinding remained a hobby for Bonet until 1924, when the decorator Matthieu Gallerey persuaded him to exhibit his works. He was presented to Henri Clouzot, the conservator at the Musée Galliera, who was preparing the exposition Art du Livre Français for the following year. Clouzot agreed to display a few of Bonet's designs, which Gallerey arranged to have executed by students at the Ecole Estienne. At the end of 1925, when further examples of his designs were accepted by the jury of the Salon d'Automne, Bonet decided to take up the craft professionally. The following year, he made his debut at the Salon of the Société des Arts Décorateurs. The public responded initially with indifference, but between 1927 and 1929 one collector in particular, R. Marty, patronized him. In 1930, a business reversal caused by the depression forced Marty to sell his entire collection. The auction, conducted by Auguste Blaizot at the Hôtel Drouot, included fifty-two Bonet bindings. The book collecting community awoke to the sudden realization of Bonet's genius.

At the 1928 Salon, Bonet gained the confidence of a second client, Carlos R. Scherrer, a businessman from Buenos Aires who spent part of each year in his Paris office. An avid collector of bindings, rather than of books *per se*, Scherrer quickly emerged as Bonet's principal client and patron, commissioning most of his major works in the 1930s. (In 1939, when war loomed, Scherrer returned to Argentina, taking his books with him. After his death years later, the Parisian book dealer Marcel Sautier went to fetch the collection, a portion of which was sold in Paris in 1963. Included were 180 of Bonet's most spectacular works.)

By 1931, Bonet was firmly established, exhibiting at Raoul Simonson's invitation in Brussels. He also bound manuscripts and Surrealist works for the Belgian collector René Gaffe. In the same year, he designed his first truly major bindings, which were bound by Ferdinand Giraldon with gold fillet work by André Jeanne.

Bonet readily acknowledged his debt to Legrain – evident in his 1920s linear designs – throughout his career. From 1930, however, his introduction of daring novel effects quickly established him as a master in his own right. His preoccupation with the letters in the book's title as the principal elements of its design, for example, was one of his major contributions to the field. He designed more than forty different covers alone for Apollinaire's *Calligrammes*, each a dynamic variation on a common theme. His Surrealist bindings, also, conveyed on photographic film the disturbing images engendered by the writings of André Breton and Paul Eluard. Equally ingenious was his creation of the irradiant design, which provided a three-dimensional optical illusion in the use of undulating lines radiating from a common center. His sculpted bindings for Picasso's *Buffon* and *Le Chef-d'oeuvre inconnu* were strikingly original.

Collaborating with *orfèvres* and jewelers (Egouville, Pierre Boit, and Gustave Miklos), Bonet introduced nickel, steel, gold, platinum, and duralumin into his covers. His leather was handled by various binders, including René Desmules, Clovis Lagadec, Henri Lapersonne, Maurice Trinckvel, and Charles Vermuyse; his gilding by Roger Arnoult, Roger Cochet, Charles Collet, Raymond Mondange, and Guy Raphaël.

As was the case with many other binders, Bonet's commissions fell off in the mid-1930s. An exhibition of his work was held in Brussels in 1933 at the Galérie Giroux but the economic recession of 1934–35 led to such a sharp reduction in bookbinding commissions that Bonet had to resort in his free time to his old profession of modeling fashion mannequins. However, the 1937 International Exposition saw new interest in and support for bookbinding as fresh clients were drawn to the medium. Bonet's exhibit charmed and astonished visitors with its new techniques and audacious designs.

During World War II, Bonet continued to execute commissions, adding designs for commercial *cartonnage* bindings to those for his private clients. In 1943, as a measure of Bonet's pre-eminence within the field, the publisher Georges Blaizot brought out a monograph on him, which coincided with an exhibition of his bindings held at the Galérie Renou et Colle. After the war, Bonet's fame increased further with his introduction of a new series of *Calligrammes* covers and, in 1949, his famous lion's head configurations.

In 1950 Bonet was appointed a Chevalier of the Legion of Honor. He was also given the first prize at the International Bookbinding Show in London and received a special award from the Société d'Encouragement à l'Art et à l'Industrie.

Bibliography

Berman, Avis, "Antiques: Bound for Glory: Rare Bookbindings of Art Deco Design," *Architectural Digest*, May 1986, p. 188*ff*

Bibliothèque reliée par Paul Bonet, Paris, 1963

Blaizot, Georges, *Masterpieces of French Modern Bindings*, New York, 1947

Catalogue de l'exposition de la reliure originale, Société de la Reliure Originale, Bibliothèque Nationale, Paris, 1947

"5 Reliures," *Mobilier et décoration*, April 1935, pp. 140–45

Clouzot, Henri, "Paul Bonet: architecte de la reliure," *Mobilier et décoration*, February 1933, pp. 66–72

Farnoux-Reynaud, Lucien, "La Reliure d'art: Triomphe du goût français," *Mobilier et décoration*, February 1938, pp. 58–78

Gaffe, René, *Connaissance de Paul Bonet*, Brussels, 1933

Lecomte, Georges, "Reliures modernes," *Plaisir de France*, December 1937, p. 65

Paul Bonet Carnets 1924–1971, Paris, 1981

T., S., "Binding for Reading," *Arts and Decoration*, February 1934, p. 52

Robert Bonfils (1886–1971)
Painter, illustrator, engraver, interior decorator, and designer of bookbindings, ceramics, tapestries, and fabrics

Bonfils entered the Ecole Germain-Pilon in Paris in 1903, three years later continuing his education in the Atelier Cormon division of the Ecole Nationale des Beaux-Arts. On graduating, he joined the furniture designer Henri Hamm, who introduced him to Paul Gallimard, the coordinator of the book section of the annual Salon d'Automne, at which Bonfils made his debut in 1909. His first book commission, *Clara d'Ellebeuse*, which he illustrated with pochoirs, was shown in 1913. Another important prewar commission was the tea-room of the large Parisian department store, Les Magasins du Printemps, which he decorated with allegorical murals depicting the Four Seasons. During World War I he illustrated with woodcuts a three-volume edition of *Les Rencontres de M. de Bréot*. He later showed his versatility by designing objects in a wide range of materials, including silks for Bianchini-Férier and ceramics for the Manufacture Nationale de Sèvres. The Musée de la Ville de Paris and the Musée d'Art Moderne today hold selections of his paintings.

In 1919, Bonfils was appointed to succeed Henri de Waroquier as a professor of design at the Ecole Estienne. He taught his students that a binding design should suggest, rather than give a precise definition of, a book's contents. He also believed that a book's surface should be flat, without sculptural detailing, incrustations, or inlaid metal plaques. His covers were therefore in leather (either plain or with inlays of color) or vellum, to which he applied in a simple linear graphic style an enchanting Art Deco imagery of fashionable young women, tribal African masks, musical instruments, and so on. His depictions of women, especially, captured the buoyant mood of the 1920s in a poignant and romantic manner. There are many charming examples, such as his covers for *Sagesse, Oeuvres de Maupassant,* and *Soyez discrèt.*

Bonfils's binding designs were executed, among others, by Cretté, Canape, and the students at the Ecole Estienne. A regular participant in bindings exhibitions, he also took part in the 1925 and 1937 International Expositions in Paris, the 1939 World's Fair in New York, and the 1957 World's Fair in Brussels. Collectors of his works included André Gillon, Oliver Sainsère, L. Comar, Henri Vever, and Pierre Hollier-Larousse.

Bibliography

Burnand, Robert, "Robert Bonfils: Peintre, Illustrateur, et Relieur," *Byblis,* Summer 1929, pp. 49–51
Catalogue de l'exposition de la reliure originale, Société de la Reliure Originale, Bibliothèque Nationale, Paris, 1947
Charpentier, Thérèse, *L'Ecole de Nancy et la reliure d'art,* Paris, 1960, p. 51
"5 Relieurs," *Mobilier et décoration,* April 1935, pp. 140–45
de Crauzat, Ernest, *La Reliure française de 1900 à 1925* (vol. 2), Paris, 1932, pp. 75–78, pls. CCLXVI-CCLXX
Deshairs, Léon, "Robert Bonfils," *Art et décoration,* February 1929, pp. 33–43
Devauchelle, Roger, *La Reliure en France de ses origines à nos jours* (vol. 3), Paris, 1961, p. 245
Farnoux-Reynaud, Lucien, "La Reliure d'art: Triomphe du goût français," *Mobilier et décoration,* February 1938, p. 67
Guignard, Jacques, "Aspects de la reliure française reliures modernes," *Art et décoration,* April 1947, p. 27
Lecomte, Georges, "Reliures modernes," *Plaisir de France,* December 1937, pp. 65–73
Quénioux, Gaston, *Les Arts décoratifs modernes 1918–1925,* Paris, 1925, p. 338
Rambosson, Yvanhoe, "Les Reliures de Robert Bonfils," *Mobilier et décoration,* February 1932, pp. 71–74

André Bruel (b. 1895)
Bookbinder

Born in Saint-Sylvain d'Anjou in Angevin, Bruel attended school in Angers before entering the Ecole Normale Supérieure in 1912. The advent of the war interrupted his tuition, and Bruel enlisted in the French infantry. Badly gassed in 1917, he was demobilized and returned to Angers where, after a spell in hospital, he married the daughter of a local book gilder, Légal, for whom he worked before establishing his own bookbinding atelier in 1919 on the rue Plantagenet. In the 1920s, while catering to a clientele of bibliophiles in nearby Anjou and Touraine, he exhibited his works at the annual Paris Salons, where he was judged the only provincial binder of major standing. In 1922 he participated in a bookbinding exhibition at the Reitlinger Gallery in Paris and, three years later, at the Exposition Universelle. In 1927 his first one-man show at the Galérie André on the rue Saints-Pères generated respectful reviews from the city's critics.

Bruel's designs were safe and harmonious, composed of large, simple images executed in the medium's traditional materials: morocco or calf. Additional detailing and color accents were introduced by the use of inlays of leather in preference to "foreign" incrustations of metal or stones. Some of his most imaginative designs, such as those for *Vie des martyrs, Les Droits de l'homme et du citoyen,* and *Le Feu,* consisted only of the letters in the book's title imposed in dynamic patterns across the entire front and back of the cover.

Bibliography

de Crauzat, Ernest, *La Reliure française de 1900 à 1925* (vol. 2), Paris, 1932, pp. 67–70
Derys, Gaston, "André Bruel," *Mobilier et décoration,* September 1932, pp. 410–13

Georges Canape (1864–1940)
Bookbinder and gilder

J. Canape *père* established his bindery at 18 rue Visconti, Paris, in 1865, where he specialized in liturgical bindings and half-bindings. In 1880, to expand his business, he purchased the inventory and client list of the last noted Second Empire bindery, Belz-Niedrée. Georges Canape succeeded his father in 1894, adding a gilding department some years later to provide the firm with full autonomy. Like his contemporaries Blanchetière, Carayon, Chambolle, and Affolter, the younger Canape soon adopted a restrained version of the Art Nouveau esthetic used by Marius-Michel at the 1900 Exposition Universelle. Many of his compositions consisted of floral emblems within rather formal borders. At the annual Paris Salons, Canape offered a new style blended with classical revival bindings, all executed with the technical precision of a long established bindery. A preference for cold-stamping distinguished his works in the prewar years.

Canape was dependent on others to provide the designs for his most important bindings, most notably Legrain, for whom he executed several covers for Doucet during World War I. Doucet's exhibition of Legrain's bindings at the 1919 Salon of the Société des Artistes Décorateurs included several fine examples by Canape, including *La Ville* by Claudel and *Portraits* by Suarès. Noted artists were commissioned to create other cover designs, including Adolphe Giraldon, Georges Lepape, George Barbier, Jules Chadel, Maurice Denis, and Robert Bonfils. Collectors of his works included Doucet, as noted, and Henri Vever, L. Comar, William Augustus Spencer, and Charles Miguet.

In 1918, Canape was nominated the President of the Syndicate of Patron Bookbinders. He turned his attention increasingly in the 1920s to the promotion of young binders by helping to modernize the apprenticeship process. In 1927 he took in a gifted young graduate from the Ecole Estienne, A. Corriez, as a partner in his firm. On his death in 1937, the firm was divided: the bindery was sold to Esparon, and the gilding department to Henri Mercher.

Bibliography

Bosquet, Emile, "La Reliure française à l'exposition," *Art et décoration,* July-December 1900, p. 47
de Crauzat, Ernest, *La Reliure française de 1900 à 1925,* Paris, 1932, (vol. 1), pp. 61*–62*; (vol. 2), pls. CCLXXIV, CCLXXV, CCLXXXII, CCLXXX, CCLXXIX
Devauchelle, Roger, *La Reliure en France de ses origines à nos jours* (vol. 3), Paris, 1961, pp. 127, 148, 153, 158, 246–47
Fleming, John F., and Juvelis, Priscilla, *The Book Beautiful and the Binding as Art* (vol. 1), New York, 1983, p. 35
Nicolle, Henri, "La Reliure moderne," *Les Arts français: la reliure d'art,* no. 36 (1919): 197
Prideaux, S.T., *Modern Bindings: Their Design and Decoration,* New York, 1906, p. 97

Emile Carayon (1843–1909)
Bookbinder

Trained in the army and then as a painter-decorator, Carayon was drawn to the binding profession by his love of books. In 1875 he established an atelier at 10 rue de Nesles in the Vieux Paris quarter, where he remained throughout his career, assisted in later years by Marie Brisson, a student of Francisque Cuzin.

Carayon built his reputation on *cartonnage,* considered an inferior form of binding and confined mainly to publishers' editions. The process consisted of a cloth or leather casing, rather than a formal leather binding, which was made separately from the book and attached to its endpapers, rather than being sewn or laced into the book's boards to integrate it fully with the text. This relatively cheap technique had been developed in the late eighteenth century by Alexis-René Bradel, who gave his name to it: *cartonnage à la Bradel.* Carayon salvaged the process from banality, interchanging morocco, calf, vellum, brocade, and even paper, enhanced with romantic watercolor or oil sketches by the period's leading artists, including Alcide Théophile Robaudi, Henriot, and Louis Morin.

Cartonnage became fashionable again among bibliophiles in the 1890s, Carayon's work reaching the peak of its popularity at the 1894 Exposition du Livre. His white vellum covers, decorated with delicate flower sprays, were particularly prized. By 1900 Carayon was one of the most versatile binders in Paris, extending his production into formal leather bindings, some of which were incised or modeled by Lucien Rudeaux and Gustave Guétant with pictorial or floral panels. From 1898, with Cuzin and Champs, he provided limited edition covers for the publisher L. Conquet. Included in Carayon's repertoire were half and full plain bindings (*reliures jansénistes*).

Bibliography

de Crauzat, Ernest, *La Reliure française de 1900 à 1925* (vol. 1), Paris, 1932, pp. 51–53
Devauchelle, Roger, *La Reliure en France de ses origines à nos jours* (vol. 3), Paris, 1961, pp. 108–9, 127
Deville, Etienne, *La Reliure française* (vol. 1), Paris, 1930, p. 41
Prideaux, S.T., *Modern Bookbindings: Their Design and Decoration,* New York, 1906, pp. 95–97

Antoinette Cerrutti
Bookbinder and gilder

Cerrutti's first binding designs were for volumes in her own library, but she gradually began to accept commissions from collectors. Legrain's display at the 1925 Exposition Universelle inspired her to enter the Ecole de Reliure division of the Ecole des Arts Décoratifs, where she studied the technical aspects of the craft for five years under Andrée Langrand. After receiving her diploma in 1930–31, Cerrutti established her atelier at 15 rue Michel Angelo.

She developed a simple, flowing style, based on the interplay of colored inlays and gold fillets, which, by the early 1940s, was closer to Bonet's than to Legrain's. Her radiating linear designs for such works as *Le Roman de Tristan et d'Iseult, L'Homme qui assassina,* and *Poèmes* evoked Bonet's first *irradiant* designs from the 1930s, but her compositions invariably had a freshness and airiness of their own. She exhibited a few examples annually at the Salons of the Société des Artistes Décorateurs.

Bibliography

Colas, Henri, "Les Reliures d'Antoinette Cerutti (sic)," *Mobilier et décoration,* January 1948, pp. 31–37
Farnoux-Reynaud, Lucien, "La Reliure d'art: Triomphe du goût français," *Mobilier et décoration,* February 1938, p. 74

René Chambolle
Bookbinder

Chambolle's father, a contemporary of Trautz, Marius-

Michel *père*, Lortic, and Cuzin, established his bindery at 20 rue de Savoie in 1873, moving later to 1 rue du Pont-de-Lodi. His specialty was plain leather bindings, sometimes lightly ornamented with gold fleur-de-lys, *guilloche* and dentilled fillets. He also perfected an inexpensive binding technique known as *faux dos fermé*. At some point he added to his own name the surname of Hippolyte Duru, the celebrated mid-century binder under whom he had been apprenticed, calling his atelier Chambolle-Duru. His son continued the business on his father's retirement in 1898, introducing a formal range of floral decoration to supplement the inspired period-revival bindings for which the firm was known.

Several of Chambolle's bindings at the turn of the century showed a cautious recognition of the capital's preoccupation with Art Nouveau. At the 1900 Exposition Universelle, for example, his display included covers decorated with garlands interspersed with gold and blind-tooled linear compositions. One example in particular, entitled *Josephine*, was well received by the critics. Others showed a distinct Persian influence. Chambolle exhibited a similar range of bindings at the St. Louis World Fair in 1904.

Bibliography

Bosquet, Emile, "La Reliure française à l'exposition," *Art et décoration*, July-December 1900, p. 52
de Crauzat, Ernest, *La Reliure française de 1900 à 1925* (vol. 2), Paris, 1932, pp. 53–55
Devauchelle, Roger, *La Reliure en France de ses origines à nos jours* (vol. 3), Paris, 1961, pp. 44–45, 48, 127
Prideaux, S.T., *Modern Bookbindings: Their Design and Decoration*, New York, 1906, p. 97

Georges Cretté (1893–1969)
Bookbinder and gilder

On the advice of the etcher Charles Jouas, Cretté attended the Ecole Estienne, where he proved a brilliant student, excelling in the course on gilding given by Godefroy and Masset and that on design by Henri de Waroquier. He graduated in 1910, but prolonged his tuition for twelve months of advanced instruction at the request of Marius-Michel, whom he joined the following year.

Cretté quickly emerged as Michel's foremost gilder, but his career was interrupted by military service and the advent of World War I. In 1919 he rejoined Marius-Michel, whose studio had been more or less inoperative due to the master's lingering ill-health. Cretté assumed control and began to direct the flow of new business, an arrangement formalized in 1923 and put into effect in April 1925, a month before Marius-Michel's death. As a mark of esteem for his former employer and mentor, Cretté added to his signature the proud imprimatur, *SUCC. de MARIUS MICHEL*. on many of the bindings which he created when he took over Marius-Michel's workshop on the rue Pierre-Nicole.

The 1925 Exposition introduced Cretté to the public as an independent binder. Adhering initially to the Art Nouveau floral esthetic which allowed him to retain Marius-Michel's old clients, he gradually began to promote his own more traditional geometric style, which was built around compositions of gold and blind-tooled fillets. His virtuosity as a gilder drew comparisons with the nineteenth-century master gilder, Trautz, and earned him the sobriquet, *maître des filets*. By 1930, he was well established as a modern binder with classical roots, one to whom collectors such as J. André, Baron Gourgaud, Aubert, Barthou, and Bussillet brought many of their volumes. His designs were often similar to those of Henri Creuzevault: crisp and in harmony with the text, composed of repeating symmetrical punched decoration, such as overlapping circles, letters, and angled or parallel lines. The incorporation of delicate images, such as ears of corn

or arabesques, added enchantment. His respect for, and mastery of, leather brought him various outside commissions, such as those from Schmied and Dunand, whose lacquered panels he bound.

Cretté's style continued to evolve after World War II, with the introduction of sharply contrasting inlays of color on to beige or tan leather grounds. He also pursued the use of recessed or sculptural definition which he had begun in the 1930s.

Bibliography

Barthou, Louis, "L'Evolution artistique de la reliure," *L'Illustration*, Christmas 1930, n.p.
Chavance, René, "Georges Cretté: artiste et artisan relieur," *Mobilier et décoration*, May 1950, pp. 21–27
"5 Reliures," *Mobilier et décoration*, April 1935, pp. 140–45
Colas, Henri, "Les Reliures de Georges Cretté," *Mobilier et décoration*, May 1946, Paris, pp. 40–45
Cretté, Georges, "Distinctive Designs in Hand-Tooled Bookbindings," *Creative Art* 7 (1930): 378–81
Farnoux-Reynaud, Lucien, "La Reliure d'art: Triomphe du goût français," *Mobilier et décoration*, February 1938, pp. 58–78
Fleming, John F., and Juvelis, Priscilla, *The Book Beautiful and the Binding as Art*, New York, 1983 and 1985; (vol. 1), p. 180; (vol. 2), p.2
Guignard, Jacques, "Les Reliures de Georges Cretté," *Mobilier et décoration*, September 1954, pp. 322-26
Lecomte, Georges, "Reliures modernes," *Plaisir de France*, December 1937, pp. 66, 69, 70
Quénioux, Gaston, *Les Arts décoratifs modernes 1918–1925*, Paris, 1925, p. 335

Henri Creuzevault (1905–1971)
Bookbinder and designer, and gilder

Born in Paris the year that his father became an independent binder, Henri Creuzevault served his apprenticeship as a gilder between 1918 and 1920, before joining the family business. He quickly propelled the *maison* Creuzevault into the front ranks of the avant-garde movement with a broad range of modernist designs executed in innovative techniques. From 1928 he was assisted by his younger brother, Louis, who bound his designs. By 1934, the workshop had moved to 159 Faubourg Saint-Honoré.

From 1925, Creuzevault bindings began to incorporate the Art Deco imagery which became popular in the decorative arts in Paris after World War I. Henri felt himself to be at one with both the new epoch and the style that dominated it. His youthful and vigorous covers took as their point of departure Legrain's revolutionary designs. His bindings for *Le Livre de la jungle* and *Les Carnets de voyage en Italie*, executed around 1926, drew praise at the Salons for their powerful imagery and robust leather covers accented with two ribs (in place of the traditional five) which protruded half an inch from the spines. With their accompanying sleeves and slip-cases, the books made an imposing and weighty package. By the early 1930s, Creuzevault was including raised or sculptural details in his covers, which were soon referred to as "architectural." His introduction of partial, or shaded, combinations of color to the surface of the leather characterized his endless pursuit of novelty. Later examples included incrustations of gold and silver (such as *La Bataille*), silver and aluminum, with blind-tooled fillets (*Le Pot au noir*), and gold with imitation lacquer (*La Rose de Bakawali*).

The death of his brother in the early 1930s had an adverse effect on Creuzevault's work for several years, but by 1937, when he was awarded both the Grand Prix and a gold medal at the Exposition Universelle, he had established himself as a contender to Adler and Bonet in the vanguard of the modernist movement in French bookbind-

ing, a position he consolidated after World War II. His covers remained remarkably fresh and experimental, combining abstract and geometric compositions with three-dimensional effects. In the same year (1937), he opened his own publishing business. After the war he continued to produce marvellous bindings, while applying himself increasingly to administrative matters within the craft. In 1946 he helped to found the society La Reliure Originale, in whose exhibitions he participated.

Around 1956 Creuzevault retired from active bookbinding, resigned from the Groupe des Grand Relieurs, and turned his attention to an art gallery that he had purchased on the avenue Matignon. At this time he also created tapestry designs for the Gobelins manufactory.

Bibliography

Barthou, Louis, "L'Evolution artistique de la reliure," *L'Illustration*, Christmas 1930, n.p.
Berman, Avis, "Antiques: Bound for Glory: Rare Bookbindings of Art Deco Design," *Architectural Digest*, May 1986, pp. 188–93, 234–35
Catalogue de l'exposition de la reliure originale, Société de la Reliure Originale, Bibliothèque Nationale, Paris, 1947
de Crauzat, Ernest, *La Reliure française de 1900 à 1925* (vol. 2), Paris, 1932, pp. 54–56
Devauchelle, Roger, *La Reliure en France de ses origines à nos jours* (vol. 3), Paris, 1961, pp. 171, 202, 210, 228
Fleming, John F., and Juvelis, Priscilla, *The Book Beautiful and the Binding as Art*, 1983 and 1985; (vol. 1), pp. 24, 28, 79, 153; (vol. 2), pp. 1, 51
Guignard, Jacques, "Aspects de la reliure française reliures modernes," *Art et décoration*, April 1947, pp. 22, 27
Henri Creuzevault: naissance d'une reliure, exhibition catalogue, Musée des Arts Décoratifs de la Ville de Bordeaux, Bordeaux, 25 November 1984
Lecomte, Georges, "Reliures modernes," *Plaisir de France*, December 1937, pp. 72, 73

Louis-Lazare Creuzevault (1879–1956)
Bookbinder

Born in Bourgogne, Creuzevault *père* moved to Paris, where he learned the craft of bookbinding under Dode, whose premises on the rue de Villejust he acquired in 1904. Specializing initially in half-bindings, Creuzevault was drawn to the Art Nouveau esthetic when it became fashionable, adding symmetrical *entrelac* and leaf ornamentation to the eighteenth-century revival bindings which he exhibited at the annual Salons. Several examples executed in 1913, and illustrated later in *La Reliure*, blended an appealing but anonymous classicism with Marius-Michel's doctrines. They resembled numerous bindings created in the French capital between 1905 and the outbreak of World War I. In fact, Creuzevault's designs always remained in the craft's mainstream. The arrival of his eldest son, Henri, in 1920 revitalized his workshop. The father retired around 1934.

Salvador David (1859–1929)
Bookbinder and gilder

David was the son of Bernard David, a noted Second Empire binder-gilder who worked for Gruel before establishing his own atelier in 1855. On his father's retirement in 1890, David took over the bindery and initially applied a similar, classically inspired range of ornaments to his covers. But by 1900, after applying himself to the production of commercial and library bindings without much success, he turned to *éditions de luxe*, which he decorated with a blend of gold fillets and garlanded flowers in a compelling and original manner. In 1907, he moved his shop from 12 rue Guénégaud to 49 rue le Peletier, where he remained until his death. Important collectors of his work included René Descamps-Scrive and Freund-Deschamps, for whom he designed bindings for *Les Liaisons dangereuses, La Mort du dauphin,* and *Mirages.*

Bibliography

de Crauzat, Ernest, *La Reliure française de 1900 à 1925* (vol. 2), Paris, 1932, pp. 55–56

Germain de Coster (b. 1895) and Hélène Dumas (b. 1896)
Designers and bookbinders

De Coster was born in Paris, the daughter of a Belgian engineer. Drawn to design at a young age, she entered the Ecole Nationale Supérieure des Arts Décoratifs, where she studied under Jules Chadel. From around 1920 she assisted Chadel for many years, designing jewelry, book plates, bindings, and so on. She was also taught by Yoshigiro Urishibora, from whom she learned the arduous Japanese technique of wood gravure. At the same time she developed an interest in interior design, theater costumes, fabrics, and posters. In the early 1920s she was appointed a professor of gravure and decoration at the Technical College of Applied Arts in the rue Duperre, where she taught until 1961. From 1934, de Coster collaborated with Hélène Dumas to create some striking bindings for books which, in many instances, she herself had illustrated. Presented to the Salon of the Société des Artistes Décorateurs by René Gabriel and Paul Bonet, de Coster later became active in the Society's administration, helping in 1954 to establish a center through which information was disseminated to members.

Born in Valance to a family of scientists, Dumas attended high school before enrolling at the Ecole des Arts Décoratifs in 1924 to study bookbinding under Henri Lapersonne. On graduating three years later, she began to work as a binder. In September 1931 she met de Coster on a sea voyage to Greece, and, three years later, joined her on the staff at the Technical College of Applied Arts as a binding instructor. In their association, de Coster provided the designs for Dumas to execute in leather with the assistance of two gilders, Raymond Mondage and André Jeanne. The pair created many striking bindings decorated with complex geometric and abstract patterns executed in gold and blind-tooled fillets. On occasion, exotic skins and stones, such as cobra, ostrich, beryls, and tourmalines, were inlaid into the base leather to provide eye-catching effects. Many of their finest works were achieved after World War II.

Bibliography

Devauchelle, Roger, *La Reliure en France de ses origines à nos jours* (vol. 3), Paris, 1961, pp. 202, 207, 210, 212, 249–50
Nicolle, Henri, "La Reliure moderne," *Les Arts français: la reliure d'art,* no. 36 (1919): 11–12
Reliure française contemporaine, exhibition catalogue, The Grolier Club, New York, 7 December 1987–30 January 1988, nos. 34–39

Marguerite de Felice
Bookbinder, gilder, and leatherworker

A graduate of the Ecole des Arts Décoratifs in Paris in 1894, de Felice had by the turn of the century become an accomplished leather modeler, creating objects such as menu holders, bags, cushions, blotter ends, music portfolios, and furniture upholstery in tooled leather decorated with Art Nouveau floral motifs.

A regular participant at the Salons of the Société des Artistes Décorateurs, de Felice was drawn to bookbinding at the request of several clients. World War I brought an abrupt halt to her commissions in leather, however, and, on the advice of René Kieffer, she began to design and print fantasy papers for use as doublures and *cartonnage* book covers in her atelier in Neuilly, where she was assisted by Mlle Picard.

As interest in Legrain's modernist bindings grew in the early 1920s, de Felice was drawn back to the medium, and was awarded a gold medal at the 1925 Exposition. Although clearly inspired by Legrain, especially in the use of the letters in the book's title to form decorative compositions, her designs showed a fresh personal interpretation. She also created a number of illuminated parchment and tinted sheepskin covers. In 1927 she accepted a teaching position at the Ecole des Arts Décoratifs, where she remained until her retirement. Larousse and Rieder were among her main clients.

Bibliography

de Crauzat, Ernest, *La Reliure française de 1900 à 1925* (vol. 2), Paris, 1932, pp. 145–47

Geneviève de Léotard (b. 1899)
Bookbinder and gilder, and gilding instructor

In 1912, at the age of thirteen, de Léotard entered the Ecole des Arts Décoratifs in Paris, where she studied book composition under Andrée Langrand and Mme René Sergent, with special emphasis on gilding. De Léotard participated in the School's book entries at the annual Salons and, on graduating, worked briefly with Pierre Legrain before becoming independent in 1925. Two years later she was the recipient of the Prix Blumenthal and returned to teach a course on gilding at the Ecole des Arts Décoratifs. She retired just before World War II.

De Léotard's covers were starkly avant-garde in their fierce linearity and choice of modern materials. Leather bindings were often inlaid with tinted snakeskin or sharkskin in a refined and seductive manner (see, for example, covers she designed for *Enfantines, Charmes,* and *Duperies*). Her graphic style was particularly exciting and varied, incorporating crisp combinations of diverging or overlapping lines interspersed with grids of *pointillé* gold or aluminum dots. Doucet and Barthou were two of the many bibliophiles who responded with warm enthusiasm to her work.

Bibliography

Adler, Rose, *Reliures, présenté par Rose Adler,* Paris, 1929, pls. 17, 23, 34, 44, 48
Barthou, Louis, "L'Evolution artistique de la reliure," *L'Illustration,* Christmas 1930, n.p.
"5 Relieurs," *Mobilier et décoration,* April 1935, p. 141
Dally, Ph., "Les Téchniques modernes de la reliure," *Art et décoration,* January 1927, pp. 19, 22
de Crauzat, Ernest, *La Reliure française de 1900 à 1925* (vol. 2), Paris, 1932, pp. 158–59
Deshairs, Léon, *Les Arts décoratifs modernes 1918–1925,* Paris, 1925, p. 186
Devauchelle, Roger, *La Reliure en France de ses origines à nos jours* (vol. 3), Paris, 1961, pp. 168, 268

Jean Dunand (1877–1942)
Metal and lacquerworker, furniture maker, and sculptor

Born in Lancy, Switzerland, to French parents, Dunand studied at the Ecole des Arts Industriels in Geneva. In 1896 he received a scholarship for advanced studies in Paris, where he met the noted sculptor Jean Dampt, who took him on as an apprentice. Until 1902 Dunand studied sculpture and mastered its materials.

Dunand appears to have established himself in a small studio near the Orleans gate in 1903, making his debut at the Société Nationale des Beaux-Arts the same year. Two years later he introduced a selection of Art Nouveau metal vases with designs in *repoussé* copper, following these with *dinanderie* objects that mixed hammered tin, nickel, lead, pewter, steel, and bronze. Dunand's transition to lacquer came in 1909, when he first saw the lacquered creations of Paris-based Japanese artisans. He was immediately drawn to the medium, recognizing its lavish gloss and vibrant colors as the ideal embellishment for his metalware. An exchange followed, Dunand trading his hammering technique for the secret formulae of lacquer application. In 1912 he became associated with the Japanese master, Sougawara, with whom Eileen Gray had worked since 1907.

After serving as a Red Cross volunteer during World War I, Dunand moved after the war to larger quarters at 70 rue Halle, which included metal, cabinetry, and lacquer workshops.

Dunand has been credited with the invention of crushed eggshell (*coquille d'oeuf*) as a decorative motif. He developed it as a dramatic substitute for the color white, which could not be obtained through vegetable dyes. The eggshell's impact was most pronounced on a red or black lacquered background.

Although Dunand tried personally to execute as many commissions as possible, he drew freely on the talents of his associates – in particular, Schmied, Lambert-Rucki, Goulden, and Jouve – to decorate his work. Infrequent collaborators were Bieler, Henri de Waroquier, Georges Dorinac, and Serge Rovinski. Clients for his furniture and metalware included the milliner Mme Agnès, the couturiers Jeanne Lanvin and Madeleine Vionnet, Ambassador Bertholet, Mme Yakoupovitch, and Mme Labourdette. Further commissions were afforded by the oceanliners *Ile-de-France, Atlantique,* and *Normandie.*

Dunand was accustomed to creating small *objets d'art,* such as jewelry, in lacquered metal, and he showed an equal facility for executing lacquered panels for the bindings of his close friend, Schmied. In most instances Dunand simply translated Schmied's sketch into lacquer, though he did create several of his own designs in bold geometric or abstract compositions, some of which covered the entire front, back, and spine of the book. Schmied and Dunand first collaborated on M. Bertraut's copy of *Le Cantique des cantiques,* which was shown both in one of their annual shows at the Georges Petit gallery and at the 1925 Exposition. The sumptuous and novel effect drew wide acclaim and led to many subsequent collaborations, including covers for *Le Livre de la jungle, Les Climats, Deux Contes, Les Chansons de Bilitis, Marrakech, La Création, Daphné,* and *Histoire de la Princesse Boudour.* Today's viewer is continually astonished by their vibrant imagery and exoticism.

In 1925 Dunand was joined by his oldest son, Bernard. The outbreak of World War II terminated the flourishing business and brought family tragedy. Bernard served in the army and was made a prisoner-of-war. The second son, Pierre, was killed in 1940. As the war progressed, raw materials became increasingly scarce, forcing Dunand to close his workshops. He died 7 June 1942.

Bibliography

Baschet, Jacques, "Les Dinanderies et les lacques de J. Dunand," *L'Illustration,* 15 October 1927, pp. 425–28
de Crauzat, Ernest, *La Reliure française de 1900 à 1925* (vol. 2), Paris, 1932, pp. 100–07
Henriot, Gabriel, "Jean Dunand," *Mobilier et décoration,* February 1926, pp. 33–47
Terrasse, Charles, "Les Reliures de Schmied et Dunand," *Byblis* (1927): 142–46

Max Fonsèque (1891–1965)
Bookbinder

The son of a Bordeaux binder, Fonsèque studied at the Ecole Estienne. His early career included working for Canape *père*, Lortic, and for his father, as well as a period in Monaco from 1920 to 1925. He eventually settled in Paris, first at 11 rue de Jean Beauvais in the Latin quarter and then at 25 rue des Feuillantines.

By 1930, Fonsèque had developed into an accomplished modernist, replacing the floral borders and architectural punches (such as plinths and cornices) of his prewar covers with a more assertive linear style. He formed arresting calligraphic patterns using the letters in the book's title. In his design for *Salammbô*, for example, he stretched the letters out in a serpentine pattern across the entire back of the book. He also often superimposed or repeated letters, or broke words in two and placed them on two lines.

Bibliography
de Crauzat, Ernest, *La Reliure française de 1900 à 1925* (vol. 2), Paris, 1932, pp. 57–58
Devauchelle, Roger, *La Reliure en France de ses origines à nos jours* (vol. 3), Paris, 1961, p.259
Fleming, John F., and Juvelis, Priscilla, *The Book Beautiful and the Binding as Art* (vol. 1), New York, 1983, p. 13

Louise-Denise Germain (1870–1936)
Leatherworker and bookbinder

Germain began her career by making small leather objects – *coffrets*, bags, cushions, and so on – in collaboration with Eugène Gaillard and Théodore Lambert. The same tooled technique prevailed in the modeled and incised bindings that she exhibited in her debut at the 1904 Salon of the Société des Artistes Décorateurs. Included were two volumes of *Pensées* bound in fawn-colored leather incrusted with bands of silver.

In the 1920s, Germain's style evolved into one of great simplicity, the leather enhanced with tones of gray and silver to evoke the spirit of the text. Occasionally, parchment (for example, *Livre d'or*) or lizard skin (*La Jeune Parque* and *Lettre à un ami*) were used in preference to leather.

Germain received a diploma of honor for her bindings at the 1925 Exposition (Class XV) and acted as a member of the Jury in Class IX. For Louis Barthou, one of her most important clients, she designed covers for *Vie de Saint Dominique, Les Climats*, and *Les Chansons de Bilitis*.

Bibliography
Barthou, Louis, "L'Evolution artistique de la reliure," *L'Illustration*, Christmas 1930, n.p.
de Crauzat, Ernest, *La Reliure française de 1900 à 1925* (vol. 2), Paris, 1932, pp. 135–37

Jean Goulden (1878–1947)
Silversmith and enamelist

Born in Charpentry (Meuse) to a prosperous Alsatian farmer, Goulden graduated in medicine from the Ecole Alsacienne, before moving to Paris in the 1890s to set up his practice. In 1908, following the publication of his thesis on the physiology of a detached heart, he was appointed a consultant to Paris's hospitals.

Goulden volunteered during World War I and was assigned to the Macedonian front. After the war he was invited to stay on by the monks at nearby Mount Athos, a sojourn that exposed him to Byzantine enamelware. On his return to Paris he sought out Jean Dunand for instruction in the technique of *champlevé* enameling. Goulden was quickly accepted into Dunand's circle, whose members included Jouve, Schmied, and Lambert-Rucki, and he participated in the group's annual exhibitions at the Galérie Georges Petit and the Galérie Charpentier. He also exhibited independently at the Salon of the Société des Artistes Décorateurs, especially from 1929, after he had transferred to Rheims to continue his medical career.

Goulden rejuvenated the technique of *champlevé* enameling, bringing to it in the late 1920s a distinctive and vigorous Cubist style. In addition to a spectacular selection of enameled silver objects – coupes, clocks, cigarette boxes, and *coffrets* – he designed several enameled silver plaques for bindings by Cretté and Schmied. A large volume on his Macedonian travels, bound by Schmied in crushed black morocco, was housed within two broad silver mounts enhanced with bands of brightly colored enameled *champs*.

Madeleine Gras (1891–1958)
Bookbinder

Born in Paris, Gras was orphaned at an early age. During World War I she dedicated herself to social work, but decided after the war to pursue a career in the arts. An aptitude for design led her to the Ecole des Arts Décoratifs, where she enrolled in the bookbinding course. On graduating in 1922, she joined Henri Noulhac, with whom she remained until around 1930, when she established her own studio.

Influenced by Legrain, Gras developed a charming modernist style in which great attention was paid to detail both in the book's binding and in its doublures and endpapers. She eliminated ribs from her spines in order to provide an unbroken design across the cover's entire surface. Several fine examples exhibited at the Salons of the Société des Artistes Décorateurs, such as *Carte blanche, Deux Contes, Pastiches et mélanges*, and *Carnets de voyage* attest to her abilities both as a designer and as a craftswoman.

In the 1930s Gras bound David-Weill's library of rare manuscripts, which was destroyed in World War II. During this time she also worked for the artists Croiza, Caplet, and La Duse. But the long interruption caused by the war disrupted her career and seems to have had an effect on the quality of her later work, which often lacked the spontaneity of her prewar designs.

Bibliography
Dally, Ph., "Les Téchniques modernes de la reliure," *Art et décoration*, January 1927, pp. 15–24
de Crauzat, Ernest, *La Reliure française de 1900 à 1925* (vol. 2), Paris, 1932, pp. 160–61
Devauchelle, Roger, *La Reliure en France de ses origines à nos jours* (vol. 3), Paris, 1961, pp. 210, 260–61
Exposition de la société de la reliure originale, exhibition catalogue, Bibliothèque Nationale, Paris, 1959
Farnoux-Reynaud, Lucien, "La Reliure d'art: Triomphe du goût français," *Mobilier et décoration*, February 1938, pp. 58–78

Léon Gruel (1841–1923)
Bookbinder and gilder

The Gruel bindery was one of the oldest in Paris. Founded in 1811 by Desforges at 418 rue Saint-Honoré, it was taken over in 1825 by Gruel's father. On the latter's death in 1846, his widow continued the business until 1850, when she married Jean Engelmann, a printer-lithographer. In 1875, when Mme Engelmann was again widowed, she turned over the administration of the workshop to her two sons, Léon Gruel and Edmond Engelmann. In 1891, Gruel became the sole owner of the workshop, which employed a large number of artisans. He was joined after 1900 by his son, Paul, who succeeded him on his death in 1923. The following year a large sale was held to dispose of Léon Gruel's library of bindings, reference materials, and tools.

In 1887 Gruel published *Manuel historique et bibliographique de l'amateur de reliures*, to which a second edition was added in 1904. The first volume included a discussion of his belief in a "synthesis of styles," in which he argued for the acceptance of non-traditional decoration for modern bindings. In practice, he matched this belief with a diverse range of emblematic and pictorial covers which antagonized the purist as much as those created by Meunier at the time. Gruel was accused of sacrificing good taste in his attempt to make his covers descriptive, and therefore commercial, by presenting a mélange of inlaid ivory medallions, *repoussé* and incised leather panels, and garish colors. Although his admirers found these artistic and appealing, most collectors did not. Gruel argued sporadically with Marius-Michel and others in the 1890s and 1900s as to where the boundaries of good taste should be drawn. Despite his progressive views, he did create numerous conventional designs in which florettes, leaves, and *entrelacs* were interspersed with fillet work in technically adept compositions. Some examples even incorporated the same range of imperial eagles, lozenges, fringes, and Persian motifs found on historic Grolier volumes.

Bibliography
Bosquet, Emile, "La Reliure française à l'exposition," *Art et décoration*, July-December 1900, pp. 48, 51, 52
de Crauzat, Ernest, *La Reliure française de 1900 à 1925*, Paris, 1932; (vol. 1), pp. 27–32; (vol. 2), pp. 44–45
Devauchelle, Roger, *La Reliure en France de ses origines à nos jours* (vol. 3), Paris, 1961, pp. 34–38, 114–15, 119, 124, 127, 144–45, 172, 261
Elek, Paul, *The Art of the French Book*, Paris, 1947, p. 146
Farnoux-Reynaud, Lucien, "La Reliure d'art: Triomphe du goût français," *Mobilier et décoration*, February 1938, pp. 58–78
Prideaux, S.T., *Modern Bindings: Their Design and Decoration*, New York, 1906
Uzanne, Octave, *L'Art dans la décoration extérieure des livres en France et à l'étranger*, Paris, 1898, pp. 168, 170, 183, 206–15

Antoine Joly (1838–1917)
and Robert Joly (1870?–1924)
Bookbinders and gilders

Born in Lamarche (Vosges) to a noted Second Empire binder, Antoine Joly was a contemporary of Gruel, Maylander, and Raparlier. Continuing the family tradition, he began his apprenticeship with a provincial binder, Clasquin, at the age of eleven, moving some years later to Paris, where he found employment with Léon Gruel. In 1874 he joined Thibaron, whom he succeeded in 1885. In 1892, he handed the business over to his son, Robert, and retired to his native Vosges. An excellent gilder like his father, Robert designed and produced a range of classical covers. In World War I he was commissioned by Henri Vever to execute bindings decorated by Jules Chadel and Adolphe Giraldon.

Bibliography
de Crauzat, Ernest, *La Reliure française de 1900 à 1925* (vol. 1), Paris, 1932, p. 76
Devauchelle, Roger, *La Reliure en France des ses origines à nos jours* (vol. 3), Paris, 1961, pp. 62, 127, 141, 144, 264

Michel Kieffer (b.1916)
Bookbinder

Born in Paris, Kieffer studied at the Ecole Estienne and the Ecole Nationale des Arts Décoratifs, before joining his father's atelier in 1935. By the time of the 1937 Exposition Universelle, at which he exhibited both independently and with his father, he had developed his own identifiable style. He was known for *décor cloisonné*, a kind of binding which included rows of jewels or glass cabochons, often framed by gold fillets, set into morocco covers in formal compositions that resembled the classical designs of Cretté and Creuzevault more than twenty years before. Kieffer had a particular affinity for three-dimensional ornamentation, achieved by the use of both recessed panels and relief applications.

After serving in the army, Kieffer returned to the family business in 1945. His style remained more crisp and geometric than that of his father. He is today still working in his bookshop on the rue Saint-André-des-Arts.

Bibliography

Devauchelle, Roger, *La Reliure en France de ses origines à nos jours* (vol. 3), Paris, 1961, pp. 264–66
Farnoux-Reynaud, Lucien, "La Reliure d'art: Triomphe du goût français," *Mobilier et décoration*, February 1938, pp. 61, 64, 73

René Kieffer (1875–1964)
Bookbinder and publisher

A member of the founding class at the Ecole Estienne in 1889, Kieffer later joined the Chambolle-Duru bindery, where he worked for ten years, specializing in gilding. In 1903 he established his own atelier at 99 boulevard Saint-Germain, later moving to 41 rue Saint-André-des-Arts, and then, in 1910, to 18 rue Séguier, where he remained until his retirement. Making his debut at the 1903 Salon des Artistes Français, Kieffer became a disciple of Marius-Michel, moving gradually away from his traditional training towards a more emblematic and modern style. His bindings at the 1909 and 1910 Salons of the Société des Artistes Décorateurs incorporate a transitional mix of flowers, vines, and rabbits in rather formal compositions. The designs were safe rather than adventurous, their Art Nouveau motifs retained within symmetrical borders that revealed his classical roots. In fact at this time, it was not so much his designs as such, but rather his preference for bright colors, such as vermilion and peacock, that set Kieffer apart from the traditionalists.

Kieffer remained in business during World War I, emerging afterwards as one of Paris's leading binders. His fine workmanship was now matched by a wide range of progressive designs inspired by Legrain (between 1917 and 1923, Kieffer executed Legrain's designs for Doucet, and therefore had first-hand knowledge of Legrain's modernist concepts). The Franchetti and Freund-Deschamps book collections, both sold at the Hôtel Drouot in the early 1920s, contained fine Kieffer bindings from the war period that showed a distinct Legrain influence. Traditional techniques, such as the use of fillets, blind-tooling, and pointillism, were mixed with colored inlays of leather to create eye-catching modern compositions. Around this time Kieffer also began to publish books, occasionally in partnership with Blaizot. At the 1925 Exposition Universelle, at which he was appointed a vice-president of Class XV, the book division, he listed himself as both a binder and a publisher. Collectors of his works in the 1920s included Dr. Henri Voisin, Henri Vever, Jacques Doucet, A. Ramuz, R. Marty, and Count de Verlet.

Kieffer's style continued to evolve in the late 1920s and 1930s. The earlier mix of figurative and decorative metal panels set into compact linear compositions was phased out. His binding for *Luxures*, by Maurice Rollinat, shown at the 1937 Exposition Universelle, for example, incorporated metal discs incrusted with cabochons of iridescent glass. Kieffer's cover for *Roman du Renart*, at the same Exposition, was inlaid with rows of red glass beads that

simulated rubies. Other examples, such as those for *Pétrone et Anacréon* and *Le Crepuscule des dieux*, incorporated silvered-metal panels and sculpted portrait medallions.

Bibliography

A-Dayot, Magdeleine, "De la Reliure: Une visite à René Kieffer," *L'Art et les artistes*, March 1935, pp. 204–8
Barthou, Louis, "L'Evolution artistique de la reliure," *L'Illustration*, Christmas 1930, n.p.
"5 Relieurs," *Mobilier et décoration*, April 1935, p. 145
Clouzot, Henri, "René Kieffer," *Mobilier et décoration*, no. 11 (1931): 195–200
de Crauzat, Ernest, *La Reliure française de 1900 à 1925*, Paris, 1932; (vol. 1), pp. 44–48; (vol. 2), p. 46–48
Derys, Gaston, "Le Vingt-Troisième Salon des artistes décorateurs," *Mobilier et décoration*, June 1933, p. 232
Devauchelle, Roger, *La Reliure en France de ses origines à nos jours* (vol. 3), Paris, 1961, pp. 127, 129, 135, 141, 144, 153, 155–57, 165, 171
Farnoux-Reynaud, Lucien, "La Reliure d'art," *Mobilier et décoration*, February 1938, pp. 58–78
Fleming, John F., and Juvelis, Priscilla, *The Book Beautiful and the Binding as Art* (vol. 1), New York, 1983, pp. 23, 42, 65, 66, 81, 82, 85, 143, 169, 201, 202
Lecomte, Georges, "Reliures modernes," *Plaisir de France*, December 1937, pp. 67, 71
Prideaux, S.T., *Modern Bindings: Their Design and Decoration*, New York, 1906
Quénioux, Gaston, *Les Arts décoratifs modernes 1918–1925*, Paris, 1925, pp. 336, 341

Jeanne Langrand
Bookbinder, gilder, and binding instructor

After four years of tuition, Langrand graduated from the Ecole des Arts Décoratifs in 1913. She returned after the war as an associate processor when her sister Andrée was appointed the School's director. In July 1934 Langrand established her own binding and gilding workshop in the Place de la Champerret. Her entries at the 1925 Exposition were well received, and she included among her clients Paul Hébert and Jacques Doucet. For the latter she created covers for *La Belle Journée* and *Ubu-Roi* in striking patterns of blind-tooled and gold fillets on red morocco.

Langrand's style was progressive: crisp linear patterns consisting of rectangles or circles of gold fillets. She emphasized the letters in the book's title to form dynamic ornamental compositions, covering the entire surface of the cover with bands of gold fillets.

Bibliography

Adler, Rose, *Reliures, présenté par Rose Adler*, Paris, 1929, pl. 28
Dally, Ph., "Les Téchniques modernes de la reliure," *Art et décoration*, January 1927, pp. 20–22
de Crauzat, Ernest, *La Reliure française de 1900 à 1925* (vol. 2), Paris, 1932
Devauchelle, Roger, *La Reliure en France de ses origines à nos jours* (vol. 3), Paris, 1961, pp. 167, 267
Michon, Marie, *La Reliure française*, Paris, 1951, p. 134
Quénioux, Gaston, *Les Arts décoratifs modernes 1918–1925*, Paris, 1925, p. 343

Charles Lanoë (1881–1959)
Bookbinder, gilder, and designer

A student of the Ecole Estienne and the Ecole des Arts Décoratifs in Paris, Lanoë was employed as a gilder first by Charles Meunier and then by Quesnel. He also worked for several months as a master gilder for Vanderwerde. In 1902 he joined Petrus Ruban, whom he succeeded eight years later. Lanoë was trained in the classical style and his

first bindings at the Salon of the Société des Artistes Français were predictably traditional. Gradually, however, he introduced a range of floral motifs into the bands of gold fillets bordering his covers, sometimes adding a central small *tableau* or bouquet to provide additional interest.

Like other Parisian binders, Lanoë was patronized during World War I by Henri Vever, who commissioned him to execute covers designed by Jules Chadel for his private collection. Notable among these were *Madame Bovary*, *Chansonnier Normand*, *Trois Eglises*, and *Chansons de Saintonge*. The collector L. Comar ordered a similar range of volumes, such as *Le Carquois*, designed by F. Siméon. In the 1920s, Lanoë appears to have turned with enthusiasm to the Art Deco style, producing many charming covers of his own design in the modernist idiom.

Bibliography

de Crauzat, Ernest, *La Reliure française de 1900 à 1925*, Paris, 1932; (vol. 1), pp. 63–68; (vol. 2), pp. 52–54
Devauchelle, Roger, *La Reliure en France de ses origines à nos jours* (vol. 3), Paris, 1961, pp. 90, 126

Jacques Anthoine-Legrain (b. 1907)
Bookbinder

The inheritor of an illustrious name, Anthoine-Legrain made his debut in 1929, the year his stepfather, Pierre Legrain, died. Installed in the family studio, he continued the Legrain tradition by applying a similar range of linear compositions and inlays of color to leather bindings, often with additional animal skin or metal accents. By the late 1930s he had won respect as a designer and technician in his own right. His cover for *Marrakech*, for example, displayed at the 1937 Exposition, drew wide praise for its delicate design and excellent execution. Other examples, such as his cover for Laurens' *Idylles*, used patterns of arabesques, circles, and curved gold fillets. For de Quincey's *L'Assassinat considéré comme un des beaux-arts*, Anthoine-Legrain conveyed the author's paradoxical style by designing the title to read from bottom to top.

Bibliography

Blaizot, Georges, *Masterpieces of French Modern Bindings*, Paris, 1947, pp. 110–17
Catalogue de l'exposition de la reliure originale, Société de la Reliure Originale, Bibliothèque Nationale, Paris, 1947
Charpentier, Thérèse, *L'Ecole de Nancy et la reliure d'art*, Paris, 1960, p. 50
Fleming, John F., and Juvelis, Priscilla, *The Book Beautiful and the Binding as Art*, New York, 1983 and 1985; (vol. 1), p. 57; (vol. 2), p. 19

Pierre Emile Legrain (1888–1929)
Book and furniture designer, illustrator, and interior decorator

Legrain was born in Levallois-Perret on the outskirts of Paris, the son of a prosperous distillery owner and a Belgian mother who entered him in the Collège Sainte-Croix in Neuilly. He began to suffer at an early age from the chronic health problems that recurred throughout his life and led to his premature death in 1929. Poor health may have contributed to his decision at twelve years of age to leave school and pursue his studies independently. In 1904, determined to become an artist, he entered the Ecole des Arts Appliqués Germain-Croix in Paris to study painting, sculpture, and theater design.

In the next four years Legrain underwent considerable hardship, caused by the failure of the family business and his father's subsequent death. But his fortunes improved in 1908 when he was invited by Paul Iribe to submit cartoons for the latter's satirical reviews, *Le Témoin*, *L'As-*

siette au beurre, Le Mot, and *La Baïonnette.* Impressed by the young man's creative skills, Iribe invited him to collaborate on various projects, including dress designs for Paquin, jewelry for Robert Linzeler, and modernist furnishings and interior settings for Iribe's progressive clientele. The latter included the commission in 1912 to decorate Jacques Doucet's apartment in the modern style.

The impending war and various differences of opinion with the couturier Paul Poiret, for whom he designed fashions, determined Iribe to leave for New York in 1914. When the hostilities began, Legrain volunteered for action but was declared medically unfit and was assigned to the home-guard in the Paris suburbs. Towards the end of 1916, after demobilization, he found himself in the capital, unemployed and without prospects or money. Remembering Doucet from the Iribe commission, he sought out the couturier to ask for work. Legrain's timing was fortuitous. Doucet had decided to bind his recently formed collection of works by contemporary authors in appropriate modernist covers, and he offered Legrain 300 francs per month to begin the project. Totally ignorant of the craft, but in desperate financial need, Legrain agreed. A makeshift studio was set up in his patron's dining room, and Legrain began to design modernist covers for works by Suarès, Gide, Jammes, Claudel, and Doucet's other favorite authors. Legrain was assisted in the afternoons by Doucet himself.

In 1919, now married and living at 9 rue de Val-de-Grace, Legrain began to accept commissions from other collectors. His liaison with Doucet had been hugely successful, but both had strong temperaments and opinions. Vehement disagreements had inevitably arisen on the suitability of certain designs, and these had strained the relationship despite Doucet and Legrain's mutual respect and common goal. At this time, also, Doucet developed a passion for surrealism and began to pursue this new interest, thus easing the way for Legrain to seek other patrons. Perhaps to facilitate this transition, Doucet exhibited twenty of his Legrain bindings at the 1919 Salon of the Société des Artistes Français. The response was unparalleled in the history of the medium. Collectors turned with renewed enthusiasm to the modern style and Legrain gained many new clients, including Baron Robert de Rothschild, Louis Barthou, Hubert de Monbrison, Baron R. Gourgaud, Georges and Auguste Blaizot, and the Americans, Florence Blumenthal and Daniel Sickles. Until 1923, Legrain's maquettes were bound by René Kieffer, after which they were distributed among Canape, Huser, David, Levitsky, Noulhac, Schroeder, and Stroobants.

In 1923 Legrain established his own studio within that of the decorators Briant et Robert at 7 rue d'Argenteuil, from where he moved in 1925 first to a basement in the avenue Percier, and then to 304 rue Saint-Jacques. During this period he gradually built up his own team of binders and gilders, including Jeanne, Collet, Desmoules, Aufschneider, Dress, Vincent, and Lordereau. In the late 1920s, hoping to extend himself into the entire field of book production as commissions continued to grow, he planned a final move to the Villa Brune, where he could house printing presses and a bindery. On 17 July 1929, the day of the scheduled move, he suffered a fatal heart attack.

In a meteoric career covering scarcely a dozen years and roughly 1,300 designs for book covers (75 completed posthumously), Legrain had single-handedly revolutionized the age-old craft, while inspiring a host of imitators. At the same time he had designed a substantial amount of furnishings in the modern idiom, first for Doucet's new studio at Neuilly, and later for friends of his mentor, including Jeanne Tachard, a noted milliner, for whom Legrain furnished two apartments at 41 rue Emile-Menier and a villa at Celle-Saint-Cloud. Another client was Pierre Meyer, for whose house on the avenue Montaigne Legrain

designed the celebrated glass and copper Pleyela piano shown at the 1929 exhibition of "Les Cinq" at the Galérie de la Renaissance. Maurice Martin du Gard (a suite of rooms), the Viscount de Noailles (a bedroom), the Princess G. de G. (a house on the rue Villejust and another at Celle-Saint-Cloud), Mme Louis Boulanger, and Suzanne Talbot provided further commissions. Small commercial commissions filled the gaps: leather camera cases for Kodak, cigarette box designs for Lucky Strike and Camel, and a desk set for the Elysée Palace.

Legrain's furniture, like his bindings, incorporated lavish materials and contrasting colors. Palmwood, with its coarse, open grain, was particularly suited to his African-inspired pieces, while highly buffed palisander and ebony brought opulence to his cubist furniture. Whenever possible, he exploited the tactile qualities of his materials. Metal or glass were juxtaposed with sharkskin or animal hides on chairs and consoles. Legrain showed examples of his furniture alongside his bindings at the annual Salons throughout the 1920s, at the 1925 Exposition, and, from 1926, at the exhibitions of "Les Cinq."

Bibliography

Barthou, Louis, "L'Evolution artistique de la reliure," *L'Illustration*, Christmas 1930, n.p.
Blaizot, Georges, *Masterpieces of French Bindings*, New York, 1947, pp. 14–66
Breck, Joseph, "Bookbindings by Legrain," *Bulletin of the Metropolitan Museum of Art*, no. 11, New York, November 1932, pp. 235–36
Brunhammer, Yvonne, *The Nineteen Twenties Style*, London, 1966
Dally, Ph., "Les Téchniques modernes de la reliure," *Art et décoration*, January-June 1927, pp. 15–17
de Crauzat, Ernest, *La Reliure française de 1900 à 1925*, Paris, 1932; (vol. 1), pp. 180–87; (vol. 2), pp. 15–31
Deshairs, Léon, *Les Arts décoratifs modernes 1918–1925*, Paris, 1925, pp. 185–88
Devauchelle, Roger, *La Reliure en France de ses origines à nos jours*, Paris, 1961, pp. 149–64, 166, 168, 170–71, 175, 200, 212, 228–29
Diehl, Edith, *Bookbinding, Its Background and Technique* (vols. 1 and 2), New York, 1946
Duncan, Alastair, *Art Deco Furniture*, London and York, 1984, pp. 117–18
Guignard, Jacques, *Pierre Legrain et la reliure: Evolution d'un style*, Paris, n.d.
Léautaud, Jean, "Modern Bindings for Modern Books," *International Studio* 84 (1926): 70–73
Michon, L.-M., *La Reliure française (arts, styles, et techniques)*, Paris, 1951
Pierre Legrain, Relieur: Repertoire descriptif et bibliographique de mille deux cent trente-six reliures, Paris, 1965
Quénioux, Gaston, *Les Arts décoratifs modernes 1918–1925*, Paris, 1925, pp. 336, 341
Rémon, G., "Groupements et regroupements," *Mobilier et décoration*, May 1926, pp. 146, 148
Rosenthal, Léon, "Pierre Legrain, relieur," *Art et décoration*, March 1923, pp. 65–70

Georges Levitsky (b. 1885)
Bookbinder

Born in the Ukraine, Levitsky studied binding in Odessa before emigrating to Paris in 1907. He worked for Proute until 1910, when he opened his own studio at 22 rue de l'Odéon. The following year he made his debut at the Salon des Artistes Français.

Well-known outside France, Levitsky applied a range of conventional designs to leather and parchment bindings for a clientele that included King Albert I of Belgium and Alexander I of Serbia. His style became increasingly dynamic and resourceful after World War I. At the 1937 Ex-

position, for example, he displayed three *tours de force:* covers for *Un Pélerin d'Angkor* (incorporating ivory, mother-of-pearl, gold, and ebony), *Marrakech* (morocco incrusted with mother-of-pearl), and *Le Paradis Musulman* (ivory and mother-of-pearl). He retired in 1965.

Bibliography

Devauchelle, Roger, *La Reliure en France de ses origines à nos jours* (vol. 3), Paris, 1961, pp. 268–69
Fleming, John F., and Juvelis, Priscilla, *The Book Beautiful and the Binding as Art* (vol. 1), New York, 1983, pp. 2, 134

Marcellin Lortic (1852–1928)
Bookbinder and gilder

The son of Pierre-Marcellin Lortic, the contemporary and equal of Trautz and Capé, Lortic *fils* worked briefly with his brother, Paul, before establishing himself independently in 1884 in the family workshop on the rue de la Monnaie. Though by temperament a traditionalist, he developed a flare for rich and elaborate covers enhanced with gold and recessed panels. These caused fierce debate among collectors and binders, who divided into opposing groups: "Lorticophiles" and "Lorticophobes." In the 1890s he embraced the Art Nouveau style, producing covers for *Tartarin de Tarascon, Le Roman de Tristan et Iseult*, and *Zadig* in patterns made up of colorful inlays and gold punches.

Lortic's clients included de Saint-Chamant, Meynial, Delacoeur, and Hirsch. During World War I he executed several covers decorated by Giraldon for Henri Vever.

Bibliography

de Crauzat, Ernest, *La Reliure française de 1900 à 1925* (vol. 1), Paris, 1932, pp. 58–59
Devauchelle, Roger, *La Reliure en France de ses origines à nos jours* (vol. 3), Paris, 1961, pp. 16, 21, 25, 28, 56–61, 64, 127, 141, 269

André Mare (1887–1932)
Painter, designer, and ensemblier

Born in Argentan (Normandie), Mare studied painting at the Académie Julian in Paris before making his debut at the Salons in the years 1903 to 1904. By 1910 an increasing emphasis on the decorative arts was evident in the work that he submitted to the Salons, which now included furniture, textiles, and bookbindings. At the outbreak of World War I, Mare volunteered for service, leaving his wife, Charlotte, to execute his designs in his absence. In 1919, Mare formalized his prewar association with the architect Louis Süe by establishing their firm, La Compagnie des Arts Français. The partnership flourished until 1928, when Mare retired to concentrate on painting.

Mare began to apply himself to bookbinding design some years before World War I. His preoccupation with parchment and vellum, rather than leather, came no doubt from their canvas-like whiteness, which he, as a painter, preferred.

Mare's bindings are highly distinctive, both in their artistry and in their technique. Drawing on the same fanciful grammar of ornament that he applied to his furnishings – in particular, baskets or garlands of summer blooms and fruit, or pairs of love-birds – Mare produced an appealing and lavish effect that echoed traditional Louis Philippe decoration as well as the designs in the prewar years of his colleagues at the Salons: André Groult (in fabric design), Paul Poiret (fashion), and Maurice Marinot (in his early enamelled glassware). Mare's palette, compared by contemporary critics to that of the Ballets Russes and German avant-garde painting, was warm and refined, with an emphasis on red, blue, and green tones.

The outlines of Mare's sketches were first engraved with a needle or burned into the surface of the bindings, after which the design was painted on in fresh watercolors or oils. The colors were contained within the dies as in *cloisonné* enamelwares. When dry, the book's entire surface was applied with a layer of varnish to protect it and to seal the image's freshness. The completed image had a richly translucent and enameled appearance.

The charm and singularity of Mare's bindings made his work greatly in demand among Paris's foremost book collectors, many of whom placed orders for their own copies of such works as *Le Temple de Gnide, Les Fioretti, La Nuit Vénitienne, Les Jardins,* and *Des Voyages et des parfums.*

Bibliography

Chantre, Ami, "Les Reliures d'André Mare," *L'Art décoratif,* July-December, 1913, pp. 251–58
de Crauzat, Ernest, *La Reliure française de 1900 à 1925* (vol. 2), Paris, 1932, pp. 90–93
Un Demi-Siècle de reliures d'art contemporain en France et dans le monde, exhibition catalogue, Bibliothèque Forney, Paris, April-June 1984
Duncan, Alastair, *Art Deco Furniture,* London and New York, 1984, pp. 166–68
Quénioux, Gaston, *Les Arts décoratifs modernes 1918–1925,* Paris, 1925, pp. 345–46

Mme Marot-Rodde (?–1935)
Bookbinder

An ex-student of Chanat, a professor at the Ecole Estienne, Marot-Rodde established her own atelier in the early 1920s at 86 boulevard Suchet. Advised by Petrus Ruban, she rapidly perfected her technique, exhibiting at the Salon d'Automne in 1924, and that of the Société des Artistes Décorateurs the following year. At the 1925 Exposition she was awarded a silver medal.

Marot-Rodde's style was highly distinctive and charming. Her use of bright inlays of colors within compact geometric or floral compositions was attractive and fresh in its respect for traditional materials blended with a modernist imagery. Book collectors responded eagerly to her creations, among them Louis Barthou (*Ballades françaises, L'Ame et la danse,* and *Marrakech*), P. Hébert (*La Leçon d'amour dans un parc* and *Scènes mythologiques*), and P. Harth (*L'Océan* and *L'Eventail*).

By 1932, assisted now by her daughter, Marot-Rodde oversaw a studio which included several binders and two gilders. A brilliant career was cut short by her premature death three years later.

Bibliography

Barthou, Louis, "L'Evolution artistique de la reliure," *L'Illustration,* Christmas 1930, n.p.
de Crauzat, Ernest, *La Reliure française de 1900 à 1925* (vol. 2), Paris, 1932, pp. 137–41
Devauchelle, Roger, *La Reliure en France de ses origines à nos jours* (vol. 3), Paris, 1961, pp. 168, 171, 269

Camille Martin (1861–1898)
Painter, decorative artist, and leatherworker

In addition to those bindings which René Wiener executed for him – in particular *L'Espagne* and *L'Argent* – Martin also created some on his own and others in collaboration with Victor Prouvé. All are distinctly "painterly," that is, transferals on to leather of his paintings on canvas. Several, such as his cover for the second volume of Gonse's *L'Art japonais* in 1893, convey a delightful *fin-de-siècle* mood mixed with a predictably Japanesque influence. In collaboration with Prouvé, he produced numerous other bindings, including *Récits de guerre, L'Estampe originale, Les Aveugles, La Pensée dans l'espace, La Melancolie d'automne,*

and *Les Harmonies du soir.* Martin's death in 1898 deprived the Nancy movement of one of its most gifted and versatile artists.

Bibliography

Charpentier, Thérèse, *L'Ecole de Nancy et la reliure d'art,* Paris, 1960, pp. 26–29, 47, 49
Le Cuir au Musée, exhibition catalogue, Musée de l'Ecole de Nancy, Nancy, 1985
Exposition Lorraine (Ecole de Nancy), exhibition catalogue, Musée de l'Union Centrale des Arts Décoratifs, Paris, 2nd series, 1903
"Modern Bookbindings and Their Designers," *The Studio,* Special Winter Issue 1899–1900, pp. 3–82
Uzanne, Octave, *L'Art dans la décoration extérieure des livres en France et à l'étranger,* Paris, 1898, p. 210

Emile Maylander (1867–1959)
Bookbinder and gilder

The son of a gilder employed by Marius-Michel *père,* Maylander apprenticed at the Gustave Bénard atelier before studying under Jules Domont, a professor at the Syndicat Patronal de la Reliure. In 1888, he joined Francisque Cuzin as a gilder. Four years later, when Cuzin died and was succeeded by Emile-Philippe Mercier, Maylander emerged as the latter's principal collaborator and one of the period's finest gilders. When, in 1910, Mercier in turn died, Maylander established his own workshop on the rue de la Harpe.

The reduction of book commissions caused by World War I forced Maylander increasingly into bindings to supplement his work in gilding. He preferred classical designs, which he executed with a faultless technique, drawing the admiration of a number of bibliophiles. Henri Vever commissioned several bindings from Maylander, which were decorated by Jules Chadel, including *Contes choisis, Au Flanc du vase, La Faune parisienne,* and *Le Puits de Sainte-Claire.*

Maylander was assisted by his two sons, and from the 1920s they gradually replaced him. Like other traditional binderies, the atelier made the transition from the prewar *fin-de-siècle* floral esthetic to the 1920s geometric style with restraint, incorporating understated variations of both, when appropriate, to its standard repertoire of gold and blind-tooled fillets and punched ornamentation.

Bibliography

de Crauzat, Ernest, *La Reliure française de 1900 à 1925* (vol. 1), Paris, 1932, p. 60
Devauchelle, Roger, *La Reliure en France de ses origines à nos jours,* Paris, 1961, pp. 144, 172, 203, 206–7, 273

Emile-Philippe Mercier (1855–1910)
Bookbinder and gilder

In 1869, Mercier was apprenticed to Charles Magnier *père,* under whom, and with the tutelage of the master gilder, Francisque Cuzin, he developed into the foremost gilder of his time. By 1890, when he succeeded Cuzin, his studio on the rue Séguier was producing a wide range of bindings which, though classical in inspiration, could not be judged merely as copies of past works. Mercier depended mainly on a mix of small punches and gold fillets for his decorative effect, which was invariably costly and lavish. Mercier's bindings, such as *La Mort amoureuse* and *Crainqueville,* often included bands of fifteen or sixteen parallel lines executed with impeccable precision. He numbered among his clients Delafosse, Descamps-Scrive, and Miguet.

In 1898, Mercier was joined by his son, Georges, who at the age of fifteen had entered the Ecole Estienne,

eventually graduating at the head of his class. Georges assisted his father until the latter's death in 1910, when he took over the workshop.

Bibliography

Bosquet, Emile, "La Reliure française à l'exposition," *Art et décoration,* July-December 1900, pp. 47–48
de Crauzat, Ernest, *La Reliure française de 1900 à 1925* (vol. 1), Paris, 1932, pp. 32–35
"Modern Bookbindings and Their Designers," *The Studio,* Special Winter Issue 1899–1900, p. 64
Nicolle, Henri, "La Reliure moderne," *Les Arts français: la reliure d'art,* no. 36 (1919): 190, 196
Prideaux, S.T., *Modern Bindings: Their Design and Decoration,* New York, 1906, pp. 62, 72, 80, 82, 84, 89–91
Uzanne, Octave, *L'Art dans la décoration extérieure des livres en France et à l'étranger,* Paris, 1898, pp. 177, 180–82, 184, 194, 204–6

Charles Meunier (1865–1940)
Bookbinder, gilder, and publisher

Born in Paris, Meunier began his apprenticeship with Gustave Bénard at the age of eleven. Five years later, after working briefly for Jules Domont and Maillard, he joined Marius-Michel's workshop, but soon became impatient with the daily routine of producing traditional bindings. In 1885, before he was fully proficient in all the technical aspects of book cover production, Meunier established his own studio in the rue Mazarine, moving shortly afterwards to 75 boulevard Malesherbes.

Contemporary criticism on Meunier was mixed. He was thought to be innovative and instinctive, with great reserves of energy and undeniable artistic talent, but he offended contemporary bibliophiles by producing vast numbers of gaudy and crudely executed covers incorporating emblematic and pictorial themes.

Drawing on both traditional and modern techniques and forms of decoration, Meunier mixed classical punches – such as quatrefoils, florettes and dentils – almost indiscriminately with newly fashionable incised and modeled leather panels. His output was prodigious; by 1897 he had produced roughly six hundred emblematic bindings, many with the book's title emblazoned on unfurled banners within compact compositions of flowers and allegorical figures. Other examples show in their use of floral decoration the influence of Marius-Michel. Some were slavish reproductions of eighteenth-century masterpieces.

The apparent ease with which Meunier moved between styles and periods offended, rather than impressed, purists, who felt that his talent lay primarily in the creation of half-bindings with decorative spines. His introduction in the late 1890s of enameled and sculpted bronze or ivory plaques into the front covers of his bindings further alienated top collectors.

Meunier declined to participate in the 1900 Exposition as he felt that the Grand Prix would automatically be awarded to Marius-Michel (which it was). He staged his own show at his studio on the boulevard Malesherbes and received as much magazine coverage as the participants at the Exposition. In the same year he launched a quarterly review, *L'Oeuvre et l'image,* which included editorials by L. Morin and J. de Marthold on all aspects of book production, in addition to watercolors and woodcut engravings. The review ceased publication in 1903, but Meunier continued periodically to publish other works, such as a set of seven albums, each containing one hundred illustrations of his finest bindings from 1893 to 1905. Publishing was by now an important aspect of his business, and included a four-volume series entitled *Réflexion d'un praticien en marge de la reliure du XIX siècle de M. Henri Béraldi* (1908), and *La Reliure du XIX siècle* and *Paroles d'un practicien pour l'art et la téchnique du relieur-doreur* (both 1918–20). In the last-mentioned, Meunier criticized the teaching methods at the Ecole Estienne.

In 1920, Meunier announced his retirement and conducted the second of two sales of his library of bindings and reference material (the first had been held in 1908). His workshop was taken over by two of Marius-Michel's artisans, Conil and Septier. At his death in 1940, Meunier was almost forgotten.

Bibliography

Bosquet, Emile, "La Reliure française à l'exposition," *Art et décoration*, July-December 1900, pp. 47, 49, 50, 53, 55

Cent Ans de reliures d'art 1880–1980, exhibition catalogue, Bibliothèque Municipale de Toulouse, Toulouse, 1981

Charpentier, Thérèse, *L'Ecole de Nancy et la reliure d'art*, Paris, 1960, p. 43

de Crauzat, Ernest, *La Reliure française de 1900 à 1925* (vol. 1), Paris, 1932, pp. 19, 35–44

Devauchelle, Roger, *La Reliure en France de ses origines à nos jours* (vol. 3), Paris, 1961, pp. 85, 98–104, 118, 126–27, 134–35

Elek, Paul, *The Art of the French Book*, Paris, 1947, pp. 141–45

"Modern Bookbindings and Their Designers," *The Studio*, Special Winter Issue 1899–1900, pp. 59, 63–64

Nicolle, Henri, "La Reliure moderne," *Les Arts français: la reliure d'art*, no. 36 (1919): 190, 196ff

Prideaux, S.T., *Modern Bindings: Their Design and Decoration*, New York, 1906, p. 93ff

Uzanne, Octave, *L'Art dans la décoration extérieure des livres en France et à l'étranger*, Paris, 1898, pp. 161, 169, 172, 174–75, 186–90

Marius-Michel (1846–1925)
Bookbinder and gilder

Christened Henri-François-Victor Michel, Marius-Michel adopted his father's name when in 1876 he joined the family workshop at 15 rue du Four. Like Trautz, Marius-Michel *père* was a Second Empire binder known for his copies of classical masterpiece bindings. The son, however, believed passionately that bookbinding needed a new vocabulary of ornamentation in order to express the mood and spirit of contemporary authors such as Hugo, de Vigny, Musset, Balzac, and Gautier. In 1881, Marius-Michel laid out his radical beliefs in a book entitled *La Reliure commerciale et industrielle depuis l'invention de l'imprimérie jusqu'à nos jours*.

From the moment that he made his debut, Marius-Michel showed remarkable initiative, applying himself with equal facility to design, research, and the technical aspects of his craft. The 1878 International Exposition became a convenient forum through which to promote his revolutionary range of decorative ornaments based on nature, *La Flore Ornamentale*. At first, his crusade faced fierce resistance from both his fellow binders and collectors, who found his youthful confidence and reformist philosophies impudent and rebellious. The general opinion was that floral motifs fell into the category of "art" rather than bindings. But the young man's fervent convictions, as well as his superb technical skills, as both a binder and a gilder, won him an increasing number of supporters. By 1885 his designs were seen as a viable alternative to traditional bindings for certain books, such as romantic novels. Other binders began to imitate his use of floral and plant motifs, bringing legitimacy to his cause. He even, on occasion, introduced on to his covers incised and modeled panels (executed by Steinlen, Lepère, or Guétant) which somehow managed to avoid the controversy surrounding the more commercial emblematic and "poster" covers (*reliures affiches*) designed at the time by Gruel, Ruban, Meunier, Raparlier, and others.

By the mid-1890s, Michel had emerged as the undisputed leader of the new movement, whose incomparable technique, harmonious selection of color, and infinite variety of plant motifs placed his work above those of his contemporaries. Michel's judicious use of color was felt to be particularly instrumental in evoking the spirit of the text.

The 1900 Exposition confirmed Michel's status as the country's supreme binder in its award of a Grand Prix and Chevalier of the Legion of Honor. Collectors such as Barthou, Béraldi, Bénard, Borderel, Descamps-Scrive, Quarré, and de Piolenc pursued him for the following two decades; only after World War I did Legrain's blend of modernism challenge his pre-eminence. Suddenly, the old revolutionary was perceived as a reactionary, his predictable floral patterns outmoded in the machine-oriented postwar society.

During World War I Marius-Michel suffered an illness which brought his workshop to a virtual standstill in 1918, but the return of Georges Cretté the following year helped to revive it. In 1925, a month before his death, Michel handed the business over to Cretté. A few months later, the International Exposition awarded Legrain top book binding honors, so providing a clean end to the Marius-Michel era.

Today, the sheer size and weight of a Marius-Michel book can make more of an impression on its handler than the realization that the binding's gentle Art Nouveau theme was once the source of huge controversy.

Bibliography

Blaizot, Georges, *Masterpieces of French Modern Bookbindings*, Paris, 1947

Bosquet, Emile, "La Reliure française à l'exposition," *Art et décoration*, July-December 1900, pp. 54–55

de Crauzat, Ernest, *La Reliure française de 1900 à 1925* (vol. 1), Paris, 1932, pp. 23–27

Devauchelle, Roger, *La Reliure en France de ses origines à nos jours* (vol. 3), Paris, 1961, pp. 117, 123, 126, 129, 135–36, 138, 143–48, 150–51, 160, 166, 168, 172, 175, 212, 269

Marius-Michel, *La Reliure française commerciale et industrielle depuis l'invention de l'imprimérie jusqu'à nos jours*, Paris, 1881

"Modern Bookbindings and Their Designers," *The Studio*, Special Winter Issue 1899–1900, p. 63

Nicolle, Henri, "La Reliure moderne," *Les Arts français: la reliure d'art*, no. 36 (1919): 190

Uzanne, Octave, *L'Art dans la décoration extérieure des livres en France et à l'étranger*, Paris, 1898, pp. 166, 184, 195, 197

Henri Noulhac (1866–1931)
Bookbinder and gilder

Noulhac was born in Chateauroux, where he served his apprenticeship as a bookbinder. In 1894 he moved to Paris, establishing his atelier at 10 rue de Buci. A superlative craftsman, Noulhac specialized initially in plain leather bindings (*reliures jansénistes*) and copies of romantic eighteenth-century bindings. By 1900 he had begun tentatively to incorporate modest floral emblems into the dentilled fillet borders on his covers. Noulhac did not attempt to create a reputation for himself as a book cover designer *per se*, a decision that he later regretted. His daughter, who had studied art under Adolphe Giraldon, joined him towards 1914 as a design collaborator.

Noulhac's clients in the early years of the century included H. Béraldi (his main patron), Belinac, Piolenc, Renevey, and Marcel Bernard. During World War I Noulhac executed several bindings designed by Jules Chadel for Henri Vever. Notable examples included *Causerie sur l'art dramatique*, *Pastels*, *Cyrano*, and *Ce Brigand d'amour*. He also executed bindings for Legrain.

In the 1920s, Noulhac developed into a fine instructor, numbering Rose Adler and Madeleine Gras among his students.

Bibliography

La Décor de la vie de 1900 à 1925, exhibition catalogue, Pavillon de Marsan, Palais du Louvre, Paris, 1937, pp. 65–67

de Crauzat, Ernest, *La Reliure française de 1900 à 1925*, Paris, 1932; (vol. 1), p. 61; (vol. 2), 49–52

Devauchelle, Roger, *La Reliure en France de ses origines à nos jours* (vol. 3), Paris, 1961, pp. 127, 141, 144, 153, 274–75

Victor Prouvé (1858–1943)
Watercolorist, decorative artist, sculptor, bookbinder, and leatherworker

Prouvé was the guiding inspiration behind the Ecole de Nancy, assuming leadership after Emile Gallé's death in 1904. While applying himself equally to many disciplines, he create a range of cushions, *portières*, plaques, caskets, and bindings in tooled and polychromed leather decorated with the flora and fauna of his native Alsace-Lorraine. His most noteworthy binding was *Salammbô*, which depicted, in a broad panorama which filled the entire cover, the splendors and cruelty of Carthage as imagined by Flaubert. Other examples, all highly Art Nouveau in spirit, included the first volume of L. Gonse's *L'Art japonais*, *Histoire de l'art décoratif*, *L'Art symboliste*, and *Le Chanson des gueux*.

A participant at the annual Champs de Mars exhibitions in Paris from 1892, and at the Cercle pour l'Art exposition staged by La Libre Esthétique in Brussels in 1894, Prouvé received an equal share with Wiener of the censure heaped on the Nanceiens for their revolutionary figurative and pictorial bindings.

Bibliography

Charpentier, Thérèse, *L'Ecole de Nancy et la reliure d'art*, Paris, 1960, pp. 7, 15, 19, 30–33, 43, 49

Le Cuir au musée, exhibition catalogue, Musée de l'Ecole de Nancy, Nancy, 1985

Exposition Lorraine (Ecole de Nancy), exhibition catalogue, Musée de l'Union Centrale des Arts Décoratifs, Paris, 2nd series, 1903

"Modern Bookbindings and Their Designers," *The Studio*, Special Winter Issue 1899–1900, pp. 3–82

Nicolle, Henri, "La Reliure moderne," *Les Arts français: la reliure d'art*, no. 36 (1919): 193

Quénioux, Gaston, *Les Arts décoratifs modernes*, Paris, 1925, p. 333

Uzanne, Octave, *L'Art dans la décoration extérieure des livres en France et à l'étranger*, Paris, 1898, p. 202

Petrus Ruban (1851–1929)
Bookbinder and gilder

Born in Villefranche (Rhône), Ruban was undecided, on completion of his training as a binder, whether to proceed with a career as a traditionalist or to follow Marius-Michel's fashionable pursuit of a new esthetic. For many years he vacillated before deciding in about 1905 to align himself with the conservative ranks of the neoclassical binders and gilders, a group headed by Emile-Philippe Mercier. Until this time, however, many of his most innovative and charming covers consisted of striking Art Nouveau floral compositions in inlays of color that used the bindings' entire surface. Ruban drew in these years on an eclectic range of styles, including neo-Egyptian, Japanesque, and traditional French influences, such as Henri II and First Empire. These he displayed at the annual Salons of the Société des Artistes Français and the Salon des Beaux-Arts. His bindings at the 1900 Exposition Universelle met with mixed reviews, some being judged too impetuous and discordant.

An important aspect of Ruban's work was his craftsmanship, described by contemporary critics as irreproachable. Drawing on all the techniques of his formal training, he mixed modeled, incised and tinted detailing with a standard formula of gold fillet and blind-tooled compositions. By 1910, the year in which he handed over his atelier to Charles Lanoë and retired to Neuilly, examples of his work had been included in all of the major book auctions in Paris, including those of the collectors Durel, Belinac, Bordes, and Piolenc. Ruban's own library, sold at the Hôtel Drouot in 1911, included further examples of his Art Nouveau covers.

Bibliography

Bosquet, Emile, "La Reliure française à l'exposition," *Art et décoration*, July-December 1900, pp. 50–51
Devauchelle, Roger, *La Reliure en France de ses origines à nos jours* (vol. 3), Paris, 1961, pp. 84, 96–98, 105, 129
Durel, A. (ed.), *Catalogue de cent relieurs d'art*, Paris, 1902
Fleming, John F., and Juvelis, Priscilla, *The Book Beautiful and the Binding as Art* (vol. 1), New York, 1983, p. 107
"Modern Bindings and Their Designers," *The Studio*, Special Winter Issue 1899–1900, p. 64
Prideaux, S.T., *Modern Bindings: Their Design and Decoration*, New York, 1906, pp. 91–92
Uzanne, Octave, *L'Art dans la décoration extérieure des livres en France et à l'étranger*, Paris, 1898, pp. 164, 167, 176, 198

François-Louis Schmied (1873–1941)
Painter, engraver, illustrator, printer, book designer, and binder

Schmied was born 6 October 1873 in Geneva, Switzerland, to an ex-colonel in the French Algerian army and his Vaudoise wife. He studied at the city's School of Industrial Arts as an apprentice wood engraver under Alfred Martin, spending his spare time researching illuminated manuscripts and incunabula at the Geneva municipal library. In 1895, after five years of tuition, he moved to Paris, where he earned a living by cutting wood blocks for the commercial house of George Auber. Joined three years later by his friend Jean Dunand, Schmied continued his career as an engraver, while developing skills as a painter and illustrator. From 1904 he exhibited wood-engravings at the Société des Beaux-Arts. In 1911, one of the exclusive French book clubs, the Société du Livre Contemporain, commissioned him to engrave and print Paul Jouve's watercolor illustrations for Rudyard Kipling's *Jungle Book*. The project, interrupted by World War I, was completed in 1919.

During the war Schmied enlisted in the French Foreign Legion, leaving his wife and three children in the custody of Dunand, a Swiss national who later joined the Red Cross. Schmied was wounded in the trenches at Capy on the Somme, losing his right eye. Demobilized, he returned to Paris to resume his career and to complete the *Jungle Book*, which was received with great acclaim by bibliophiles for its precise color reproductions of Jouve's sketches. To achieve such precision, Schmied established his own printing plant, purchasing a Stanhope platen hand-press which was operated by an expert pressman, Pierre Bouchet. Sometimes twenty to twenty-five colors were used in a single illustration, each requiring a separate image engraved on a wood block. Examples of this caliber

included *Marrakech*, *Les Climats*, *Daphné*, and *Le Cantique des cantiques*. Some books, such as *Le Paradis musulman*, even contained illustrations consisting of more than forty different colors. A single page of these books took almost a month to print.

After the war Schmied applied himself increasingly to the total production of *éditions de luxe*; their illustrations, typography, typesetting, page design and printing. He did not, however, bind all of his works. Many were published in unbound sheets enclosed in a slipcase in the normal manner of French illustrated books, allowing the purchaser to select his own preferred binder. For this reason, some of Schmied's books contain bindings by other binders, such as Cretté. Some bindings – those for *Le Cantique des cantiques*, for example – became a collaboration between Schmied, Dunand, and Cretté.

By 1925, Schmied's atelier at 12 rue Friant, Paris, had become too small to house his expanding operation, and he moved into larger premises at 74 *bis*, rue Halle. His eldest son, Théo, himself an accomplished engraver, supervised the firm's four or five wood engravers. In addition to the Stanhope hand-press, there were now four Italian Nebiolo printing presses.

The 1920s witnessed Schmied's most sumptuous works, often issued in editions of between 25 and 100 for members of France's elite book clubs. The distinctly exotic graphic style of several of these, such as *Paysages méditerranéens*, *Sud-Marocain*, *La Fête Arabe*, and *Mille et une nuits*, showed the artist's fascination with North Africa and Orientalism. The earlier works, in particular, were exuberant in their use of vibrant colors and fantastic imagery. Some of Schmied's illustrations, such as those for *Histoire de la Princesse Boudour*, were hand-colored in Dunand's atelier. Others were colored by pochoir by Saude. Artists such as Goulden, Barbier, Jouve, Bergue, and Sureda were commissioned to provide illustrations for books which Schmied did not himself illustrate.

During this period, Schmied participated in several exhibitions, in particular the annual shows staged at the Georges Petit Gallery by himself, Dunand, Goulden, and Jouve. He also took part in the Salons of the Société Nationale des Beaux-Arts and the Société des Artistes Décorateurs. In 1927, he held a one-man exhibition of paintings and bindings at the Arnold Seligmann Galleries in New York. One or two of the most elaborate volumes were priced at roughly $10,000, with others around $4–5,000. Several of these works had been in production for three to four years. Schmied's clients included Vever, Barthou, Miguet, Chouanard, and, one of his favorite authors, Dr. Mardrus.

The collapse of the world economy following the 1929 Wall Street crash had drastic financial repercussions for Schmied. The demand for expensive books diminished sharply. In addition, examples of his earlier works began to appear on the second-hand market. To protect their value (and, thereby, his reputation), Schmied attempted to repurchase as many of these as he could, which contributed to his impending bankruptcy. Among the first items that he was forced to sell was his yacht, *Le Peau brun*. Matters deteriorated rapidly, and by 1935 the studio on the rue Halle was closed. In April of the same year, an auction of Schmied's books was held at the Hôtel Drouot in Paris. Schmied decided to exile himself, settling in Tahanaout, an outpost in the Moroccan desert south of Marrakesh, where he transformed a deserted fort into a miniature palace. The bookbinder Lucie Weill was among the last to see him there. During his years in exile he returned to Paris on several occasions to oversee the execution of outstanding book commissions, including *Faust* and *Le Tapis de prière*.

Bibliography

Barthou, Louis, "L'Evolution artistique de la reliure," *L'Illustration*, Christmas 1930, n.p.

Berman, Avis, "Antiques: Bound for Glory: Rare Bookbindings of Art Deco Design," *Architectural Digest*, May 1986, p. 188ff
Catalogue des oeuvres de F.-L. Schmied. . ., exhibition catalogue, Pavillon de Marsan, Paris, January, 1934
de Bormans, Pierre, "Un Artiste du livre: F.-L. Schmied," *Revue des deux mondes*, 15 May 1932, pp. 436–47
de Crauzat, Ernest, *La Reliure française de 1900 à 1925* (vol. 2), Paris, 1932, pp. 100–07
François-Louis Schmied, auction catalogue, Hôtel Drouot, Paris, 30 April 1975
François-Louis Schmied (1873–1941), exhibition catalogue, Schweiz Landesbibliothek, Berne, Switzerland, November 1976
Marcel, Roland, "F.-L. Schmied: peintre, graveur, imprimeur," *La Renaissance de l'art français*, April 1928, pp. 149–56
Marcilhac, Félix, *Des Reliures pour F.-L. Schmied*, exhibition catalogue, Schmuckmuseum, Pforzheim, 1975
Rémon, Georges, "F.-L. Schmied," *Mobilier et décoration*, June 1932, pp. 309–10
Ritchie, Ward, *François-Louis Schmied: Artist, Engraver, Printer*, Tucson, Arizona, 1976
"Seligmann Shows Schmied's Books," *The Art News*, 19 March 1927, p. 3
Terrasse, Charles, "Les Reliures de Schmied et Dunand," *Byblis* 6 (1927): 142–46

Germaine Schroeder (1889–1983)
Bookbinder

Schroeder incorporated brilliant colors into inlays of leather, parchment, and vellum covers. Her compositions were invariably harmonious and delicate, often including large heart motifs, such as that for *Les Amours de Psyché et de Cupidon*.

Little is recorded of her upbringing and early career, but by 1925 Schroeder had attracted the admiration of a substantial number of collectors, including Marcel Bernard, Louis Barthou, Dr. Jaltrain, Lecointe, and Lazard.

Bibliography

Dally, Ph., "Les Téchniques modernes de la reliure," *Art et décoration*, January 1927, pp. 18, 22
de Crauzat, Ernest, *La Reliure française de 1900 à 1925* (vol. 2), Paris, 1932, pp. 141–42
Nicolle, Henri, "La Reliure moderne," *Les Arts français: la reliure d'art*, no. 36 (1919): 199
Quénioux, Gaston, *Les Arts décoratifs modernes*, Paris, 1925, pp. 339, 342

Marcellin Semet (b. 1894) and Georges Plumelle (b. 1902)
Bookbinders and gilders

Semet served his apprenticeship with Chambolle-Duru during World War I. His later partner, Plumelle, was trained first by the gilder Pagnier and then by Maylander. The two became acquainted at the Gruel atelier after the war, and formed an association in 1925 to take over the maison Pinardon, at 19 rue Guisarde, where they remained until 1955. They rapidly acquired a reputation for excellence, blending impeccable binding techniques with a fresh modernist vocabulary of design. Many volumes bear witness to their expertise, including *A. O. Barnabooth*, *Les Fleurs du mal*, *Poésies*, and *Le Siège de Jerusalem*.

At their finest, bindings by Semet and Plumelle consist of flowing lines or arabesques on subtle two- or three-color grounds. It is often difficult today to determine when these were executed as their style remained consistent for many years. The problem is compounded by the fact that their bindings were often undertaken many years after the book's publication. Semet retired in 1955 to the south of France. Plumelle continued working until 1980, in most part creating bindings for friends and a select clientele.

Bibliography

Devauchelle, Roger, *La Reliure en France de ses origines à nos jours* (vol. 3), Paris, 1961, pp. 204, 206–07, pl. XCII
Fleming, John F., and Juvelis, Priscilla, *The Book Beautiful and the Binding as Art*, New York, 1983 and 1985; (vol. 1), p. 113, (vol. 2) pp. 21, 24, 30

Vermorel (?–1925)

Born in Lyon, Vermorel settled in Paris in 1887, where he was apprenticed by Edouard Pagnant. In 1894 he established himself in the Faubourg Saint-Honoré, moving in 1912 to the Place de l'Etoile. His initial specialty was liturgical books, to which he later added half- and full-bindings. Vermorel's son, a designer, assisted him with the designs for his covers until 1914, when he was conscripted and killed in the final battle of the war. Alone again, Vermorel turned to modern composition. Following Legrain's example, he introduced linear designs into his new works at the Salons. His new style was pleasing and fresh, though lacking the verve and impetuosity of the younger generation of binders with whom he exhibited. Collectors responded with enthusiasm, however, commissioning fine examples of such volumes as *Autour de nos moulins*, *Antar*, *Le Livre de la jungle*, and *Mireille*.

Bibliography

de Crauzat, Ernest, *La Reliure française de 1900 à 1925* (vol. 1), Paris, 1932, pp. 69–70
Devauchelle, Roger, *La Reliure en France de ses origines à nos jours* (vol. 3), Paris, 1961, pp. 278–79

Lucie Weill (b. 1901)
Bookbinder and illustrator

Weill was born in Paris and worked initially as a bookseller before opening her own atelier in 1930 at 6 rue Bonaparte, where she remained until 1978. In addition to de luxe bindings, she specialized in modern illustrated books.

An administrator of numerous bookbinding exhibitions, both in France and abroad, Weill participated in the 1937 Exposition Universelle, and, in 1949, in "The French Art of the Book" Exhibition held at the California Palace of the Legion of Honor in San Francisco.

Bibliography

Devauchelle, Roger, *La Reliure en France de ses origines à nos jours* (vol. 3), Paris, 1961, pp. 206–7, 279
Lecomte, Georges, "Les Relieurs d'art français à l'exposition de Paris," *La Chronique graphique*, Brussels, 1938, p. 3931

René Wiener (1855–1940)
Bookbinder

Born into the book and stationery business – his grandfather and father in turn ran a *papeterie* and print shop at 53 rue des Dominicains in Nancy – Wiener was initially drawn to binding in 1883 by Victor Prouvé and Camille Martin, who commissioned him to execute their designs for book covers. Trained in magazine printing and gilding, he was not a binder by profession, but his artisanship was clearly of a sufficient standard for him to be subsequently retained by several members of the Ecole de Nancy and the Art Nouveau community in Paris and Brussels, including Georges Auriol, Louis Guignot, Emile Friant, Carlos Schwabe, Toulouse-Lautrec, Eugène Grasset, Paul Berthon, Jacques Gruber, Théophile Alexandre Steinlen, and Georges de Feure. He also executed a range of other objects in tooled leather, such as buckles, box covers, purses, and screens.

The fact that Wiener was not a binder *per se*, in the sense that Marius-Michel or Meunier were, no doubt helped to intensify the fury of the Parisian book community when the Ecole Lorraine d'Art Décoratif (renamed the Ecole de Nancy in 1901) first participated in the Salon of the Société Nationale des Beaux-Arts at the Champs de Mars in Paris in 1892. "Wienerism" became a term of abuse, used to describe the most commercial aspects of book cover design. Today this seems unfair, since the designs were not his own, but those of his fellow Nanceiens.

Wiener retired abruptly in 1900, at the time of the International Exposition. Two years later, when his only daughter died, he abandoned the craft altogether. He later bequeathed his book collection and binding documentation to the Musée Lorrain.

Bibliography

Le Bulletin des Sociétés artistiques de l'est. 1892-1900
Charpentier, Thérèse, *L'Ecole de Nancy et la reliure d'art*, Paris, 1960, pp. 6, 8–10, 12–14, 21, 24, 38–39, 42
Le Cuir au musée, exhibition catalogue, Musée de l'Ecole de Nancy, Nancy, 1985
Exposition Lorraine (Ecole de Nancy), exhibition catalogue, Musée de l'Union Centrale des Arts Décoratifs, Paris, 2nd series, 1903
"Modern Bookbindings and Their Designers," *The Studio*, Special Winter Issue 1899–1900, pp. 57, 60, 61, 64
Nicolle, Henri, "La Reliure moderne," *Les Arts français: la reliure d'art*, no. 36 (1919): 191
Prideaux, S.T., *Modern Bindings: Their Design and Decoration*, New York, 1906
La Revue des arts décoratifs, 1892-1900
Uzanne, Octave, *L'Art dans la décoration extérieure des livres en France et à l'étranger*, Paris, 1898, pp. 202–9

Yseux (?–1951)
Bookbinder

After working for many years for Durvand, Yseux associated himself in 1908 with Thierry, the successor of Petit-Simier, whose workshop at 7 quai de Conti he acquired in 1916. Moving later to 18 rue Dauphine, he maintained a small family studio in which to create jansenist and half-bindings ornamented with punches he had acquired from Thierry's inventory. He specialized after World War I in inlays of leather and white vellum romantic bindings, some enhanced with oils by Théophile Gautier. Yseux was succeeded on his retirement by Barbance.

Bibliography

de Crauzat, Ernest, *La Reliure française de 1900 à 1925* (vol. 2), Paris, 1932, pp. 59–60

GENERAL BIBLIOGRAPHY

1. Books

Adler, Rose, *Reliures, présenté par Rose Adler*, Paris, 1929
Blaizot, Georges, *Masterpieces of French Modern Bindings*, New York, 1947
Brunhammer, Yvonne, *The Nineteen Twenties Style*, London, 1966
Cain, Julien, *Bibliothèque reliée par Paul Bonet*, Paris, 1963
Catalogue de cent reliures d'art, Paris, 1902
Charpentier, Thérèse, *L'Ecole de Nancy et la reliure d'art*, Paris, 1960
Conceptions personnelles sur le problème de la décoration du livre, Paris, 1950
de Crauzat, Ernest, *La Reliure française de 1900 à 1925*, 3 vols., Paris, 1932
Deshairs, Léon, *Les Arts décoratifs modernes*, Paris, 1925, pp. 185–89
Devauchelle, Roger, *La Reliure en France de ses origines à nos jours* (vols. 2 and 3), Paris, 1961
Devaux, Yves, *La Reliure en France*, Paris, 1981

Deville, Etienne, *La Reliure française* (vols. 1 and 2), Paris, 1930–31
Diehl, Edith, *Bookbinding: Its Background and Technique* (vol. 1), New York, 1946
Duncan, Alastair, *Art Deco*, London, 1988
——— (ed.), *The Encyclopedia of Art Deco*, New York, 1988
Elek, Paul, *The Art of the French Book*, Paris, 1947, pp. 141–45
Encyclopédie des arts décoratifs et industriels modernes au XXème siècle (vol. 7), Paris, 1925, pp. 58–60
L'Evolution professionnelle et téchnique de 1870 à 1899, Paris, 1956
Fleming, John F., and Juvelis, Priscilla, *The Book Beautiful and the Binding as Art* (vols. 1 and 2), New York, 1983, 1985
Guignard, Jacques, *Pierre Legrain et la reliure: Evolution d'un style*, Paris
Lejard, André (ed.), *The Art of the French Book from Early Manuscripts to the Present Time*, London, 1947

Lewis, Roy Harley, *Fine Bookbinding in the Twentieth Century*, New York, 1984
Marius-Michel, *La Reliure française commerciale et industrielle depuis l'invention de imprimérie jusqu'à nos jours. . .*, Paris, 1881
Michon, Marie, *La Reliure française*, Paris, 1951, pp. 131–40
Modern Book Production, London, 1928
Moutard-Uldry, Renée (ed.), *Documents Paul Bonet 1889*, Paris, 1960
Prideaux, S.T., *Modern Bookbindings: Their Design and Decoration*, New York, 1906
Quénioux, Gaston, *Les Arts décoratifs modernes 1918–1925*, Paris, 1925
Recueil des reliures de Paul Bonet pour les calligrammes d'Apollinaire, Paris, 1949
La Reliure originale, Paris, 1961
Ritchie, Ward, *François-Louis Schmied: Artist, Engraver, Printer*, Tucson, Arizona, 1976
Saunier, Charles, *Les Décorateurs du livre*, Paris, 1922

Taylor, E.A., *The Art of the Book in France*, London, 1914

Uzanne, Octave, *L'Art dans la décoration extérieure des livres en France et à l'étranger*, Paris, 1898

Valéry, Paul, *et al.*, *Paul Bonet*, Paris, 1945

2. Catalogues

The Artist and the Book: 1860–1960 (in Western Europe and the United States), Museum of Fine Arts, Boston, 1961

Catalogue de l'exposition de la reliure originale, Société de la Reliure Originale, Bibliothèque Nationale, Paris, 1947

Catalogue des oeuvres de F.L. Schmied, Pavillon de Marsan, Paris, January, 1934

Cent Ans de reliures d'art 1880–1980, Bibliothèque Municipale de Toulouse, Toulouse, 1981

Le Décor de la vie de 1900 à 1925, Pavillon de Marsan, Palais du Louvre, Paris, 1937

Un Demi-Siècle de reliures d'art contemporain en France et dans le monde, Exposition Internationale, La Chambre Syndicale Nationale de la Reliure Brochure Dorure, Paris, 1984

L'Exposition d'art français contemporain à Bucharest, Paris, August, 1928, pp. 86–130

Exposition de la Société de la Reliure Originale, Bibliothèque Nationale, Paris, 1959

Exposition Lorraine (Ecole de Nancy) au Musée de l'Union Centrale des Arts Décoratifs, Paris, 2nd series, 1903

François-Louis Schmied, Hôtel Drouot, Paris, 30 April 1975

Henri Creuzevault: naissance d'une reliure, Musée des Arts Décoratifs de la Ville de Bordeaux, Bordeaux, November, 1984

Pascal, Georges, *La Reliure, le livre, et l'illustration*, Paris, May-October, 1935

Reliure française contemporaine, La Société Française les Amis de la Reliure Originale, The Grolier Club, New York, 7 December 1987 – 30 January 1988

3. Articles

Alfassa, Mme. Jane, "Le Nouveau Visage de l'art: chez le reliure Legrain," *Conferencia*, no.7 (1928):375–83

"L'Art décoratif au Salon d'Automne, les grandes ventes," *L'Art vivant*, 1 December 1926, pp. 900–901

Barthou, Louis, "L'Evolution artistique de la reliure," *L'Illustration*, Christmas, 1930

Berman, Avis, "Antiques: Bound for Glory: Rare Bookbindings of Art Deco Design," *Architectural Digest*, May 1986, pp. 188–93, 234–35

Bosquet, Emile, "La Reliure française à l'exposition," *Art et décoration*, July 1900, pp. 46–55

"Les Cinq," *Mobilier et décoration*, July 1928, pp. 43–51

"5 Relieurs," *Mobilier et décoration*, April 1935, pp. 140–45

Clément-Janin, "Exposition internationale des arts décoratifs: le livre et ses éléments," *L'Art vivant*, 15 August 1925, pp. 25–32

Cretté, Georges, "Distinctive Designs in Hand-Tooled Book-Bindings," *Creative Art* 7 (1930):378–81

Dally, Ph., "Les Téchniques modernes de la reliure," *Art et décoration*, January 1927, pp. 15–24

"De la reliure," *Le Livre et ses amis*, no.13, (1946):47–51

de Ricci, Seymour, "Les Expositions – reliures de Pierre Legrain," *Beaux-Arts*, 15 November 1923, p. 303

Derys, Gaston, "Le Vingt-Troisième Salon des Artistes Décorateurs," *Mobilier et décoration*, June 1933, pp. 201–72

"Des Incunables aux reliures de Pierre Legrain," *L'Art vivant*, May 1931, p. 243

Dormoy, Marie, "L'Exposition des arts décoratifs et industriels de 1925, les tendances générales," *L'Amour de l'art*, August 1925, pp. 283–99

———, "Les Reliures de Legrain à la Bibliothèque Jacques-Doucet," *Le Portique*, no.3 (1946):121–31

"L'Exposition des reliures au Musée des Arts Décoratifs," *L'Art décoratif*, 1906, pp. 193–98

Farnoux-Reynaud, Lucien, "La Reliure d'art: Triomphe du goût français," *Mobilier et décoration*, February 1938, pp. 58–78

Flavigny, Bertrand Galimard, "Apollinaire le bien-aimé," *La Gazette*, no.30 (1987):18–19

Gonon, A.J., "De la Reliure et de quelques relieurs," *Arts et métiers graphiques*, no.59 (1937):55–63

"Le Groupe des Cinq," *Les Echos des industries d'art*, April 1927, pp. 29–31

"Groupe des cinq," *Mobilier et décoration*, April 1929, pp. 121–24

Guignard, Jacques, "Aspects de la reliure française," *Art et décoration*, April 1947, pp. 22–29

"History of Bookbindings," *Le Crapouillot*, Christmas 1927, pp. 57–60

Léautaud, Jean, "Modern Bindings for Modern Books," *International Studio* 84 (1926):70–73

Lecomte, Georges, "Les Relieurs d'art français à l'Exposition de Paris," *La Chronique graphique*, Paris, pp. 3930–4011

———, "Reliures modernes," *Plaisir de France*, December 1937, pp. 65–73

Lièvre, Pierre, "Pierre Legrain," *L'Amour de l'art*, June 1922, pp. 170–72

Megret, Jacques, "Pierre Legrain," *Arts et métiers graphiques*, November 1929, pp. 839–42

Migennes, P., "Reliure et photographie," *Art et décoration*, November 1934, pp. 427–29

"Modern Bookbindings and Their Designers," *The Studio*, Special Winter Number 1899–1900, pp. 3–82

Mourey, Gabriel, "Histoire générale de l'art français," *L'Art décoratif*, 1922, pp. 243

Moutard-Uldry, Renée, "Paul Bonet," *L'Art et les artistes*, March 1937, pp. 203–7

———, "Documents Paul Bonet 1889," *Ecole française*, no.99 (1960)

———, "Paul Bonet, relieur," *Art et décoration*, September-October 1938, pp. 301–7

———, "Le Rayon de la reliure: exposition de la reliure originale," *Cahiers du bibliophile*, no.7 (1953):16–18

Nicolle, Henri, "La Reliure moderne," *Les Arts français: la relieure d'art*, no.36 (1919):199

"Pierre Legrain, relieur," *Mobilier et décoration*, March 1925, pp. 11–16

Rambosson, Yvanhoe, "Madame Anita Conti, relieur," *Mobilier et décoration*, September 1932, pp. 379–83

"La Reliure," *Les Echos des industries d'art*, October 1928, pp. 31–34

"Les Reliures de Pierre Legrain," *Mobilier et décoration*, March 1927, pp. 87–92

Rémon, Georges, "Jean Lambert, relieur," *Mobilier et décoration*, April 1932, pp. 160–62

———, "Un Petite Exposition après la grande, groupements et regroupements," *Mobilier et décoration*, May 1926, pp. 143–48

"Rose Adler," *Le Jardin des arts*, no.77 (1961):53–55

"Salon d'Automne," *Le Crapouillot*, 15 November 1923, pp. 19–20

"Le Salon d'Automne," *Mobilier et décoration*, December 1926, pp. 151–74

Saunier, Charles, "La Reliure moderne," *L'Art décoratif*, March 1901, pp. 253–63

T., S., "Binding for Reading," *Art et décoration*, February 1934, pp. 52, 54

Terrasse, Charles, "Les Reliures de Schmied et Dunand," *Byblis* 6 (1927):142–46

Vauxcelles, Louis, "L'Art décoratif," *L'Amour de l'art*, October 1921, pp. 306–8

Vitry, Paul, "Le Caractère français," *Beaux-Arts*, 15 September 1925, pp. 256–61

Zervos, Christian, "Les Reliures de Pierre Legrain," *Byblis* 4 (1925):36–38

INDEX